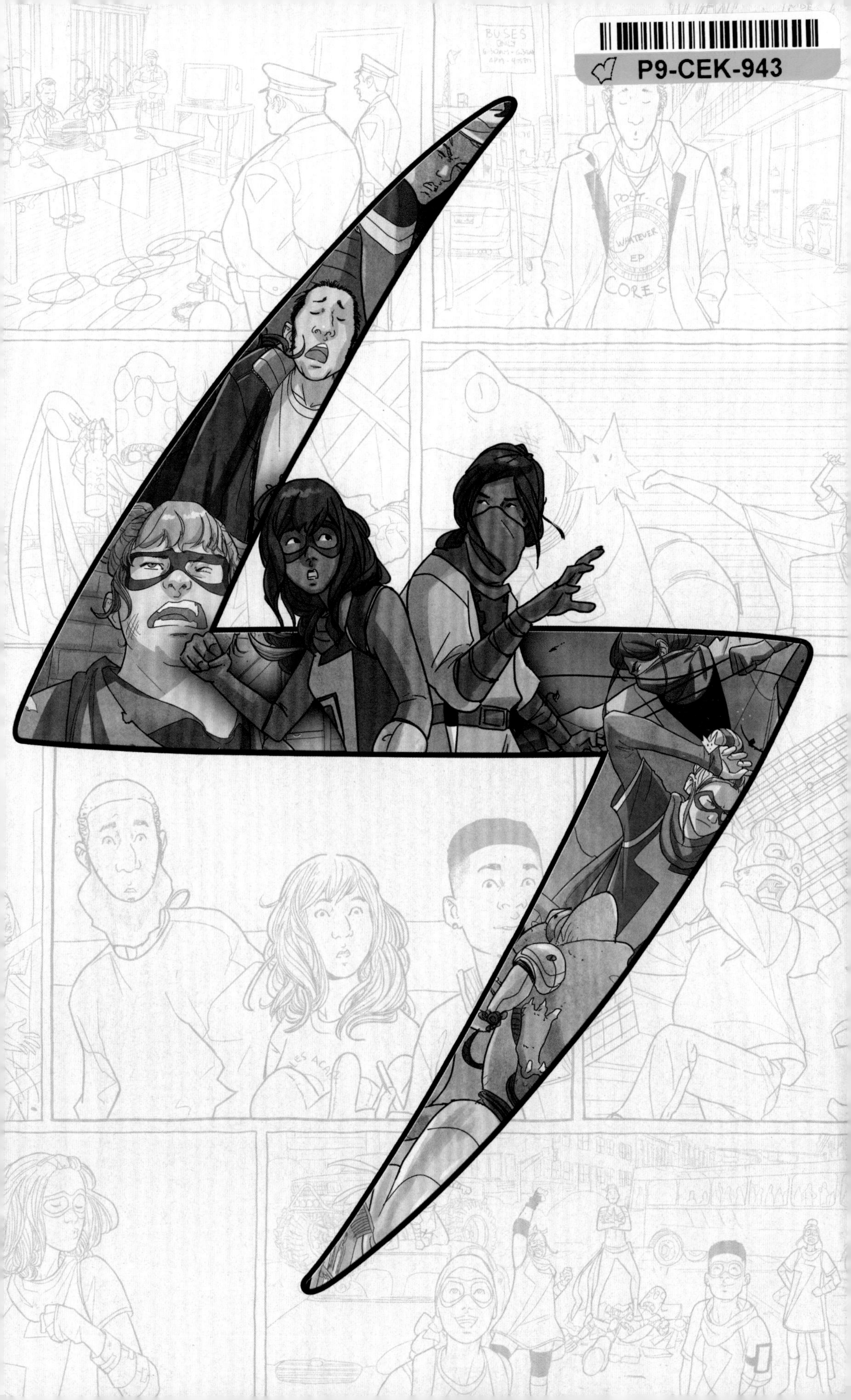
BUSES ONLY
WHATEVER
EP
CORES

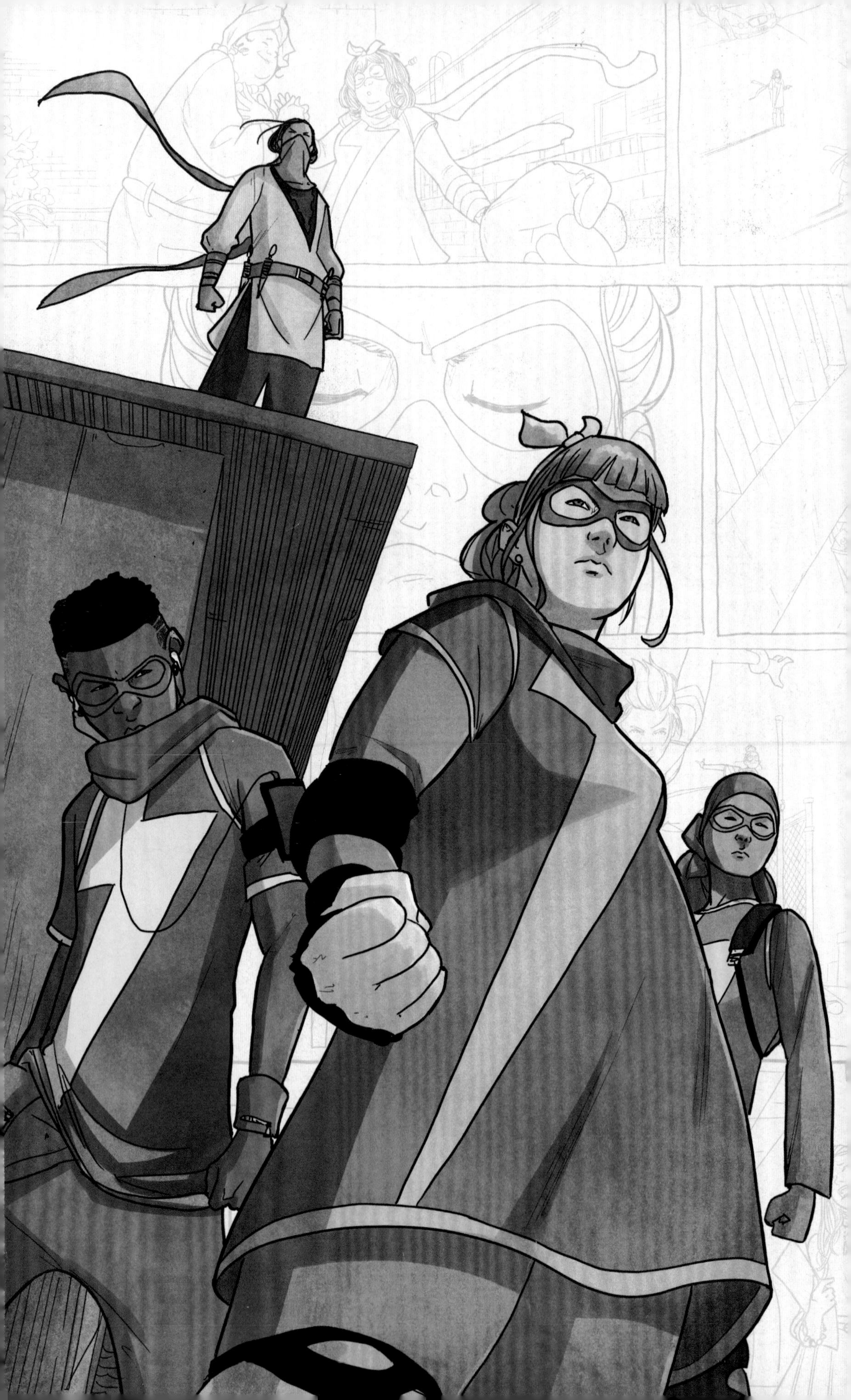

MS. MARVEL

TEENAGE WASTELAND

writer
G. WILLOW WILSON

artist
NICO LEON

color artist
IAN HERRING

letterer
VC's JOE CARAMAGNA

cover art
VALERIO SCHITI & RACHELLE ROSENBERG

associate editor
MARK BASSO

editor
SANA AMANAT

collection editor
JENNIFER GRÜNWALD

assistant editor
CAITLIN O'CONNELL

associate managing editor
KATERI WOODY

editor, special projects
MARK D. BEAZLEY

vp production & special projects
JEFF YOUNGQUIST

svp print, sales & marketing
DAVID GABRIEL

editor in chief
C.B. CEBULSKI

chief creative officer
JOE QUESADA

president
DAN BUCKLEY

executive producer
ALAN FINE

MS. MARVEL VOL. 9: TEENAGE WASTELAND. Contains material originally published in magazine form as MS. MARVEL #25-30. First printing 2018. ISBN 978-1-302-91078-5. Published by MARVEL WORLDWIDE, INC., a subsidiary of MARVEL ENTERTAINMENT, LLC. OFFICE OF PUBLICATION: 135 West 50th Street, New York, NY 10020. Copyright © 2018 MARVEL No similarity between any of the names, characters, persons, and/or institutions in this magazine with those of any living or dead person or institution is intended, and any such similarity which may exist is purely coincidental. **Printed in Canada.** DAN BUCKLEY, President, Marvel Entertainment; JOHN NEE, Publisher; JOE QUESADA, Chief Creative Officer; TOM BREVOORT, SVP of Publishing; DAVID BOGART, SVP of Business Affairs & Operations, Publishing & Partnership; DAVID GABRIEL, SVP of Sales & Marketing, Publishing; JEFF YOUNGQUIST, VP of Production & Special Projects; DAN CARR, Executive Director of Publishing Technology; ALEX MORALES, Director of Publishing Operations; DAN EDINGTON, Managing Editor; SUSAN CRESPI, Production Manager; STAN LEE, Chairman Emeritus. For information regarding advertising in Marvel Comics or on Marvel.com, please contact Vit DeBellis, Custom Solutions & Integrated Advertising Manager, at vdebellis@marvel.com. For Marvel subscription inquiries, please call 888-511-5480. **Manufactured between 5/25/2018 and 6/26/2018 by SOLISCO PRINTERS, SCOTT, QC, CANADA.**

10 9 8 7 6 5 4 3 2 1

PREVIOUSLY

WHEN A STRANGE TERRIGEN MIST DESCENDED UPON JERSEY CITY, KAMALA KHAN WAS IMBUED WITH POLYMORPH POWERS. USING HER NEW ABILITIES TO FIGHT EVIL AND PROTECT JERSEY CITY, SHE BECAME THE ALL-NEW

MS. MARVEL

HER LIFE WAS CHANGED FOREVER... AND SO WERE THE LIVES OF HER FAMILY AND FRIENDS.

BUT THINGS HAVEN'T BEEN GOING SO WELL FOR KAMALA. HER BEST FRIEND BRUNO MOVED TO WAKANDA. SHE'S FALLEN OUT WITH HER SUPER HERO COLLEAGUES AND MENTORS LIKE CAROL DANVERS AND TONY STARK. A NEW HERO FROM PAKISTAN, THE RED DAGGER, HAS RELOCATED TO JERSEY CITY, AND AFTER ALL HE'S BEEN ABLE TO DO IN THE SHORT TIME HE'S BEEN THERE, IT'S ONLY ADDED TO A NAGGING THOUGHT IN HER MIND: IS MS. MARVEL NO LONGER NEEDED?

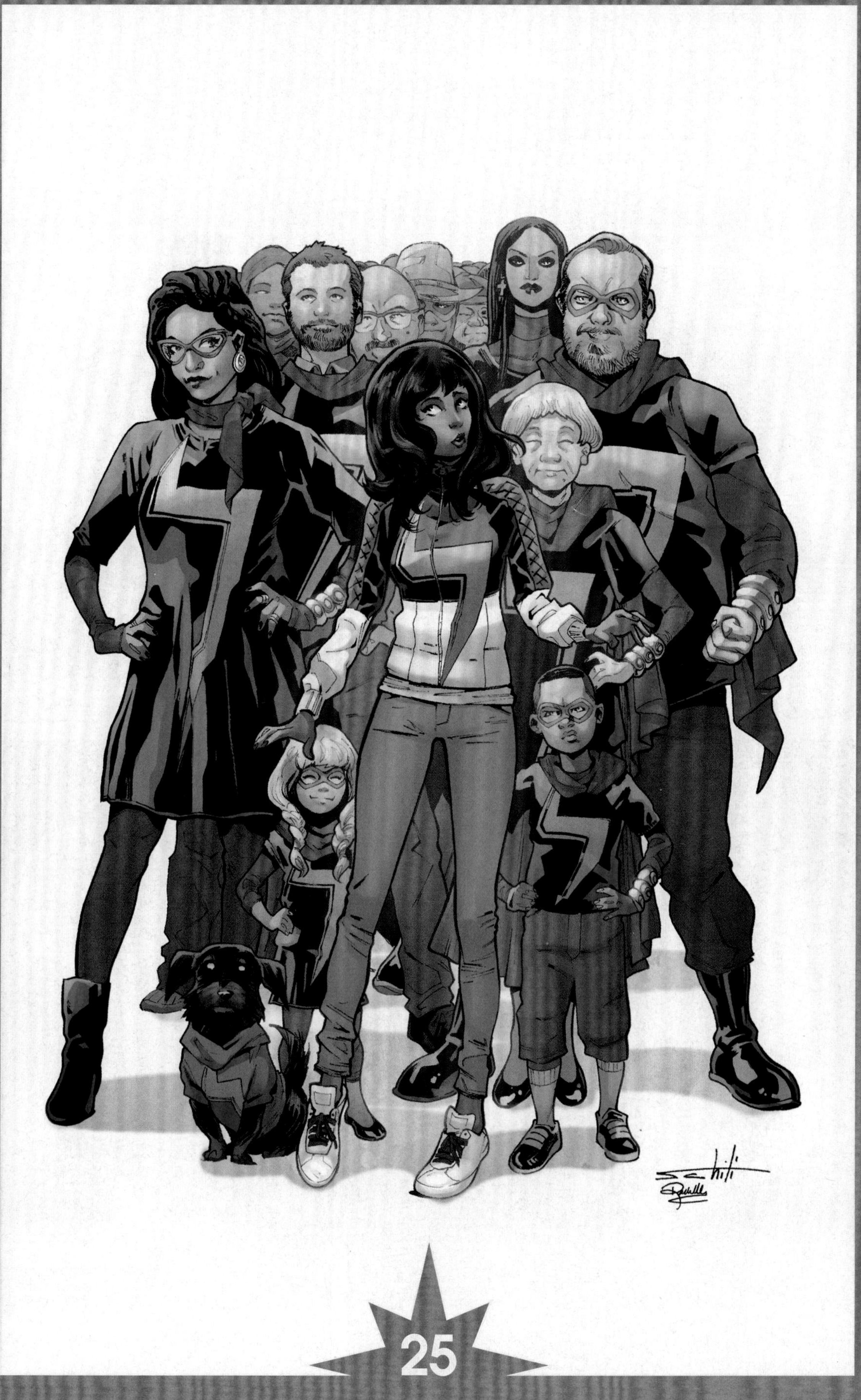
25

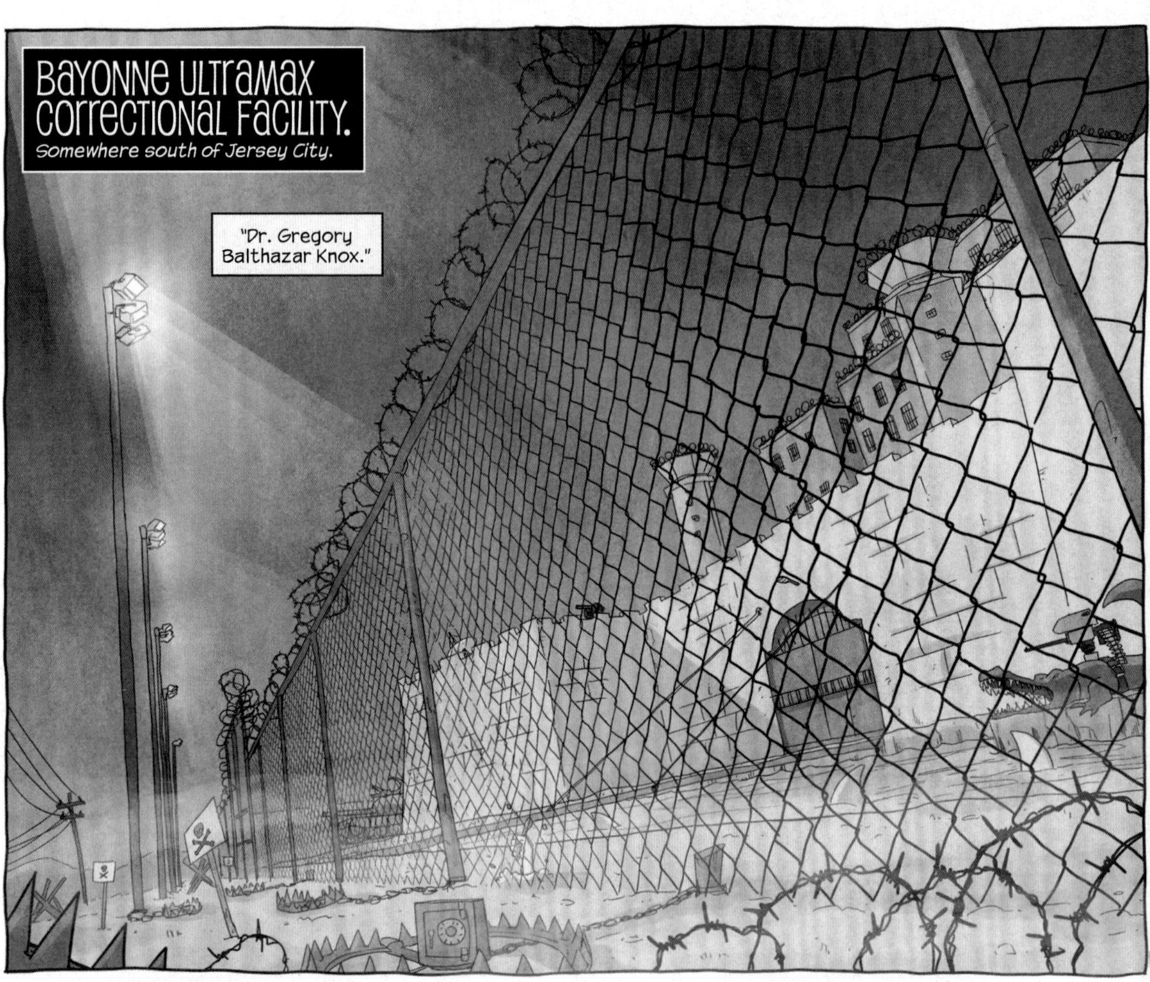
BAYONNE ULTRAMAX CORRECTIONAL FACILITY.
Somewhere south of Jersey City.
"Dr. Gregory Balthazar Knox."

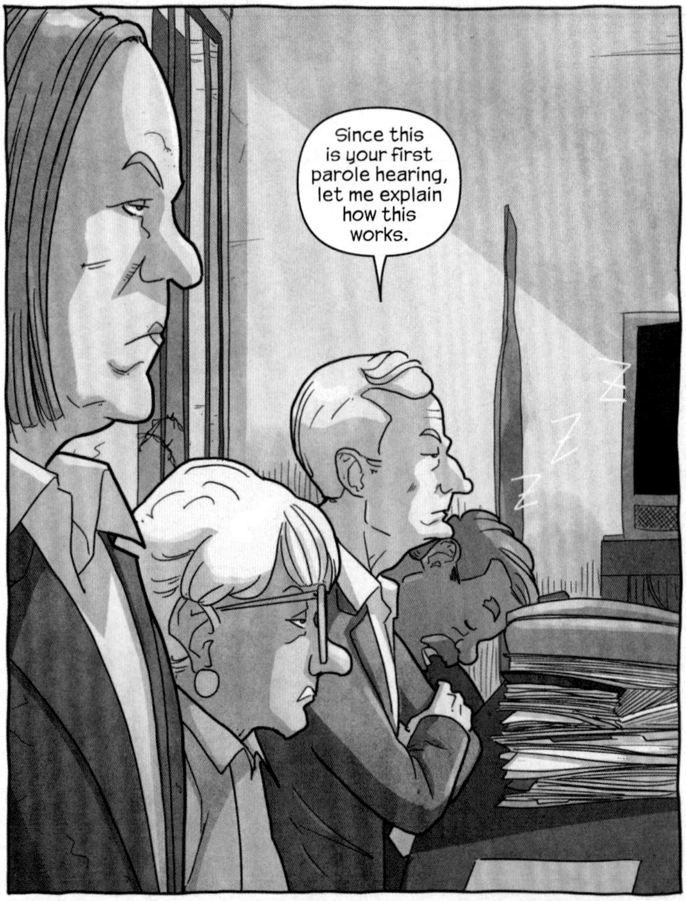
Since this is your first parole hearing, let me explain how this works.
Z Z Z

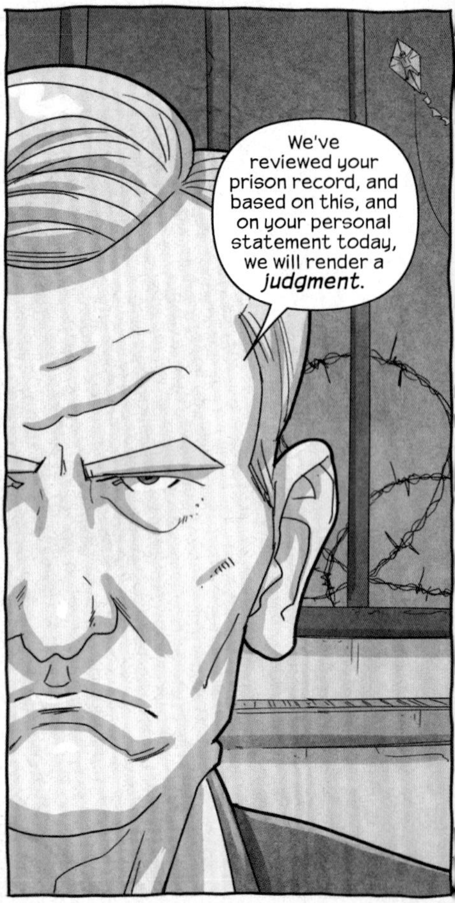
We've reviewed your prison record, and based on this, and on your personal statement today, we will render a *judgment*.

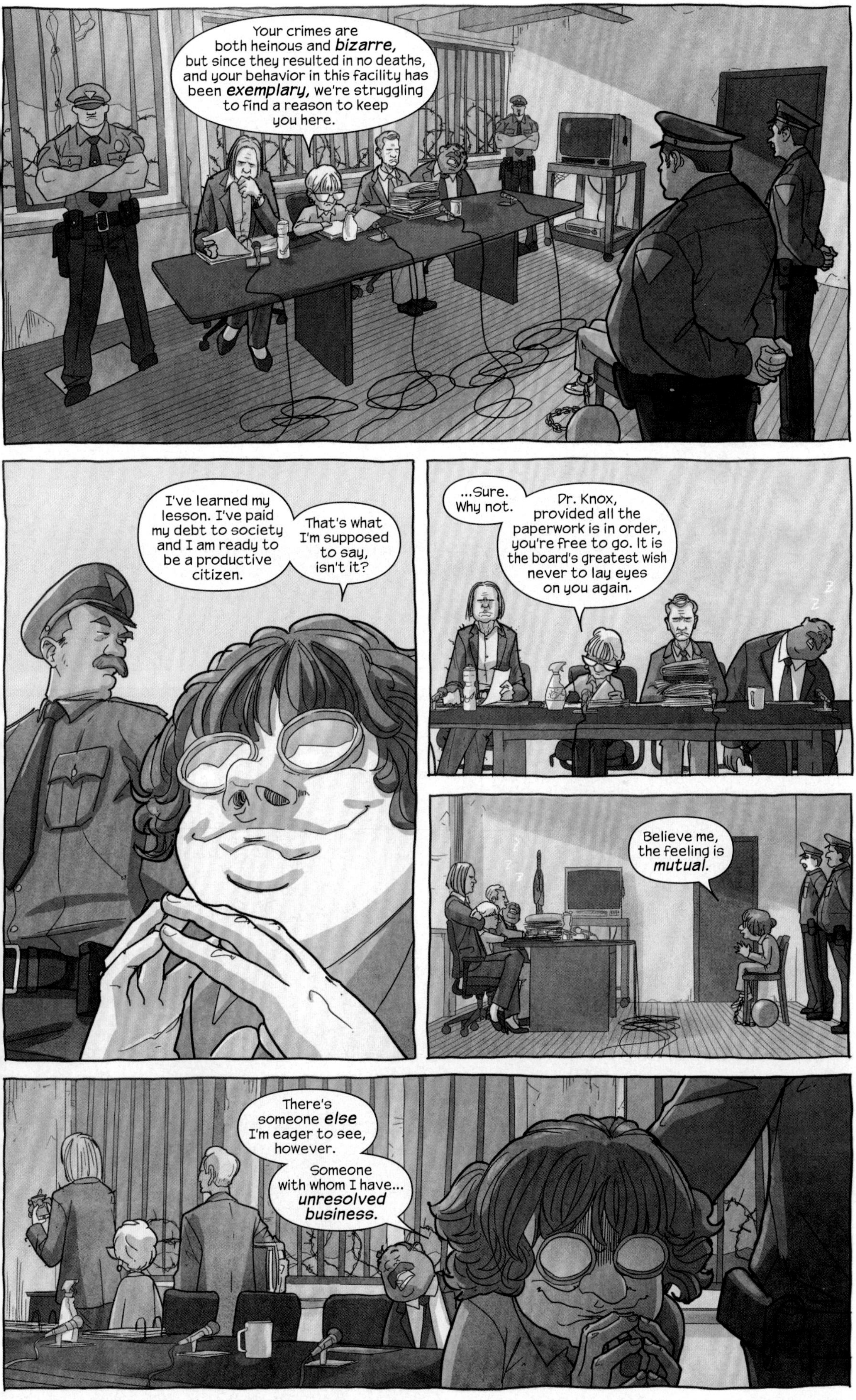
Your crimes are both heinous and *bizarre,* but since they resulted in no deaths, and your behavior in this facility has been ***exemplary,*** we're struggling to find a reason to keep you here.
I've learned my lesson. I've paid my debt to society and I am ready to be a productive citizen.
That's what I'm supposed to say, isn't it?
...Sure. Why not.
Dr. Knox, provided all the paperwork is in order, you're free to go. It is the board's greatest wish never to lay eyes on you again.
Z Z
Believe me, the feeling is *mutual.*
There's someone *else* I'm eager to see, however.
Someone with whom I have... ***unresolved business.***

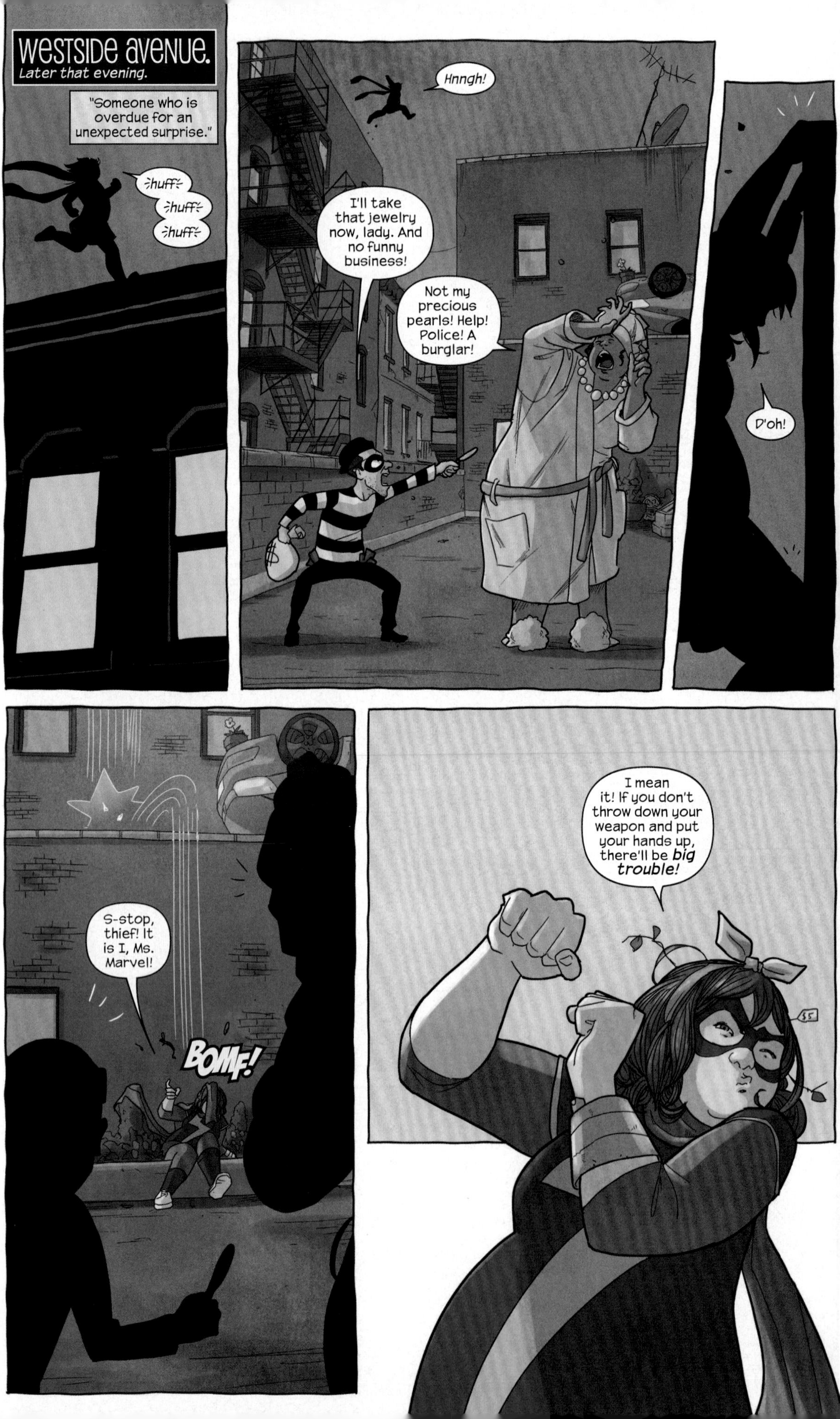
WESTSIDE AVENUE.
Later that evening.
"Someone who is overdue for an unexpected surprise."
huff
huff
huff
Hnngh!
I'll take that jewelry now, lady. And no funny business!
Not my precious pearls! Help! Police! A burglar!
D'oh!
S-stop, thief! It is I, Ms. Marvel!
BOMF!
I mean it! If you don't throw down your weapon and put your hands up, there'll be *big trouble!*

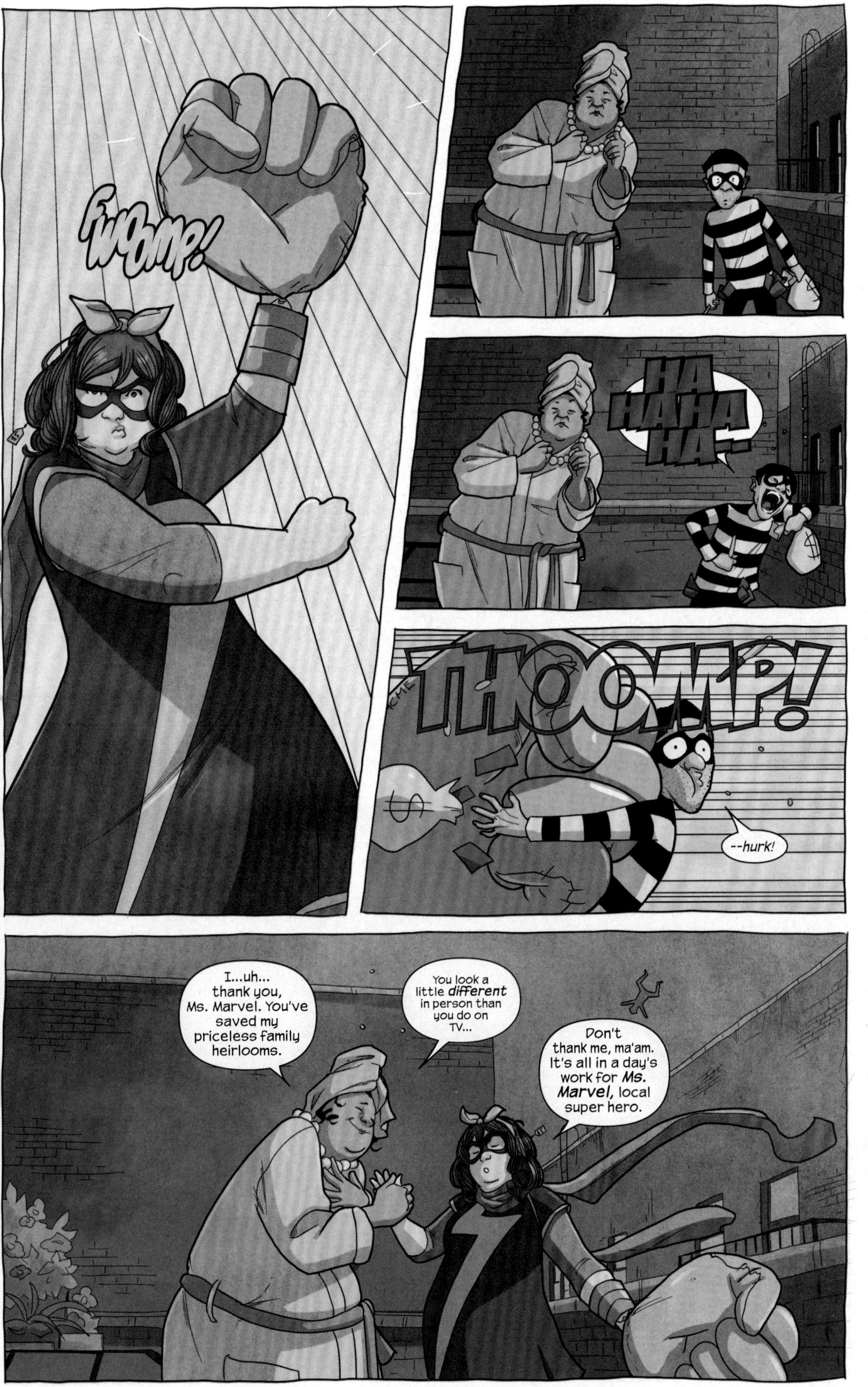
FWOOMP!
HA HA HA HA HA--
THOOMP!
--hurk!
I...uh... thank you, Ms. Marvel. You've saved my priceless family heirlooms.
You look a little different in person than you do on TV...
Don't thank me, ma'am. It's all in a day's work for Ms. Marvel, local super hero.

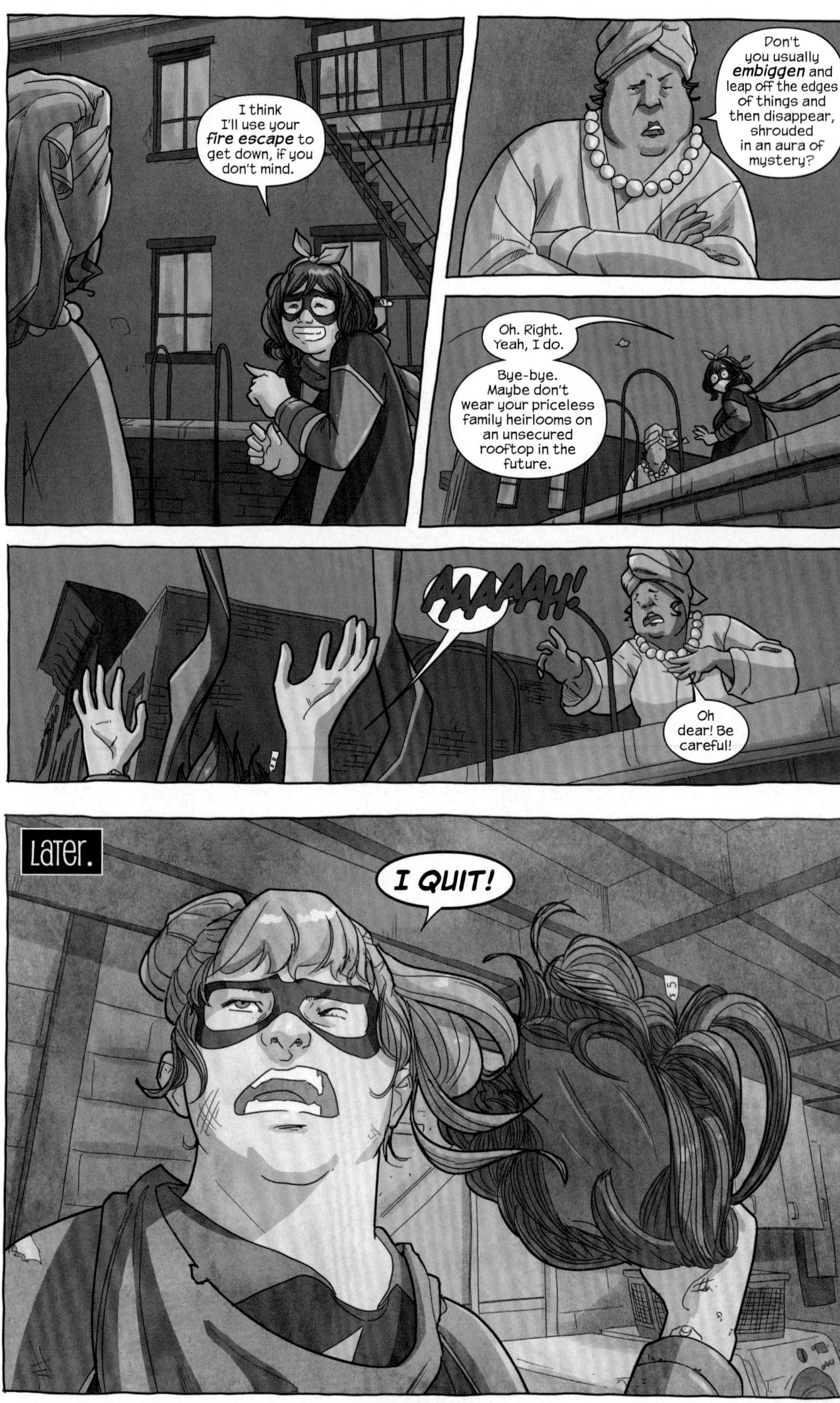
I think I'll use your *fire escape* to get down, if you don't mind.
Don't you usually ***embiggen*** and leap off the edges of things and then disappear, shrouded in an aura of mystery?
Oh. Right. Yeah, I do.
Bye-bye. Maybe don't wear your priceless family heirlooms on an unsecured rooftop in the future.
AAAAAH!
Oh dear! Be careful!
LATER.
I QUIT!

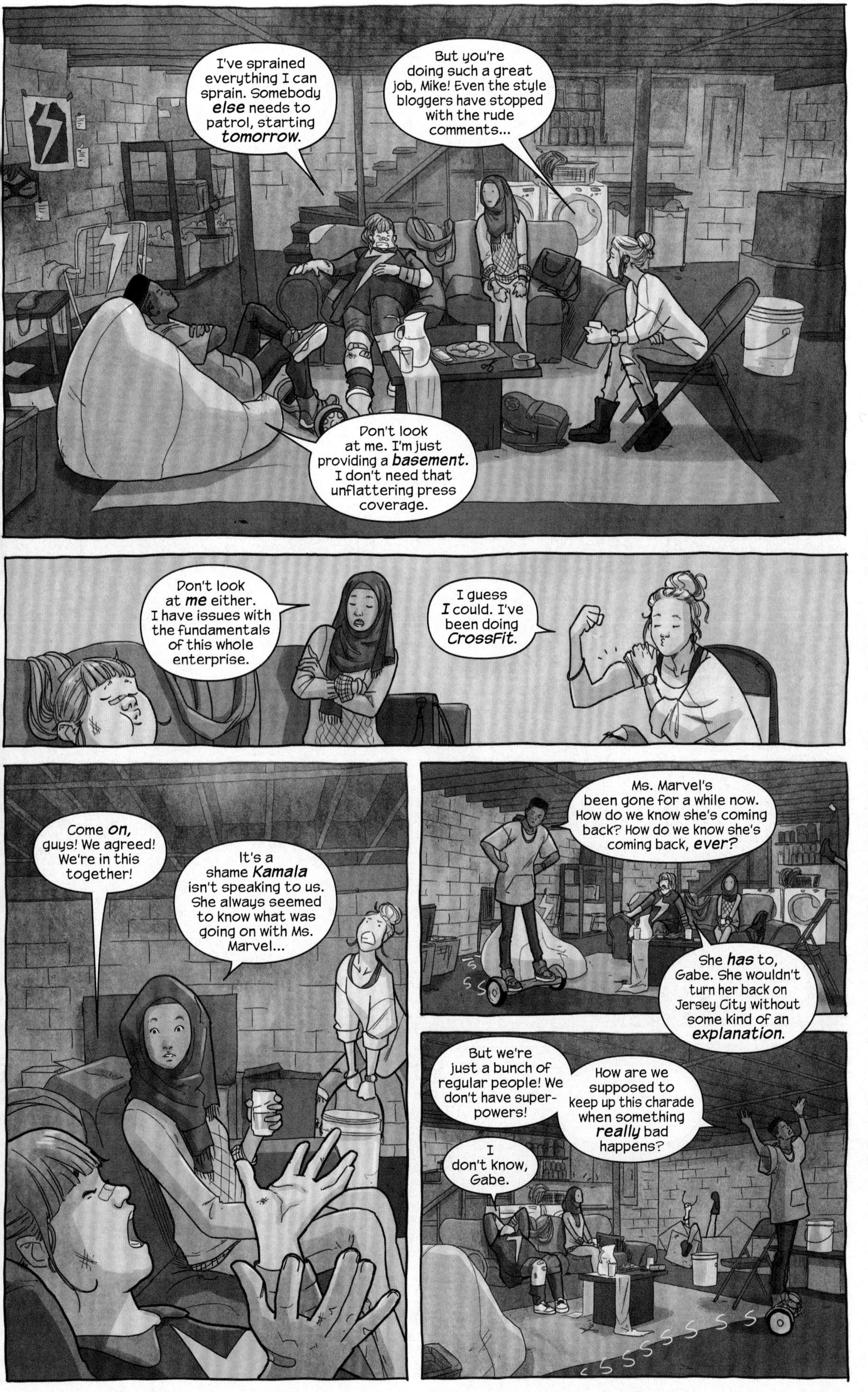
I've sprained everything I can sprain. Somebody else needs to patrol, starting tomorrow.
But you're doing such a great job, Mike! Even the style bloggers have stopped with the rude comments...
Don't look at me. I'm just providing a basement. I don't need that unflattering press coverage.
Don't look at me either. I have issues with the fundamentals of this whole enterprise.
I guess I could. I've been doing CrossFit.
Come on, guys! We agreed! We're in this together!
It's a shame Kamala isn't speaking to us. She always seemed to know what was going on with Ms. Marvel...
Ms. Marvel's been gone for a while now. How do we know she's coming back? How do we know she's coming back, ever?
She has to, Gabe. She wouldn't turn her back on Jersey City without some kind of an explanation.
But we're just a bunch of regular people! We don't have super-powers!
How are we supposed to keep up this charade when something really bad happens?
I don't know, Gabe.

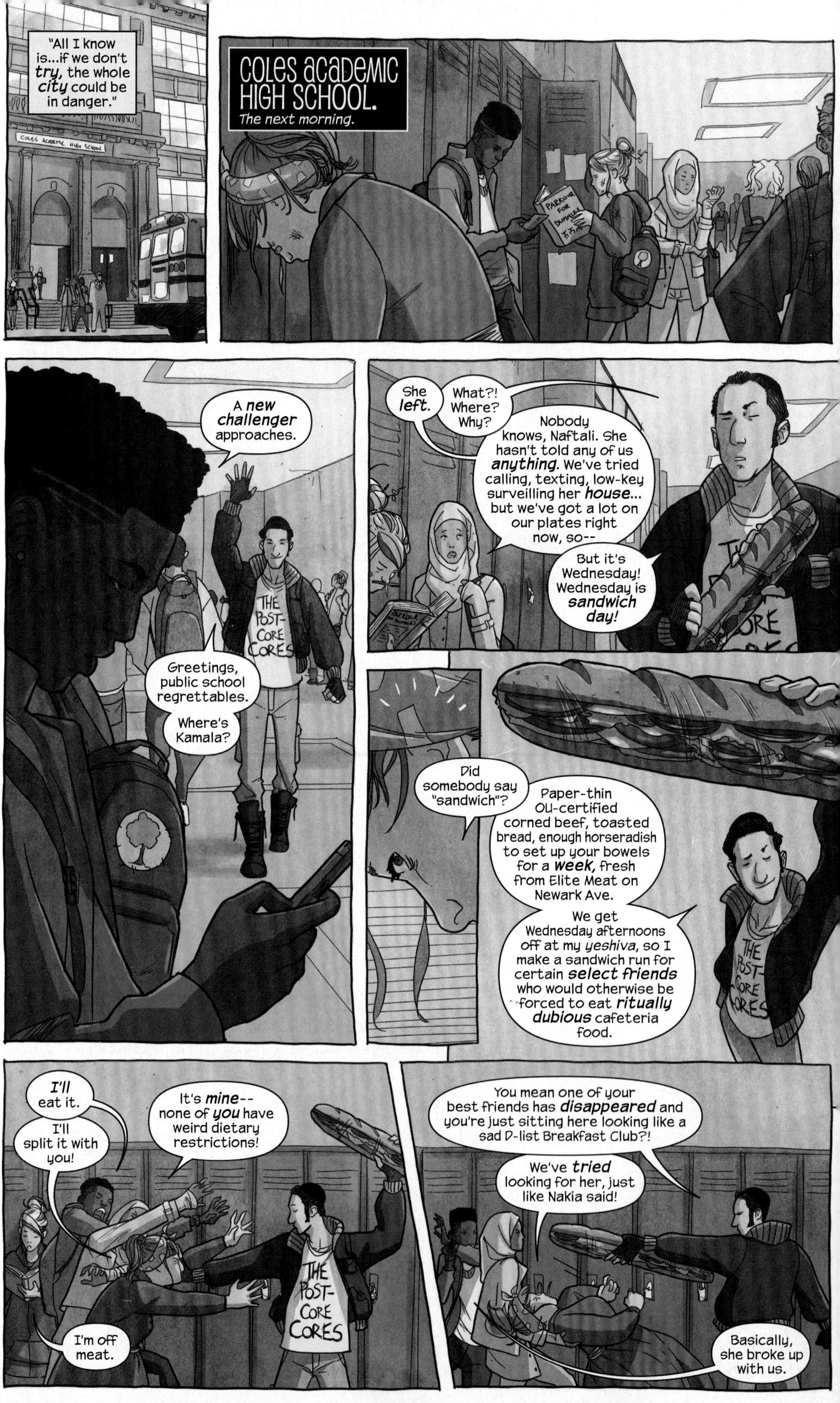
"All I know is...if we don't try, the whole city could be in danger."
COLES ACADEMIC HIGH SCHOOL
COLES ACADEMIC HIGH SCHOOL. The next morning.
PARKOUR FOR DUMMIES
A new challenger approaches.
Greetings, public school regrettables.
Where's Kamala?
THE POST-CORE CORES
She left.
What?! Where? Why?
Nobody knows, Naftali. She hasn't told any of us anything. We've tried calling, texting, low-key surveilling her house... but we've got a lot on our plates right now, so--
But it's Wednesday! Wednesday is sandwich day!
Did somebody say "sandwich"?
Paper-thin OU-certified corned beef, toasted bread, enough horseradish to set up your bowels for a week, fresh from Elite Meat on Newark Ave.
We get Wednesday afternoons off at my yeshiva, so I make a sandwich run for certain select friends who would otherwise be forced to eat ritually dubious cafeteria food.
I'll eat it.
I'll split it with you!
It's mine-- none of you have weird dietary restrictions!
I'm off meat.
THE POST-CORE CORES
You mean one of your best friends has disappeared and you're just sitting here looking like a sad D-list Breakfast Club?!
We've tried looking for her, just like Nakia said!
Basically, she broke up with us.

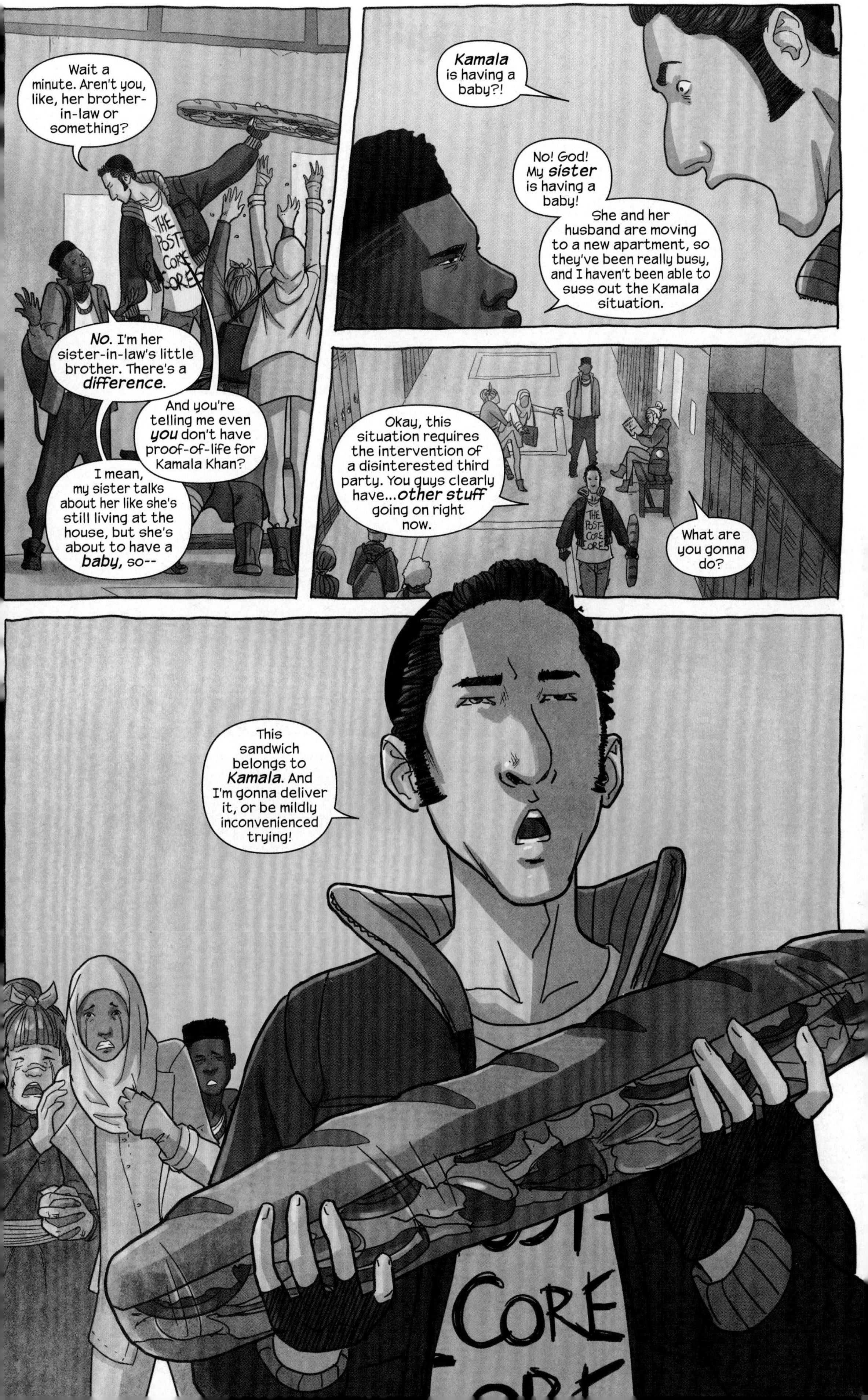
Wait a minute. Aren't you, like, her brother-in-law or something?
THE POST-CORE CORE
No. I'm her sister-in-law's little brother. There's a difference.
And you're telling me even you don't have proof-of-life for Kamala Khan?
I mean, my sister talks about her like she's still living at the house, but she's about to have a baby, so--
Kamala is having a baby?!
No! God! My sister is having a baby!
She and her husband are moving to a new apartment, so they've been really busy, and I haven't been able to suss out the Kamala situation.
Okay, this situation requires the intervention of a disinterested third party. You guys clearly have...other stuff going on right now.
THE POST-CORE CORE
What are you gonna do?
This sandwich belongs to Kamala. And I'm gonna deliver it, or be mildly inconvenienced trying!
CORE

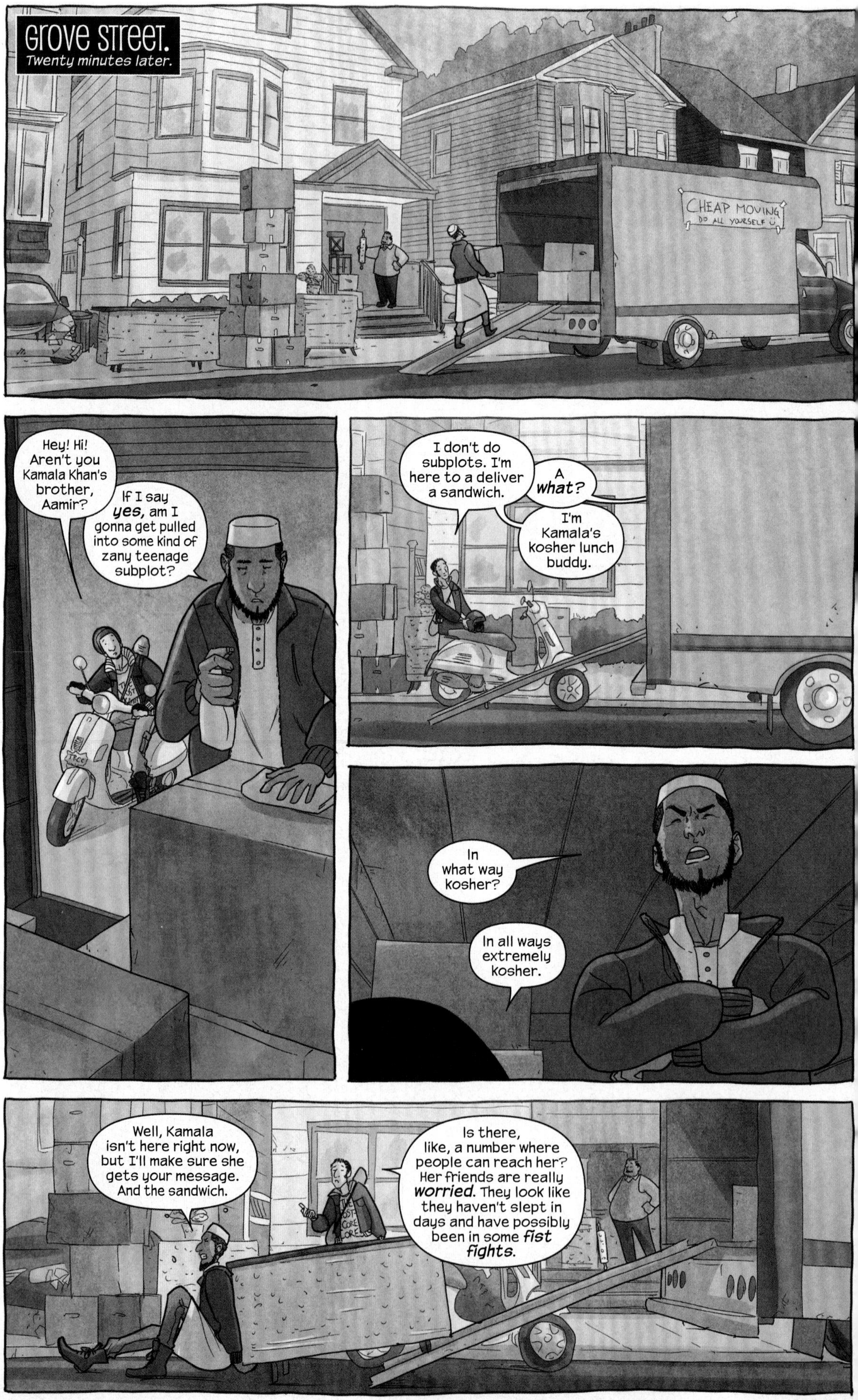
GROVE STREET.
Twenty minutes later.
CHEAP MOVING
DO ALL YOURSELF
Hey! Hi! Aren't you Kamala Khan's brother, Aamir?
If I say yes, am I gonna get pulled into some kind of zany teenage subplot?
I don't do subplots. I'm here to a deliver a sandwich.
A what?
I'm Kamala's kosher lunch buddy.
In what way kosher?
In all ways extremely kosher.
Well, Kamala isn't here right now, but I'll make sure she gets your message. And the sandwich.
Is there, like, a number where people can reach her? Her friends are really worried. They look like they haven't slept in days and have possibly been in some fist fights.

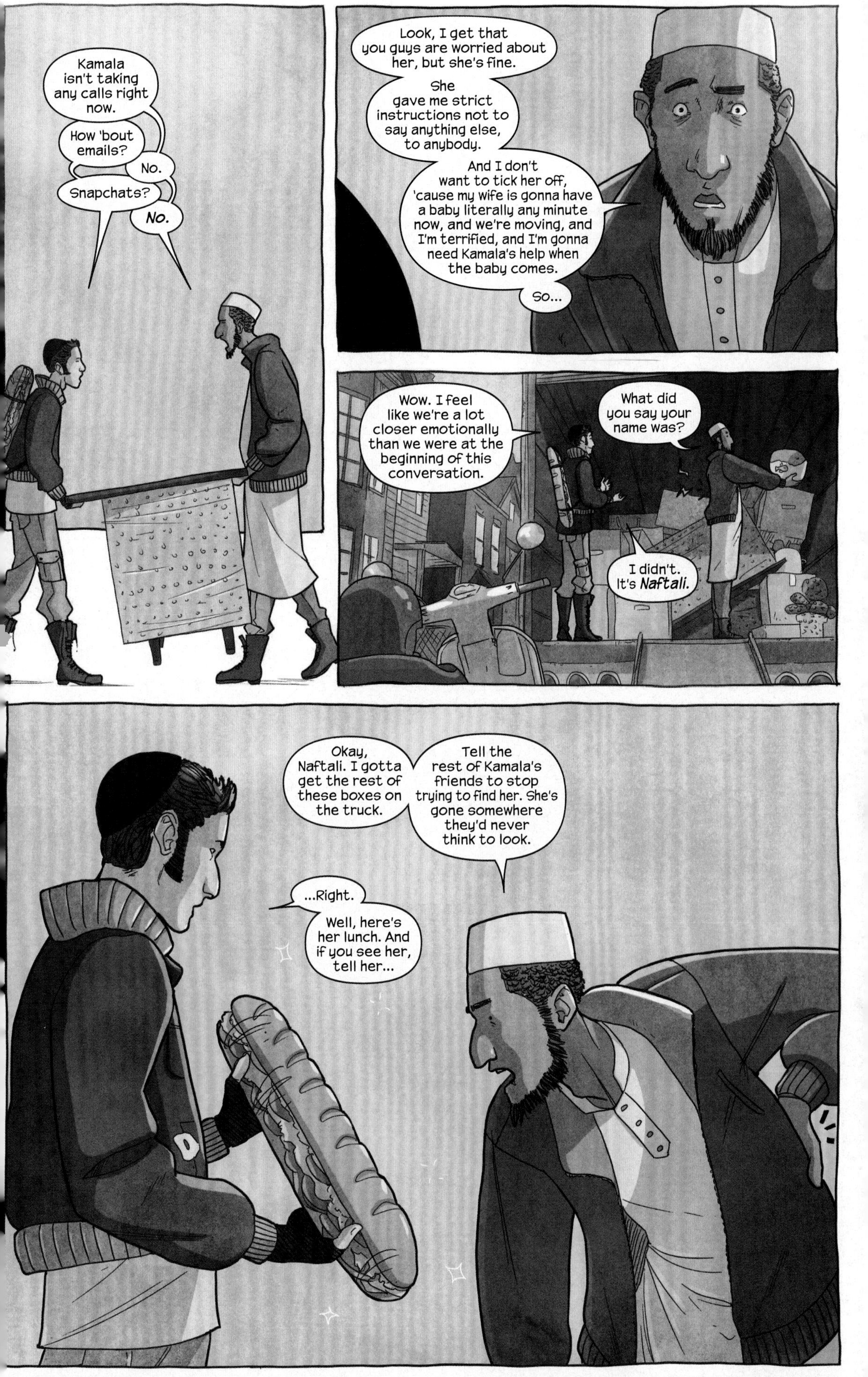
Kamala isn't taking any calls right now.
How 'bout emails?
No.
Snapchats?
No.
Look, I get that you guys are worried about her, but she's fine.
She gave me strict instructions not to say anything else, to anybody.
And I don't want to tick her off, 'cause my wife is gonna have a baby literally any minute now, and we're moving, and I'm terrified, and I'm gonna need Kamala's help when the baby comes.
So...
Wow. I feel like we're a lot closer emotionally than we were at the beginning of this conversation.
What did you say your name was?
I didn't. It's *Naftali.*
Okay, Naftali. I gotta get the rest of these boxes on the truck.
Tell the rest of Kamala's friends to stop trying to find her. She's gone somewhere they'd never think to look.
...Right.
Well, here's her lunch. And if you see her, tell her...

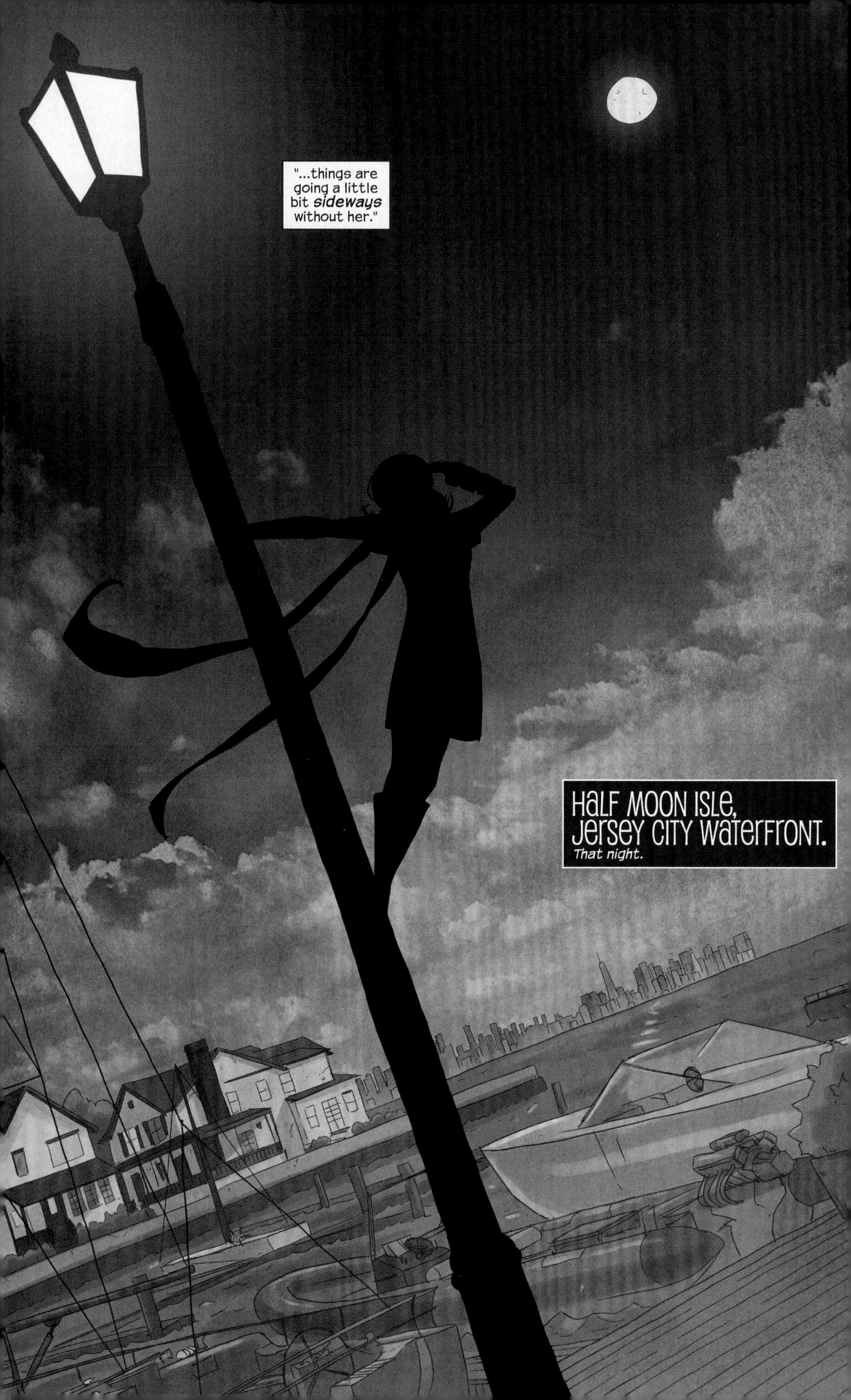
"...things are going a little bit *sideways* without her."
HALF MOON ISLE, JERSEY CITY WATERFRONT.
That night.

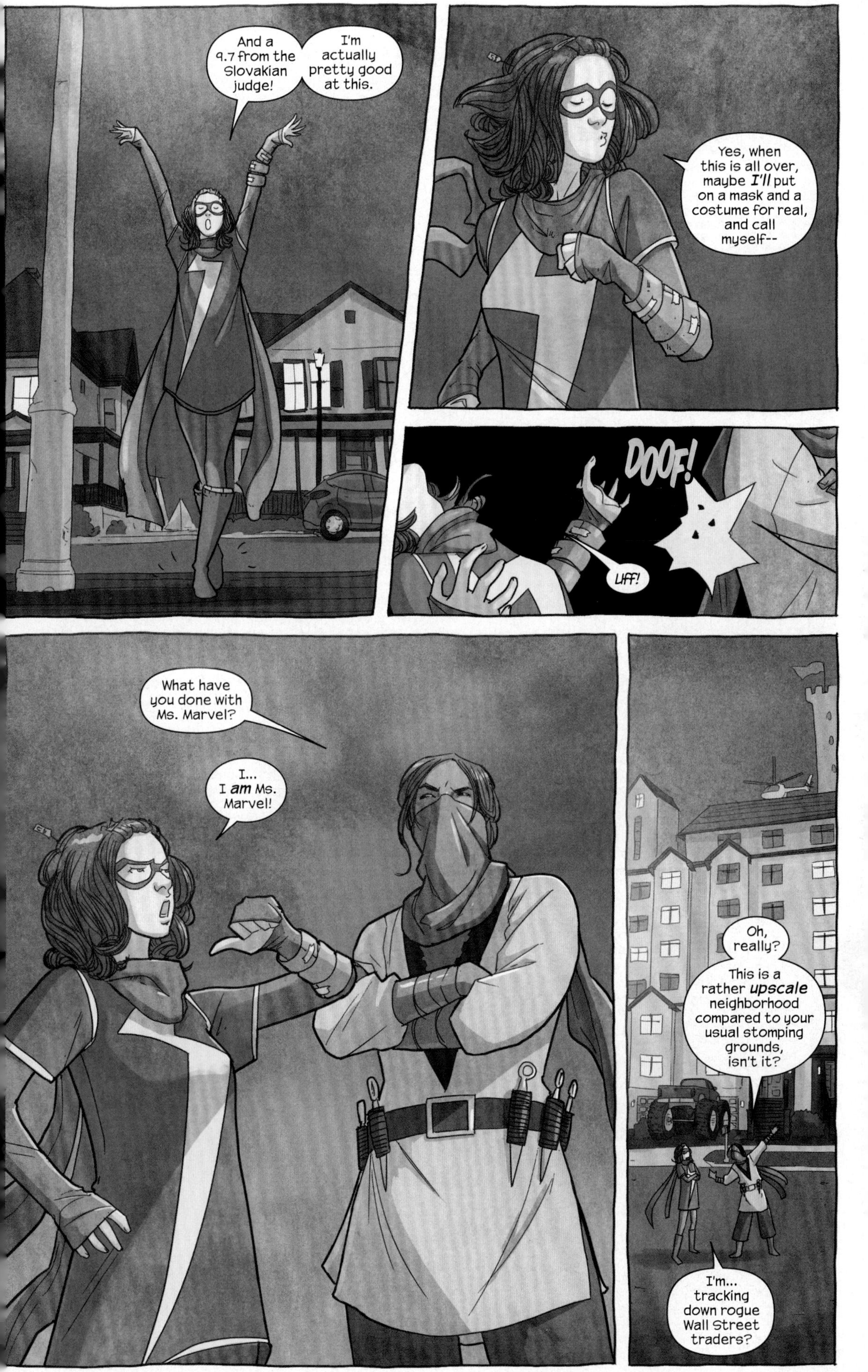
And a 9.7 from the Slovakian judge!
I'm actually pretty good at this.
Yes, when this is all over, maybe *I'll* put on a mask and a costume for real, and call myself--
DOOF!
UFF!
What have you done with Ms. Marvel?
I... I *am* Ms. Marvel!
Oh, really?
This is a rather *upscale* neighborhood compared to your usual stomping grounds, isn't it?
I'm... tracking down rogue Wall Street traders?

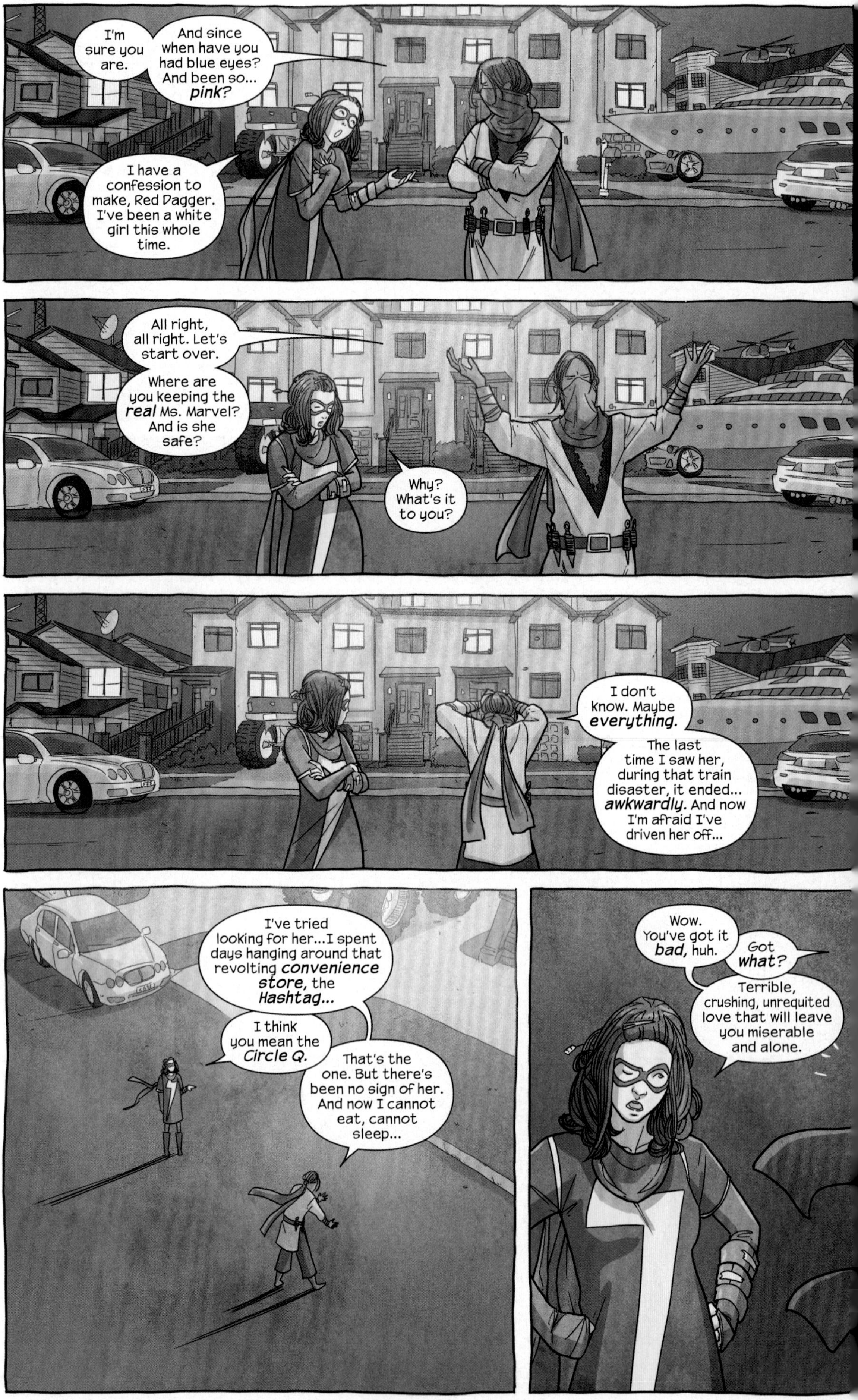
I'm sure you are.
And since when have you had blue eyes? And been so... pink?
I have a confession to make, Red Dagger. I've been a white girl this whole time.
All right, all right. Let's start over.
Where are you keeping the real Ms. Marvel? And is she safe?
Why? What's it to you?
I don't know. Maybe everything.
The last time I saw her, during that train disaster, it ended... awkwardly. And now I'm afraid I've driven her off...
I've tried looking for her...I spent days hanging around that revolting convenience store, the Hashtag...
I think you mean the Circle Q.
That's the one. But there's been no sign of her. And now I cannot eat, cannot sleep...
Wow. You've got it bad, huh.
Got what?
Terrible, crushing, unrequited love that will leave you miserable and alone.

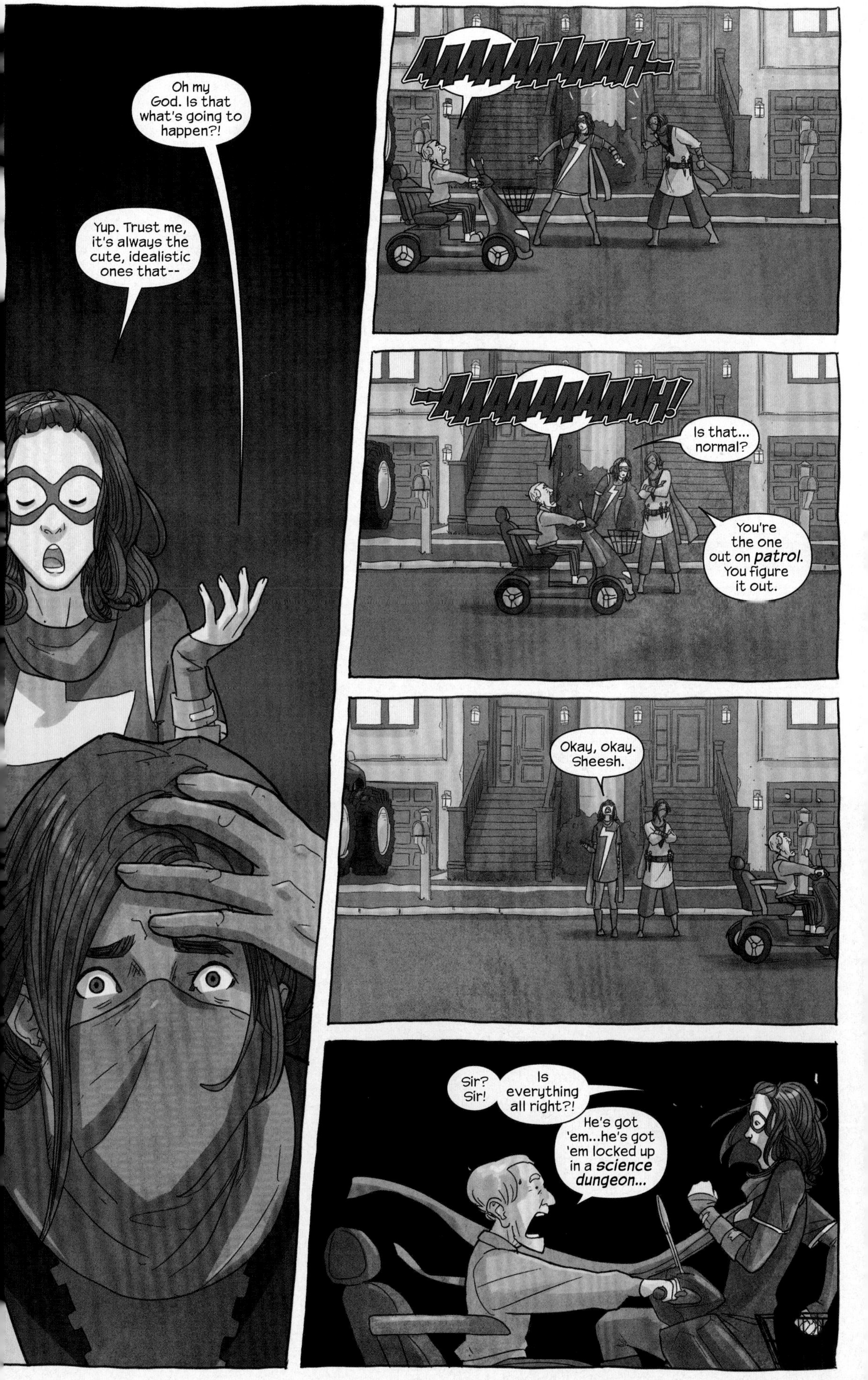
Oh my God. Is that what's going to happen?!
Yup. Trust me, it's always the cute, idealistic ones that--
AAAAAAAAAH--
-AAAAAAAAAH!
Is that... normal?
You're the one out on *patrol*. You figure it out.
Okay, okay. Sheesh.
Sir? Sir!
Is everything all right?!
He's got 'em...he's got 'em locked up in a *science dungeon...*

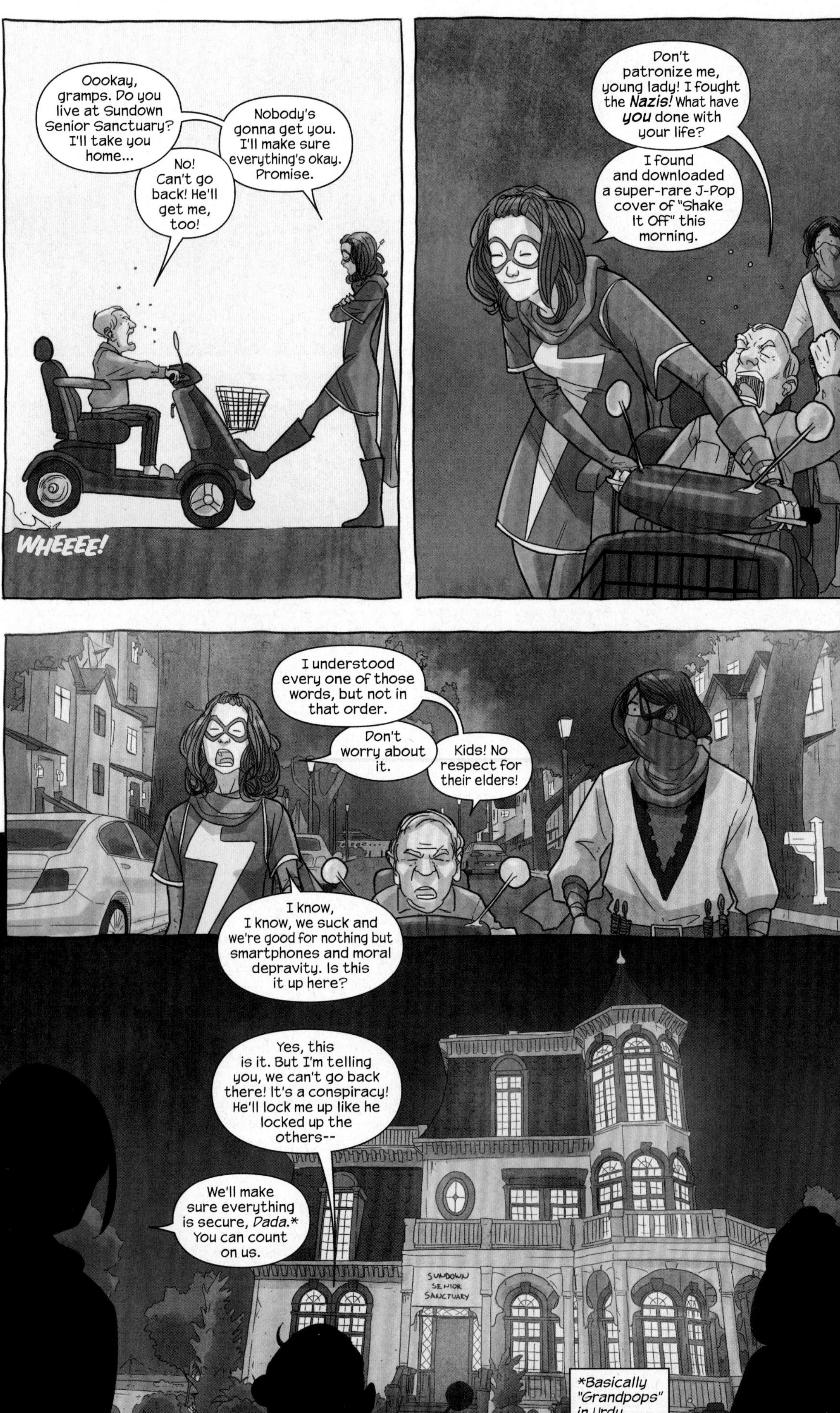
Oookay, gramps. Do you live at Sundown Senior Sanctuary? I'll take you home...
No! Can't go back! He'll get me, too!
Nobody's gonna get you. I'll make sure everything's okay. Promise.
WHEEEE!
Don't patronize me, young lady! I fought the Nazis! What have you done with your life?
I found and downloaded a super-rare J-Pop cover of "Shake It Off" this morning.
I understood every one of those words, but not in that order.
Don't worry about it.
Kids! No respect for their elders!
I know, I know, we suck and we're good for nothing but smartphones and moral depravity. Is this it up here?
Yes, this is it. But I'm telling you, we can't go back there! It's a conspiracy! He'll lock me up like he locked up the others--
We'll make sure everything is secure, Dada.* You can count on us.
SUNDOWN SENIOR SANCTUARY
*Basically "Grandpops" in Urdu.

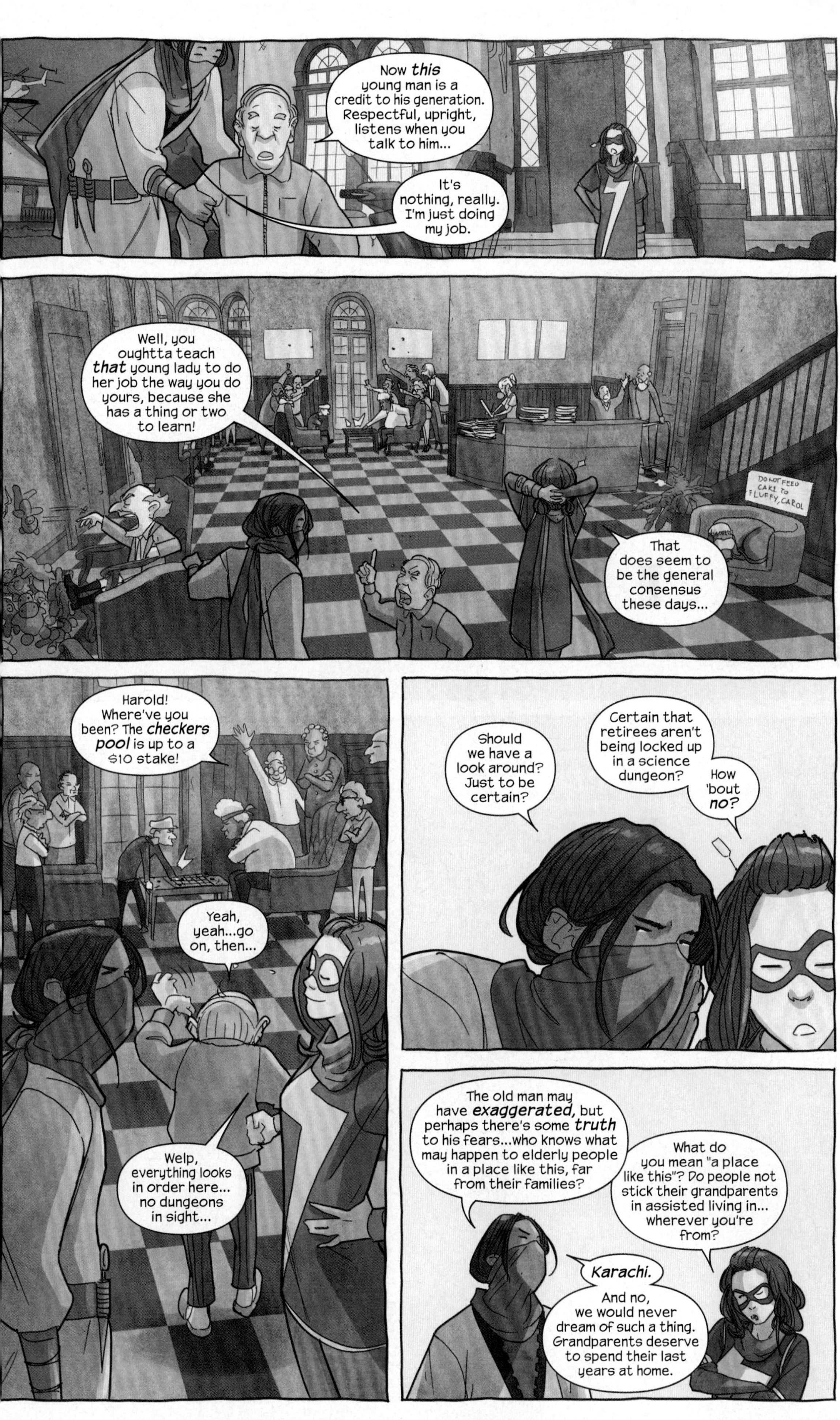

Now this young man is a credit to his generation. Respectful, upright, listens when you talk to him...
It's nothing, really. I'm just doing my job.
Well, you oughtta teach that young lady to do her job the way you do yours, because she has a thing or two to learn!
That does seem to be the general consensus these days...
DO NOT FEED CAKE TO FLUFFY, CAROL
Harold! Where've you been? The checkers pool is up to a $10 stake!
Yeah, yeah...go on, then...
Welp, everything looks in order here... no dungeons in sight...
Should we have a look around? Just to be certain?
Certain that retirees aren't being locked up in a science dungeon?
How 'bout no?
The old man may have exaggerated, but perhaps there's some truth to his fears...who knows what may happen to elderly people in a place like this, far from their families?
What do you mean "a place like this"? Do people not stick their grandparents in assisted living in... wherever you're from?
Karachi.
And no, we would never dream of such a thing. Grandparents deserve to spend their last years at home.

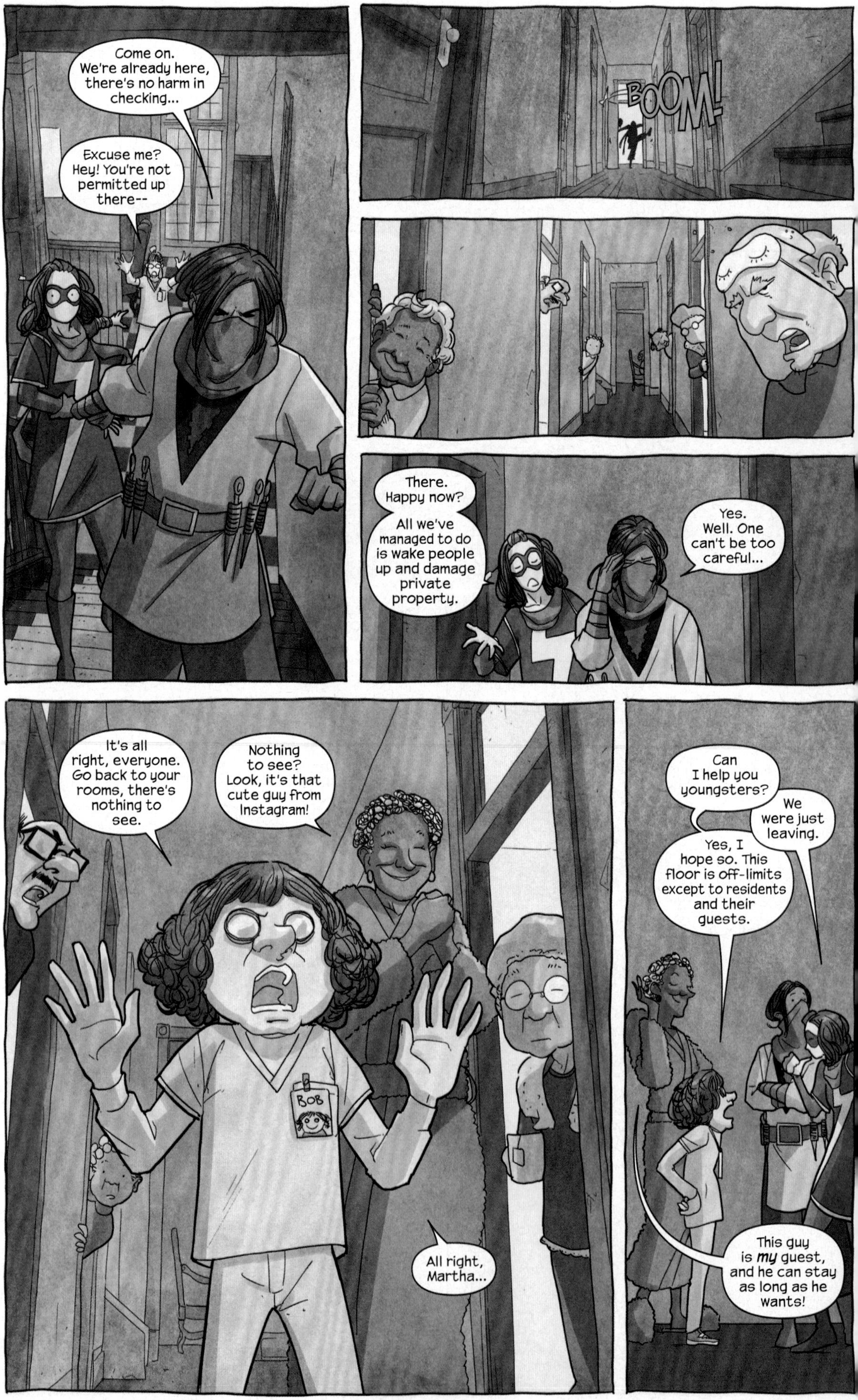
Come on. We're already here, there's no harm in checking...
Excuse me? Hey! You're not permitted up there--
BOOM!
There. Happy now?
All we've managed to do is wake people up and damage private property.
Yes. Well. One can't be too careful...
It's all right, everyone. Go back to your rooms, there's nothing to see.
Nothing to see? Look, it's that cute guy from Instagram!
BOB
All right, Martha...
Can I help you youngsters?
We were just leaving.
Yes, I hope so. This floor is off-limits except to residents and their guests.
This guy is *my* guest, and he can stay as long as he wants!

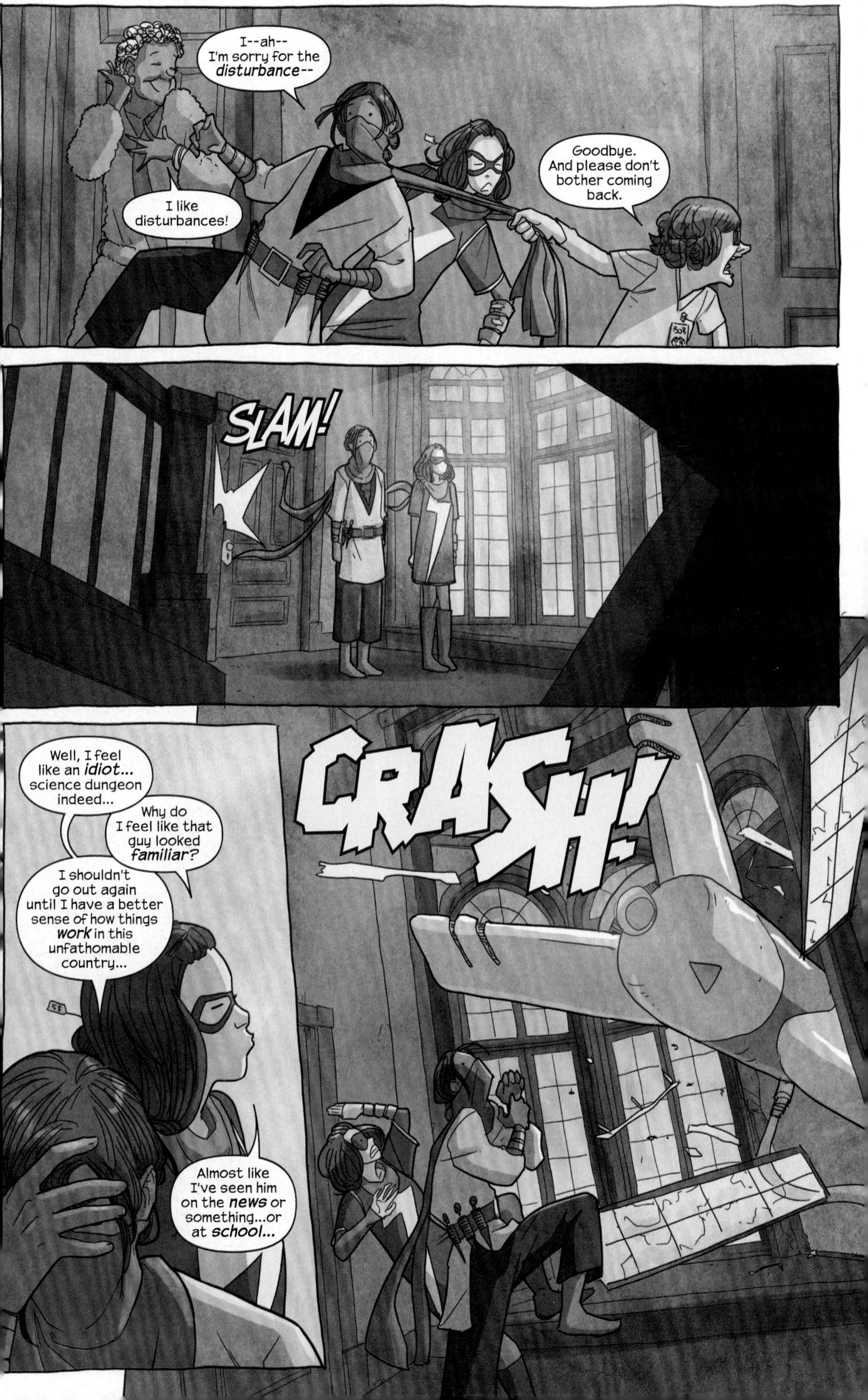
I--ah--
I'm sorry for the disturbance--
I like disturbances!
Goodbye. And please don't bother coming back.
SLAM!
CRASH!
Well, I feel like an idiot... science dungeon indeed...
Why do I feel like that guy looked familiar?
I shouldn't go out again until I have a better sense of how things work in this unfathomable country...
Almost like I've seen him on the news or something...or at school...

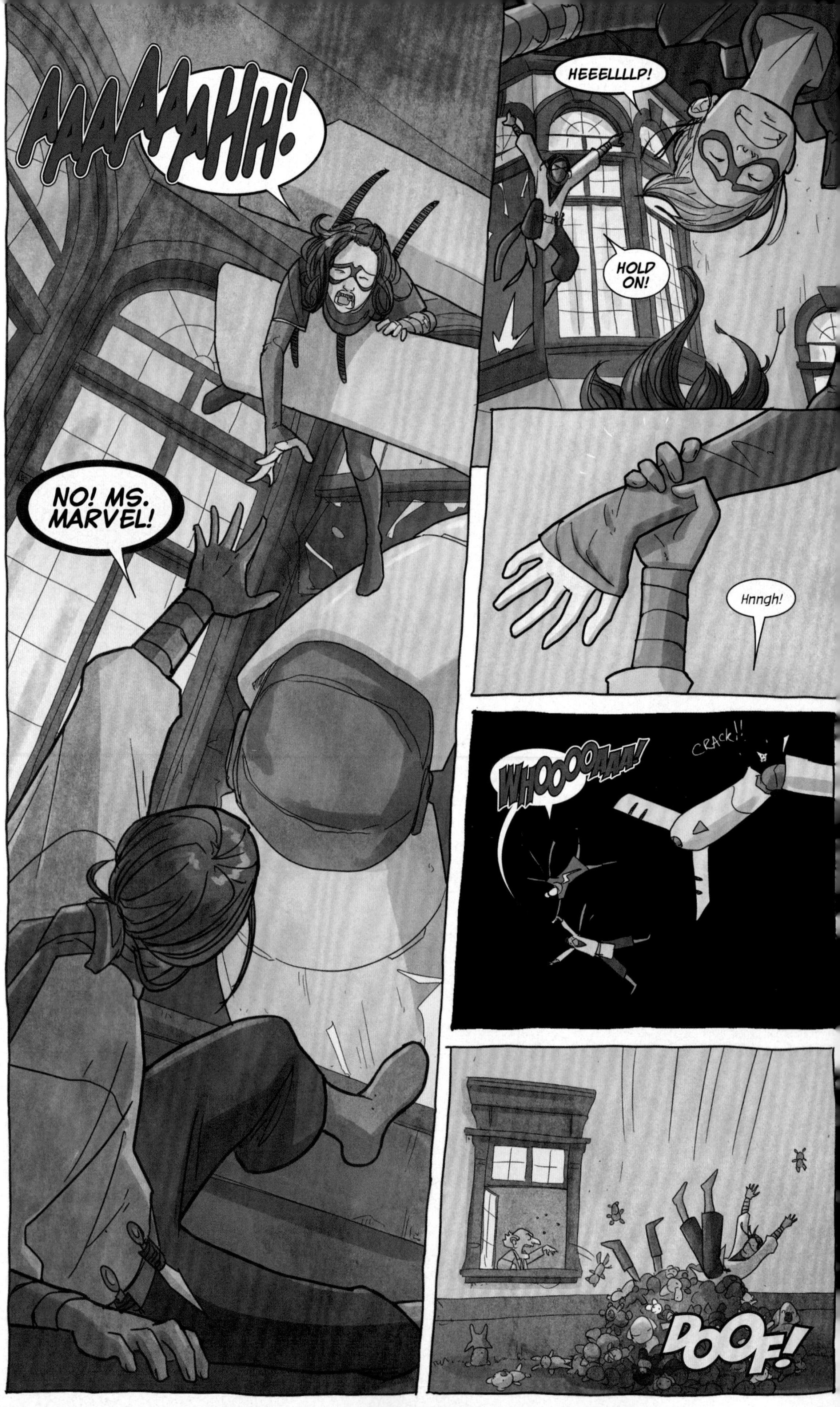
AAAAAAHH!
NO! MS. MARVEL!
HEEELLLLP!
HOLD ON!
Hnngh!
WHOOOOAAA!
CRACK!!
DOOF!

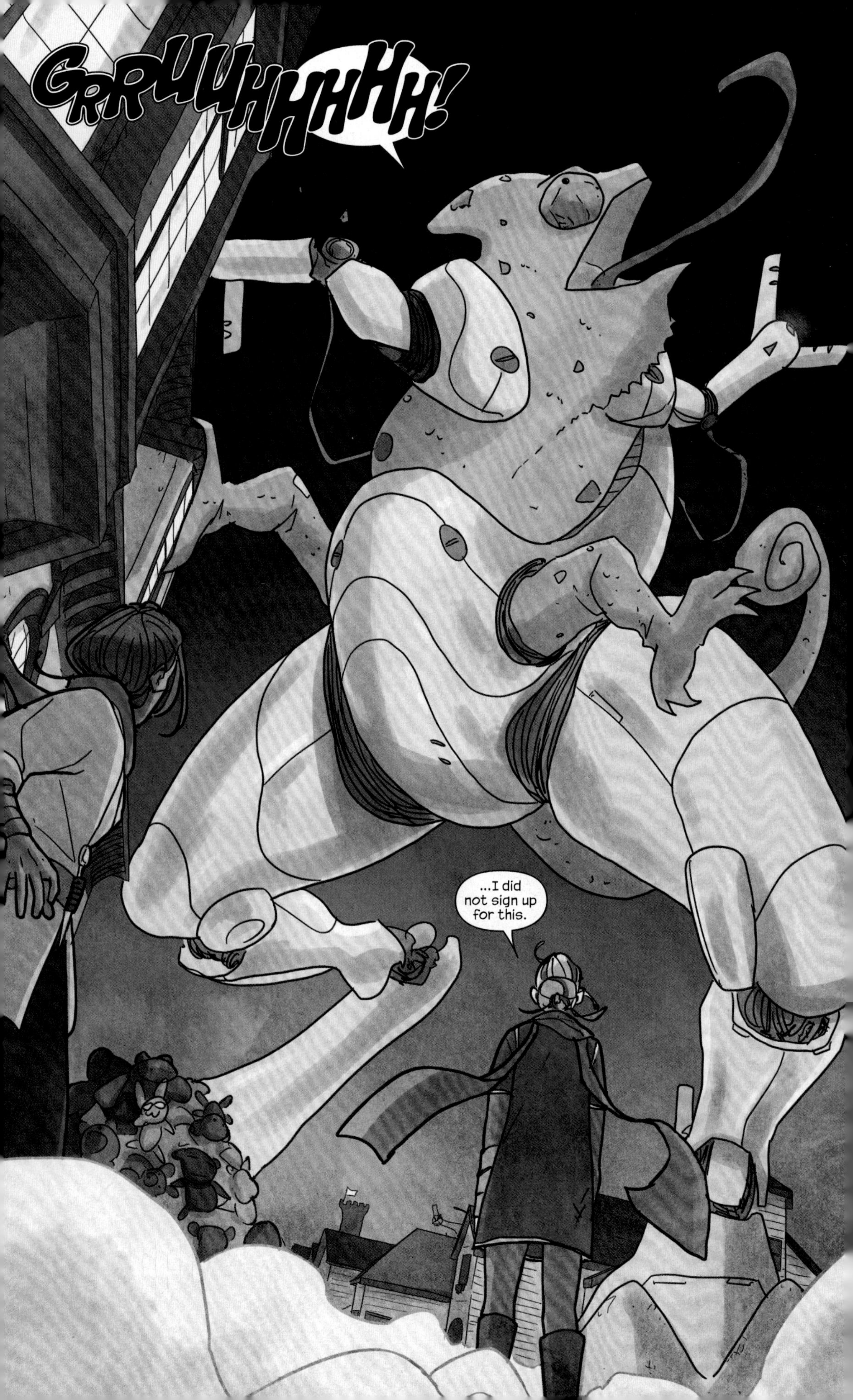
GRRUUHHHHHH!
...I did not sign up for this.

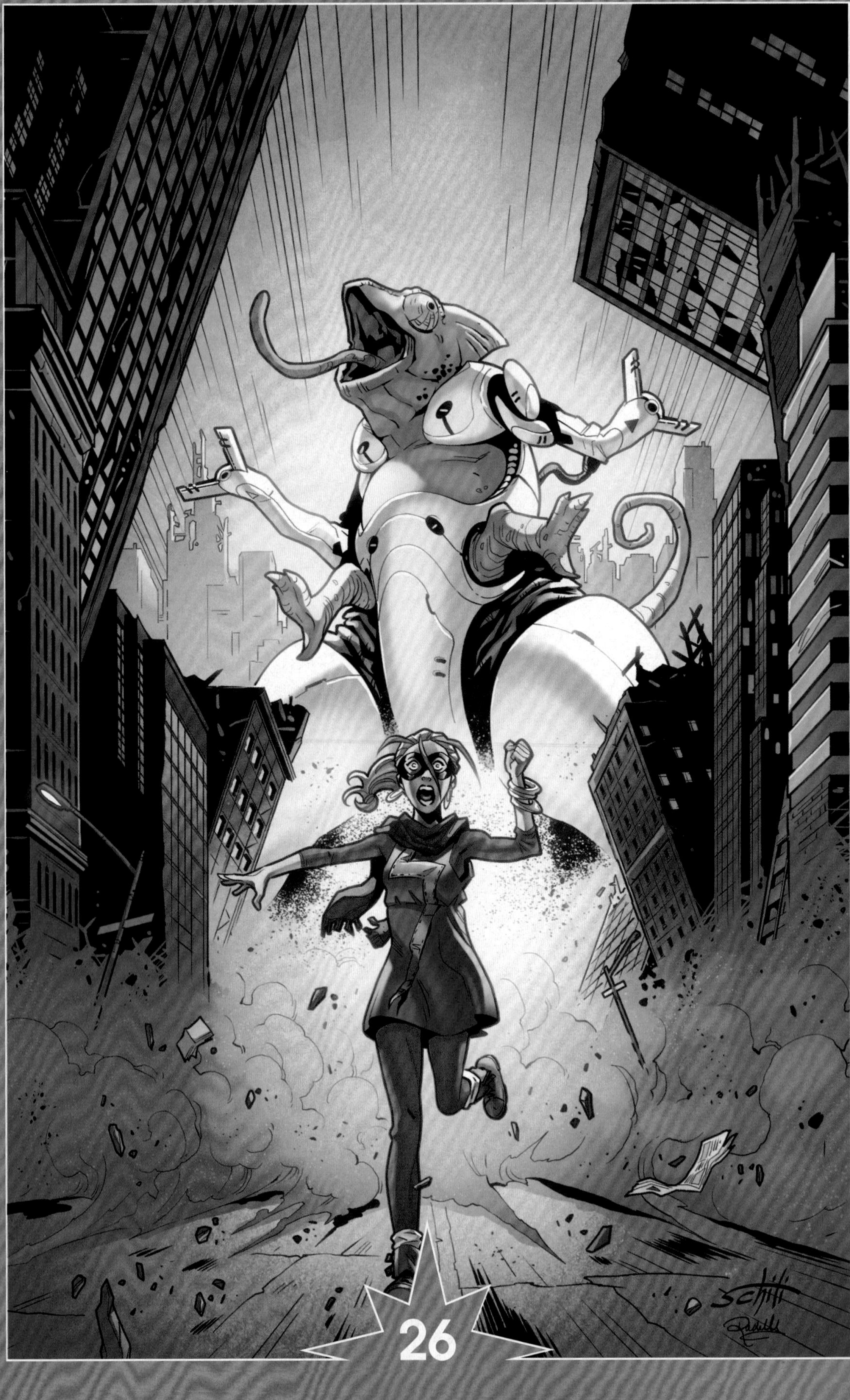

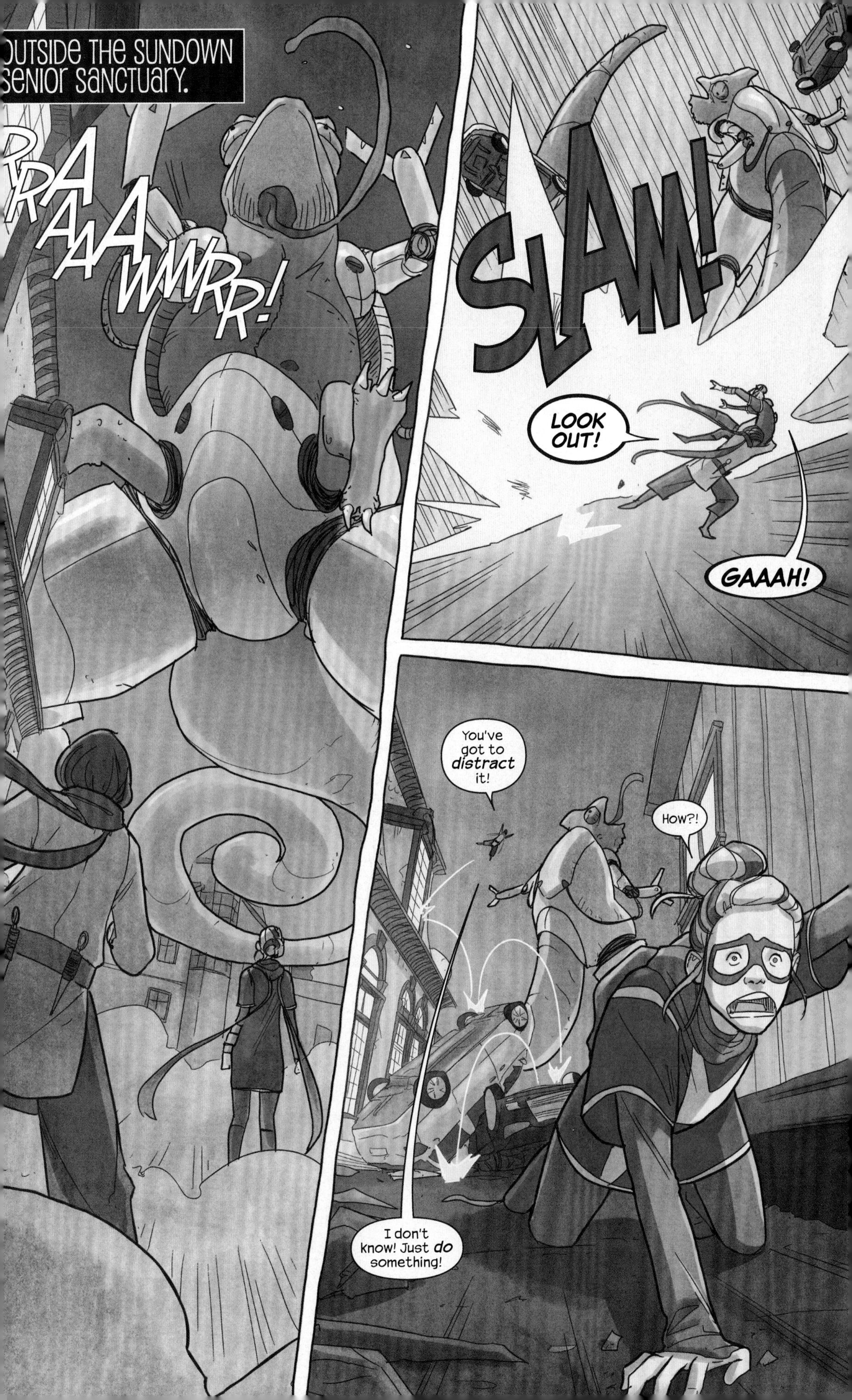
OUTSIDE THE SUNDOWN SENIOR SANCTUARY.
RRAAAAWWRRR!
SLAM!
LOOK OUT!
GAAAH!
You've got to distract it!
How?!
I don't know! Just do something!

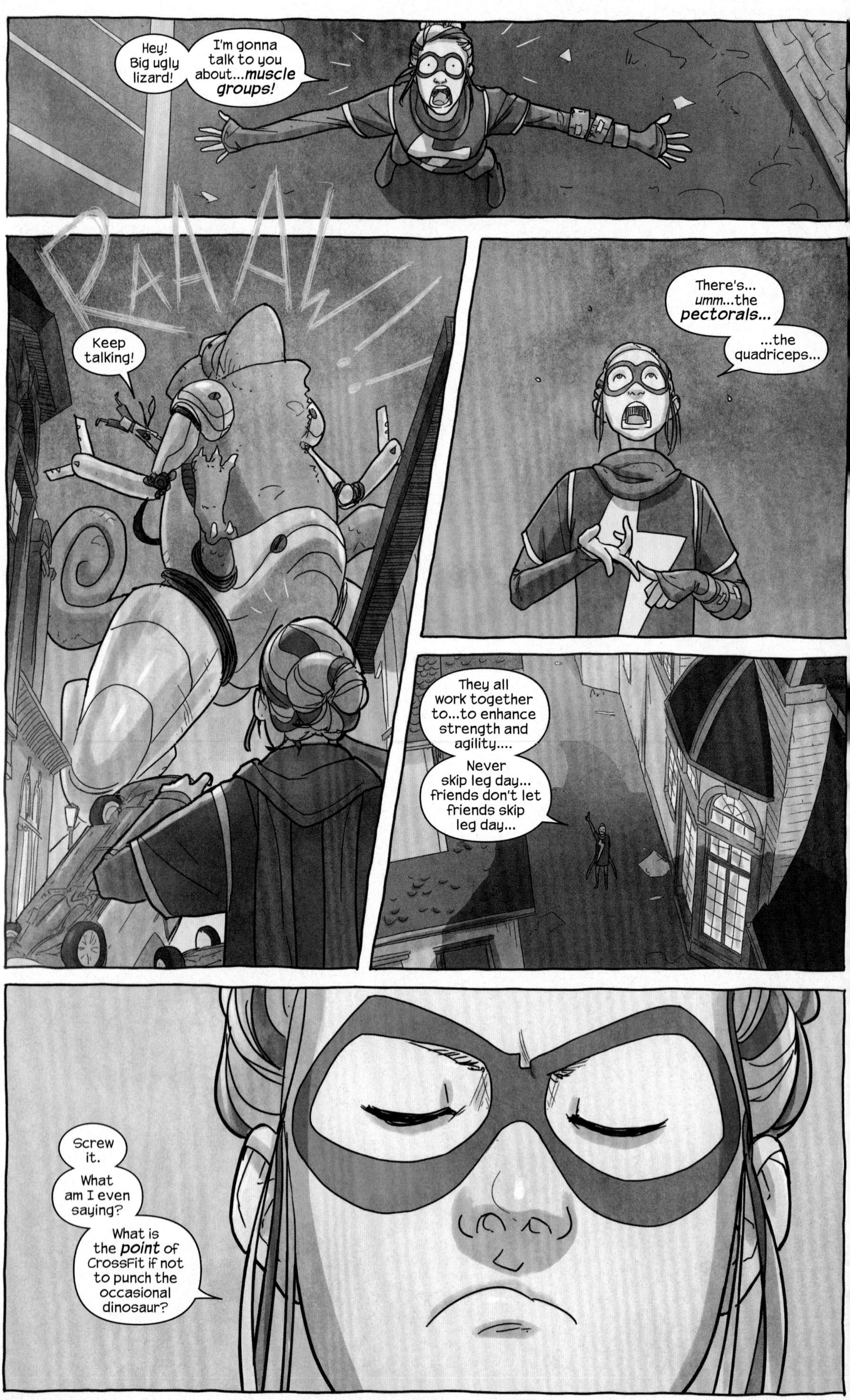
Hey! Big ugly lizard!
I'm gonna talk to you about...*muscle groups!*
RAAAW
Keep talking!
There's... *umm*...the *pectorals...*
...the quadriceps...
They all work together to...to enhance strength and agility....
Never skip leg day... friends don't let friends skip leg day...
Screw it.
What am I even saying?
What is the *point* of CrossFit if not to punch the occasional dinosaur?

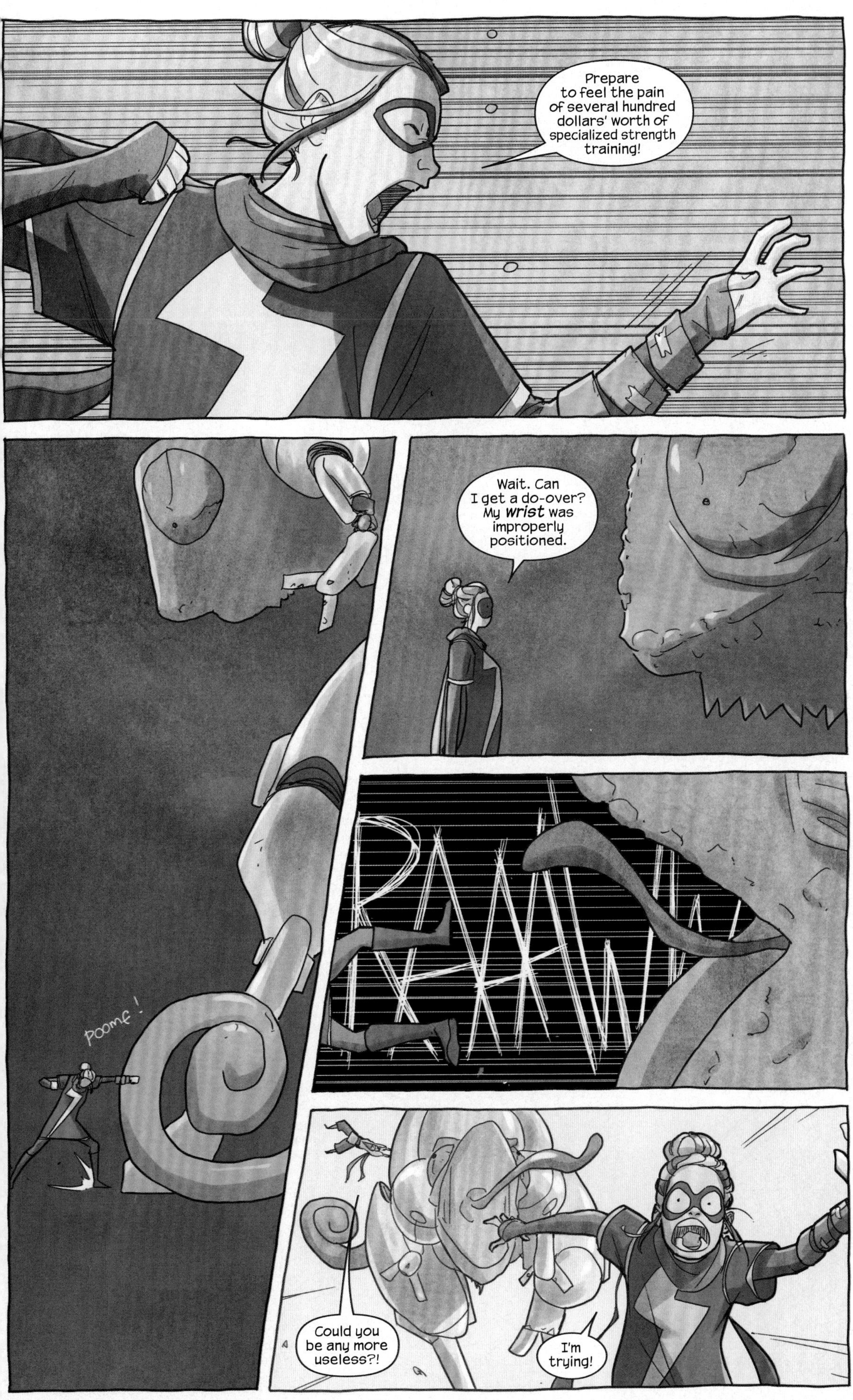
Prepare to feel the pain of several hundred dollars' worth of specialized strength training!
Wait. Can I get a do-over? My wrist was improperly positioned.
POOMF!
RAAWR
Could you be any more useless?!
I'm trying!

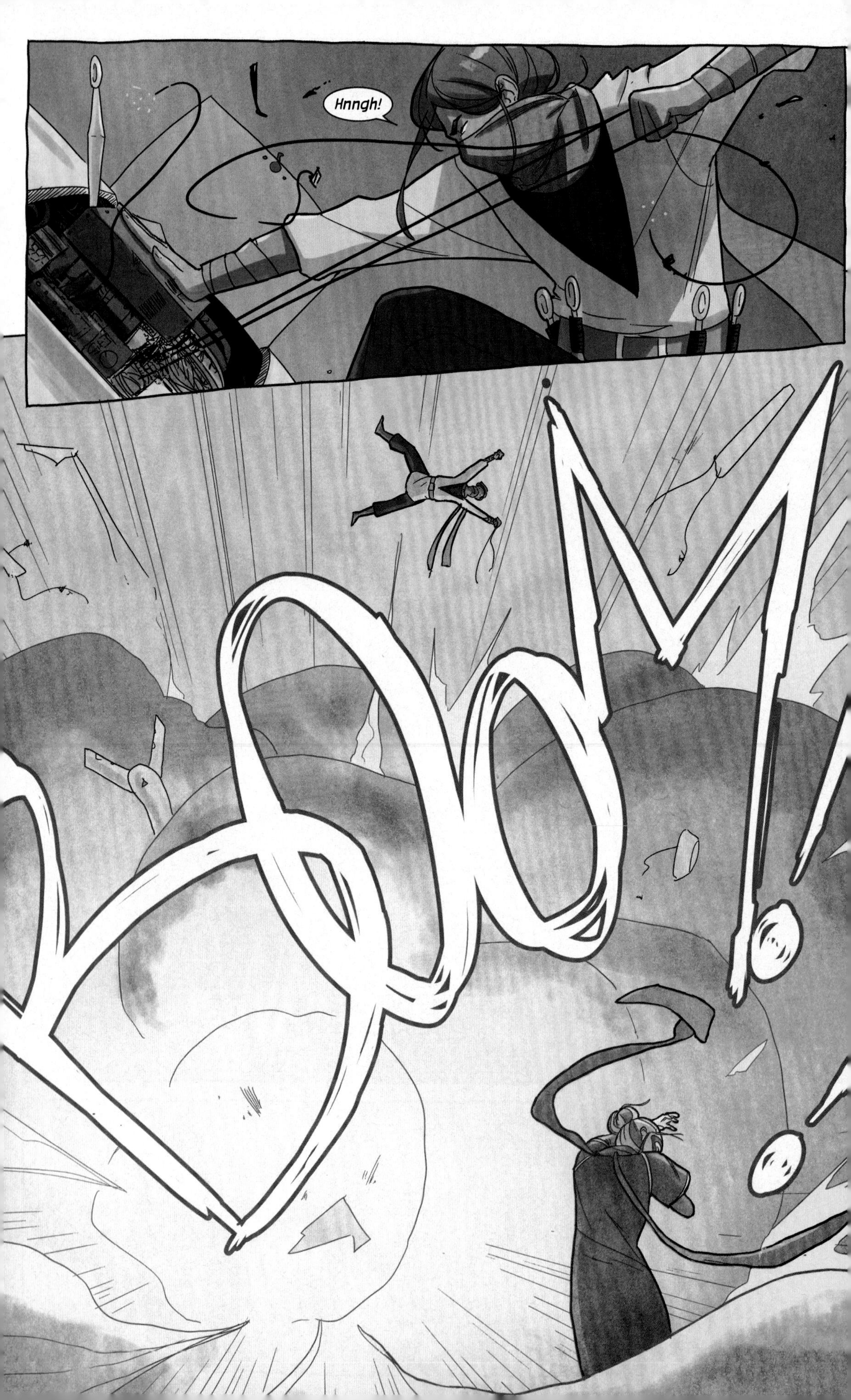
Hnngh!
BOOOM!!

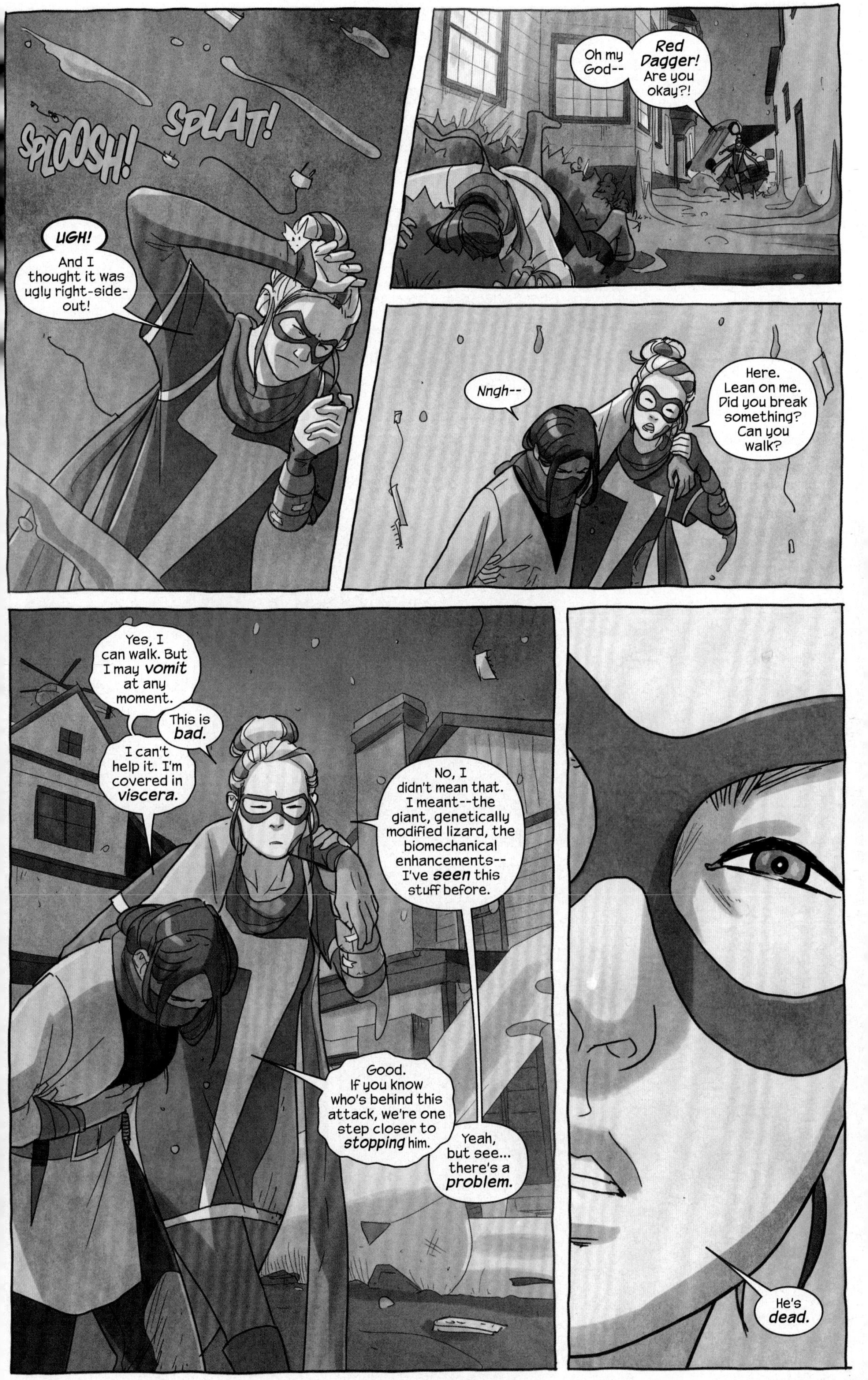
SPLOOSH!
SPLAT!
UGH! And I thought it was ugly right-side-out!
Oh my God--
Red Dagger! Are you okay?!
Nngh--
Here. Lean on me. Did you break something? Can you walk?
Yes, I can walk. But I may vomit at any moment.
This is bad.
I can't help it. I'm covered in viscera.
No, I didn't mean that. I meant--the giant, genetically modified lizard, the biomechanical enhancements-- I've seen this stuff before.
Good. If you know who's behind this attack, we're one step closer to stopping him.
Yeah, but see... there's a problem.
He's dead.

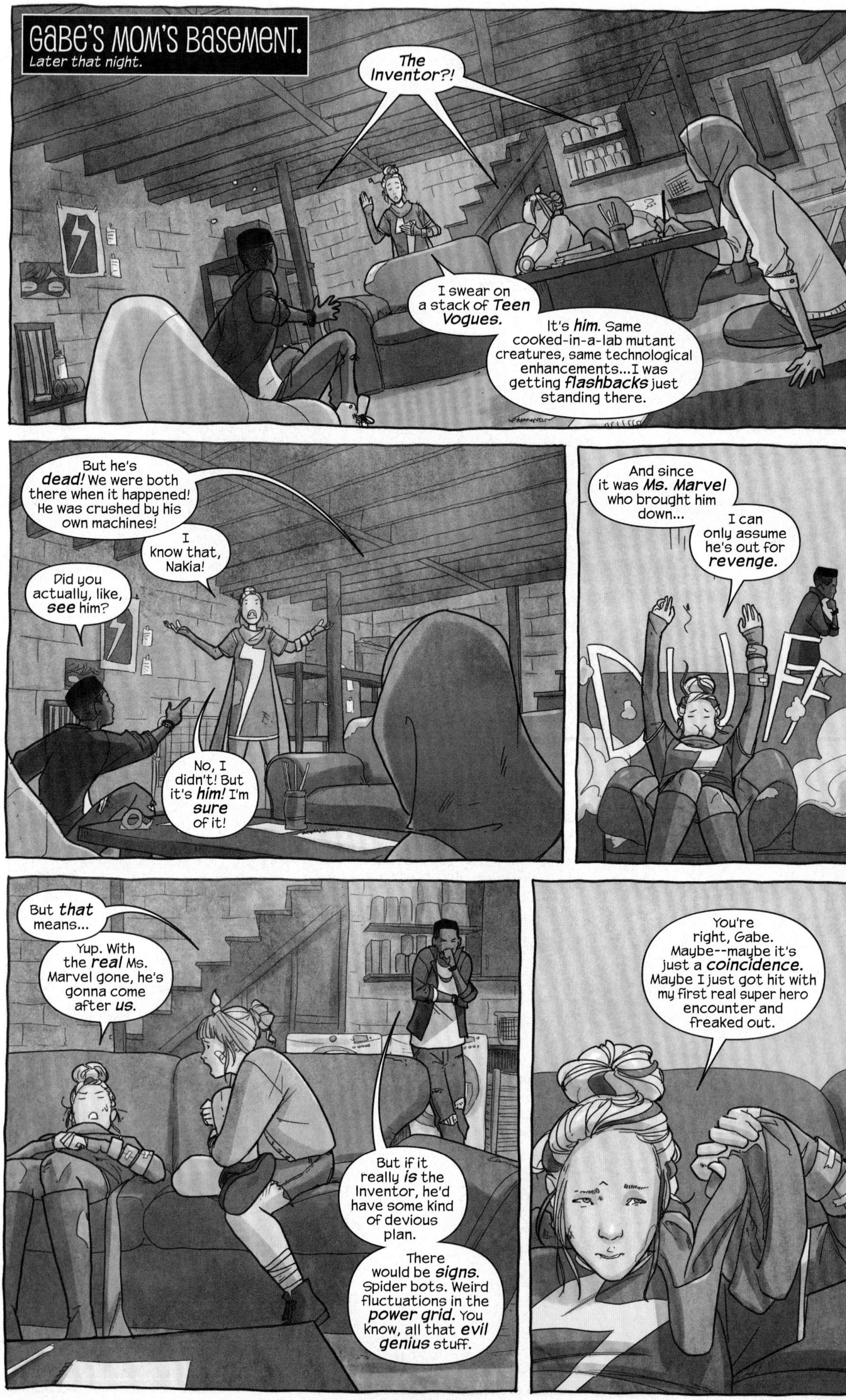

GABE'S MOM'S BASEMENT.
Later that night.
The Inventor?!
I swear on a stack of Teen Vogues.
It's him. Same cooked-in-a-lab mutant creatures, same technological enhancements...I was getting flashbacks just standing there.
But he's dead! We were both there when it happened! He was crushed by his own machines!
I know that, Nakia!
Did you actually, like, see him?
No, I didn't! But it's him! I'm sure of it!
And since it was Ms. Marvel who brought him down...
I can only assume he's out for revenge.
DUFF
But that means...
Yup. With the real Ms. Marvel gone, he's gonna come after us.
But if it really is the Inventor, he'd have some kind of devious plan.
There would be signs. Spider bots. Weird fluctuations in the power grid. You know, all that evil genius stuff.
You're right, Gabe. Maybe--maybe it's just a coincidence. Maybe I just got hit with my first real super hero encounter and freaked out.

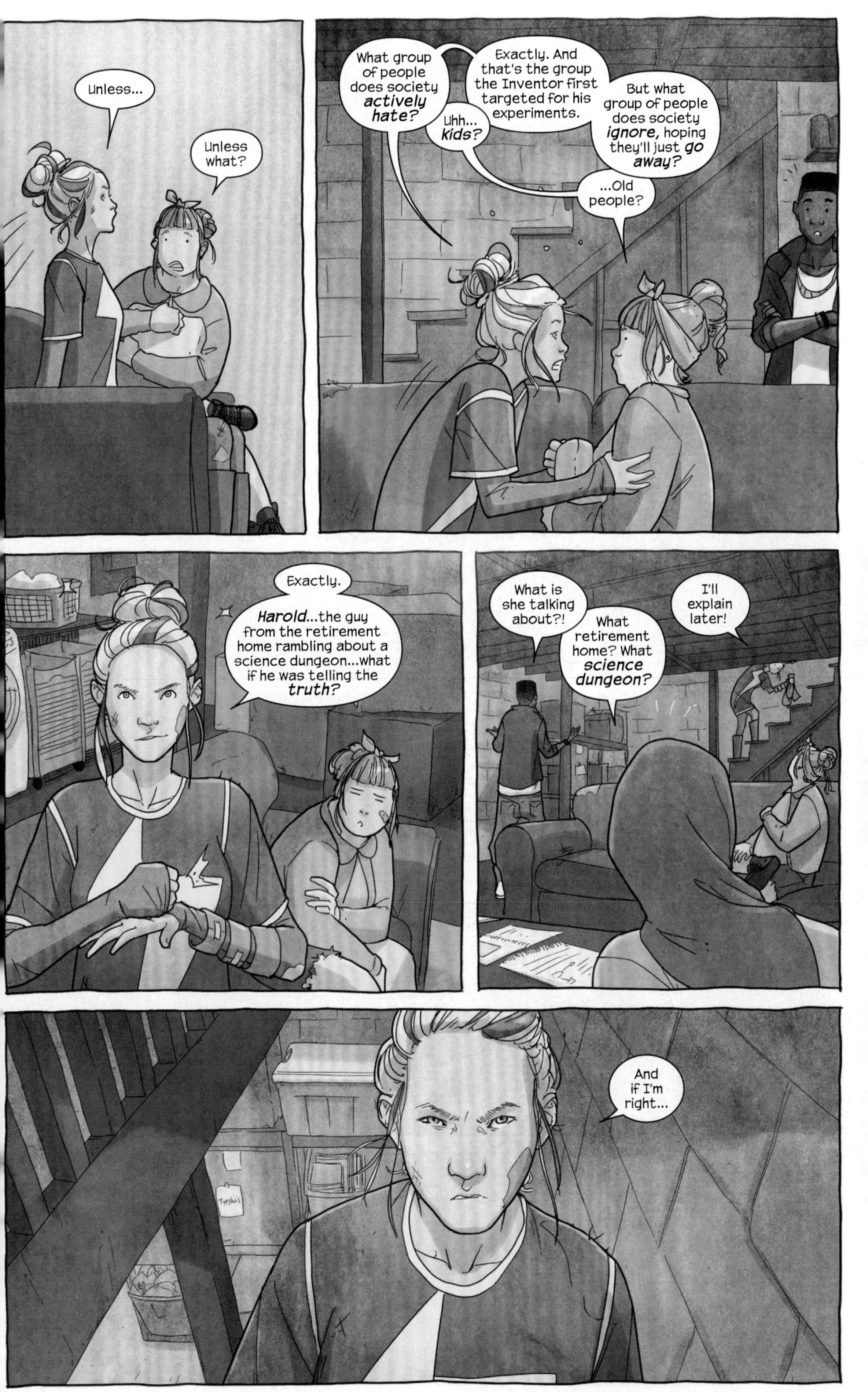
Unless...
Unless what?
What group of people does society *actively hate?*
Uhh... *kids?*
Exactly. And that's the group the Inventor first targeted for his experiments.
But what group of people does society *ignore,* hoping they'll just *go away?*
...Old people?
Exactly.
Harold...the guy from the retirement home rambling about a science dungeon...what if he was telling the *truth?*
What is she talking about?!
What retirement home? What *science dungeon?*
I'll explain later!
And if I'm right...

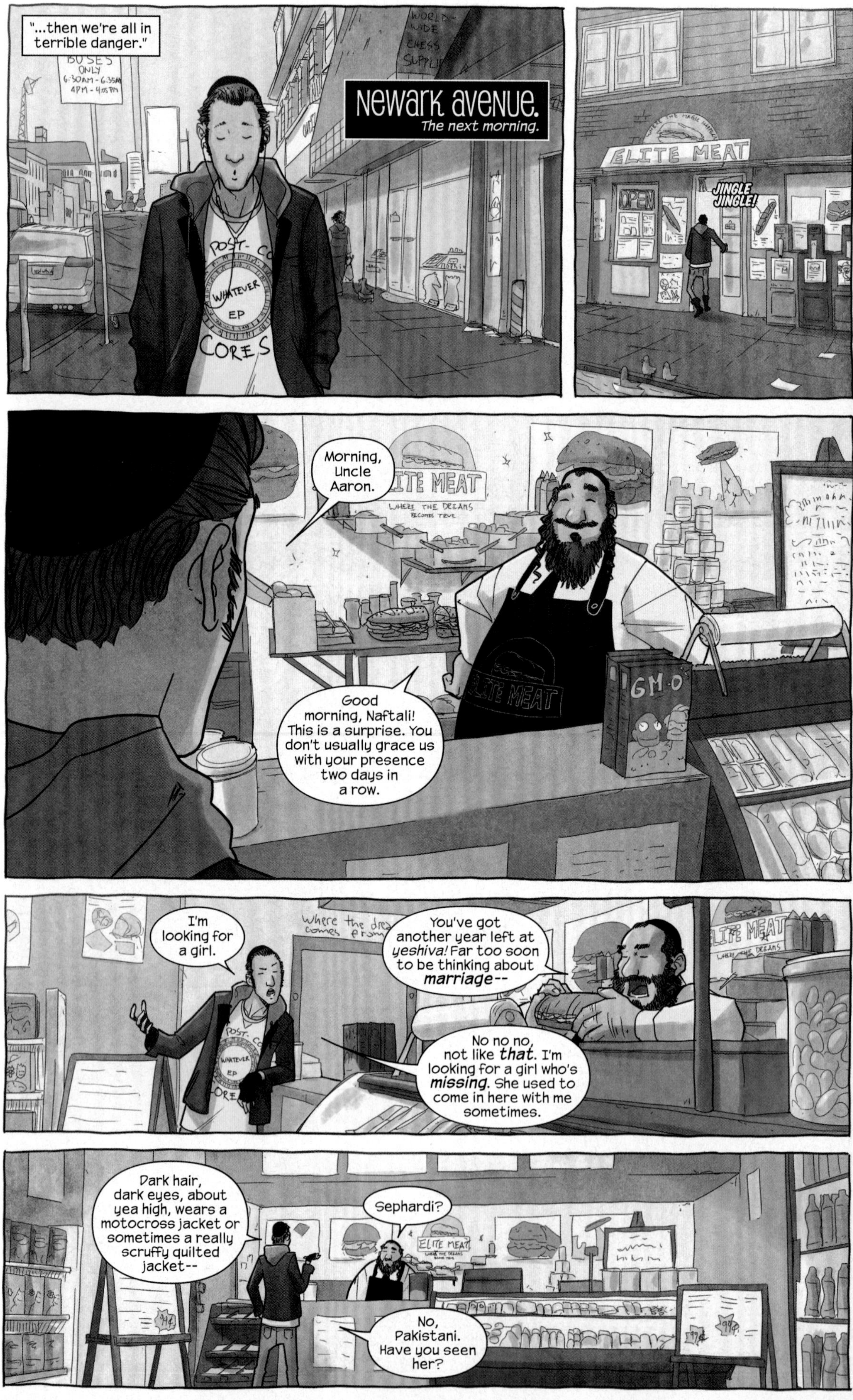
"...then we're all in terrible danger."
BUSES ONLY 6:30AM - 6:35AM 4PM - 4:05PM
WORLD-WIDE CHESS SUPPLIES
Newark avenue.
The next morning.
POST-CO WHATEVER EP CORES
ELITE MEAT
OPEN
JINGLE JINGLE!
Morning, Uncle Aaron.
ELITE MEAT
WHERE THE DREAMS BECOMES TRUE
Good morning, Naftali! This is a surprise. You don't usually grace us with your presence two days in a row.
ELITE MEAT
GMO
I'm looking for a girl.
You've got another year left at *yeshiva!* Far too soon to be thinking about ***marriage***--
No no no, not like ***that***. I'm looking for a girl who's ***missing***. She used to come in here with me sometimes.
Dark hair, dark eyes, about yea high, wears a motocross jacket or sometimes a really scruffy quilted jacket--
Sephardi?
No, Pakistani. Have you seen her?

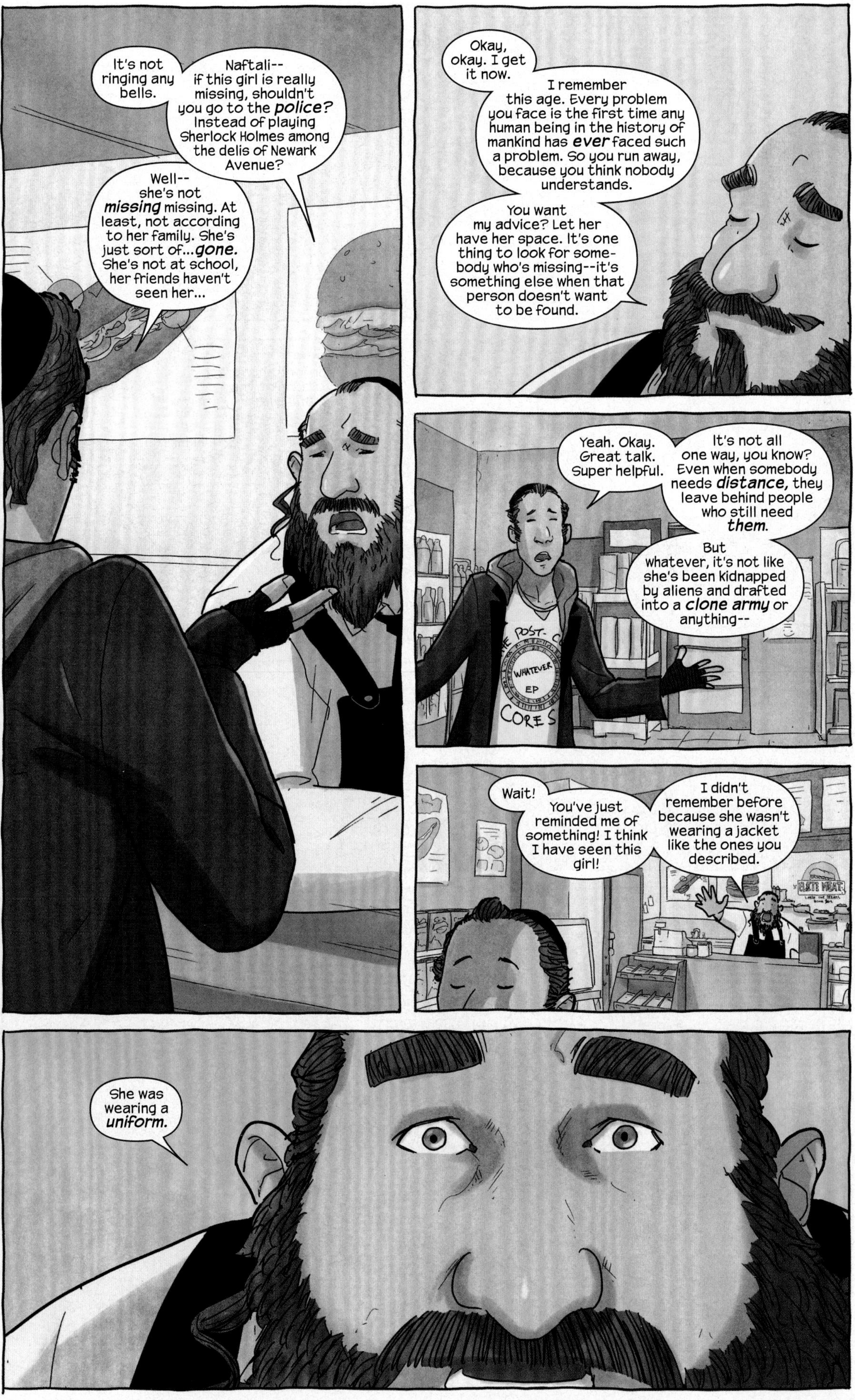
It's not ringing any bells.
Naftali-- if this girl is really missing, shouldn't you go to the **police?** Instead of playing Sherlock Holmes among the delis of Newark Avenue?
Well-- she's not **missing** missing. At least, not according to her family. She's just sort of...**gone.** She's not at school, her friends haven't seen her...
Okay, okay. I get it now.
I remember this age. Every problem you face is the first time any human being in the history of mankind has **ever** faced such a problem. So you run away, because you think nobody understands.
You want my advice? Let her have her space. It's one thing to look for somebody who's missing--it's something else when that person doesn't want to be found.
Yeah. Okay. Great talk. Super helpful.
It's not all one way, you know? Even when somebody needs **distance,** they leave behind people who still need **them.**
But whatever, it's not like she's been kidnapped by aliens and drafted into a **clone army** or anything--
WHATEVER
EP
Wait!
You've just reminded me of something! I think I have seen this girl!
I didn't remember before because she wasn't wearing a jacket like the ones you described.
She was wearing a **uniform.**

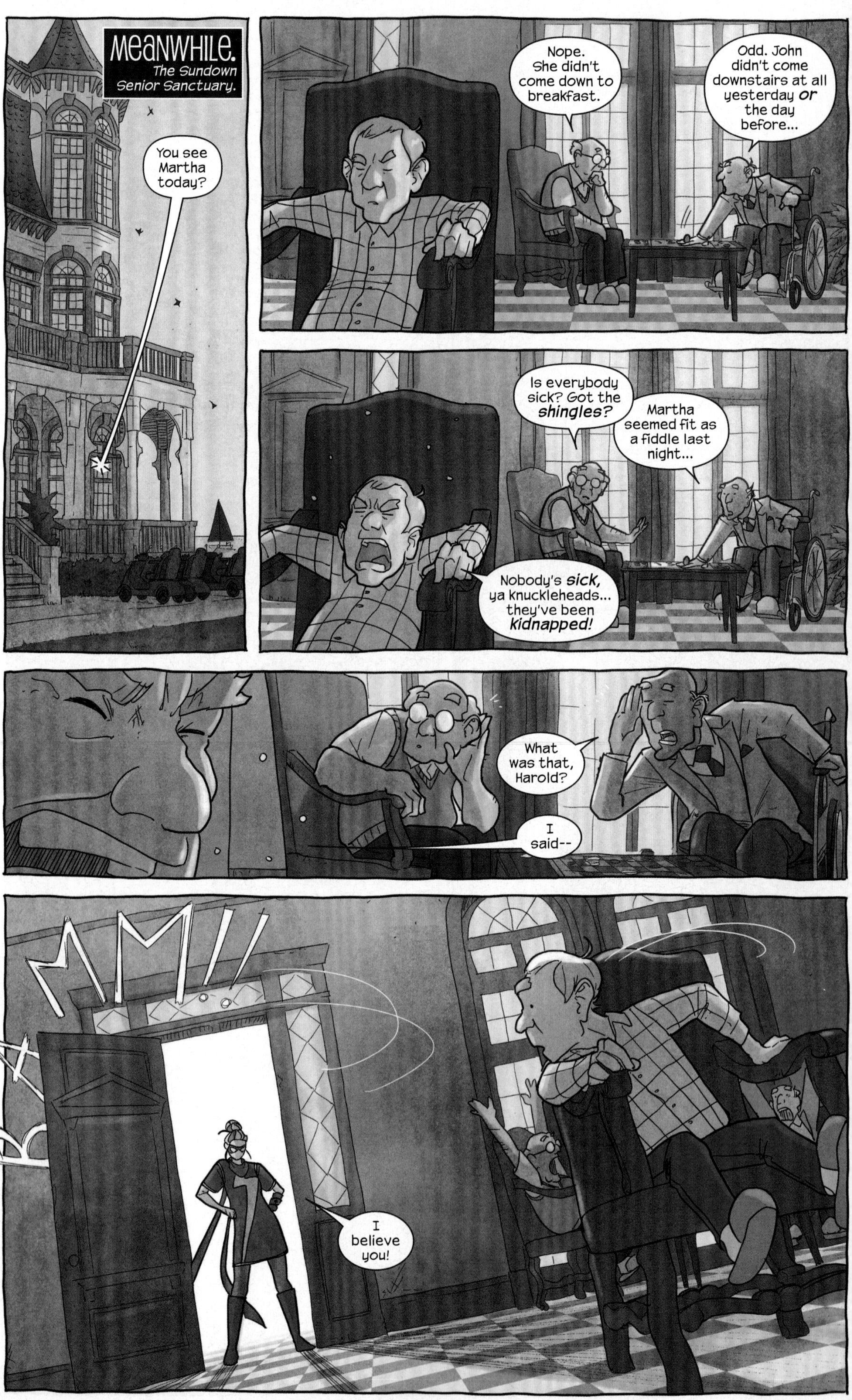
MEANWHILE.
The Sundown Senior Sanctuary.
You see Martha today?
Nope. She didn't come down to breakfast.
Odd. John didn't come downstairs at all yesterday *or* the day before...
Is everybody sick? Got the *shingles?*
Martha seemed fit as a fiddle last night...
Nobody's *sick,* ya knuckleheads... they've been *kidnapped!*
What was that, Harold?
I said--
BAMM!!
I believe you!

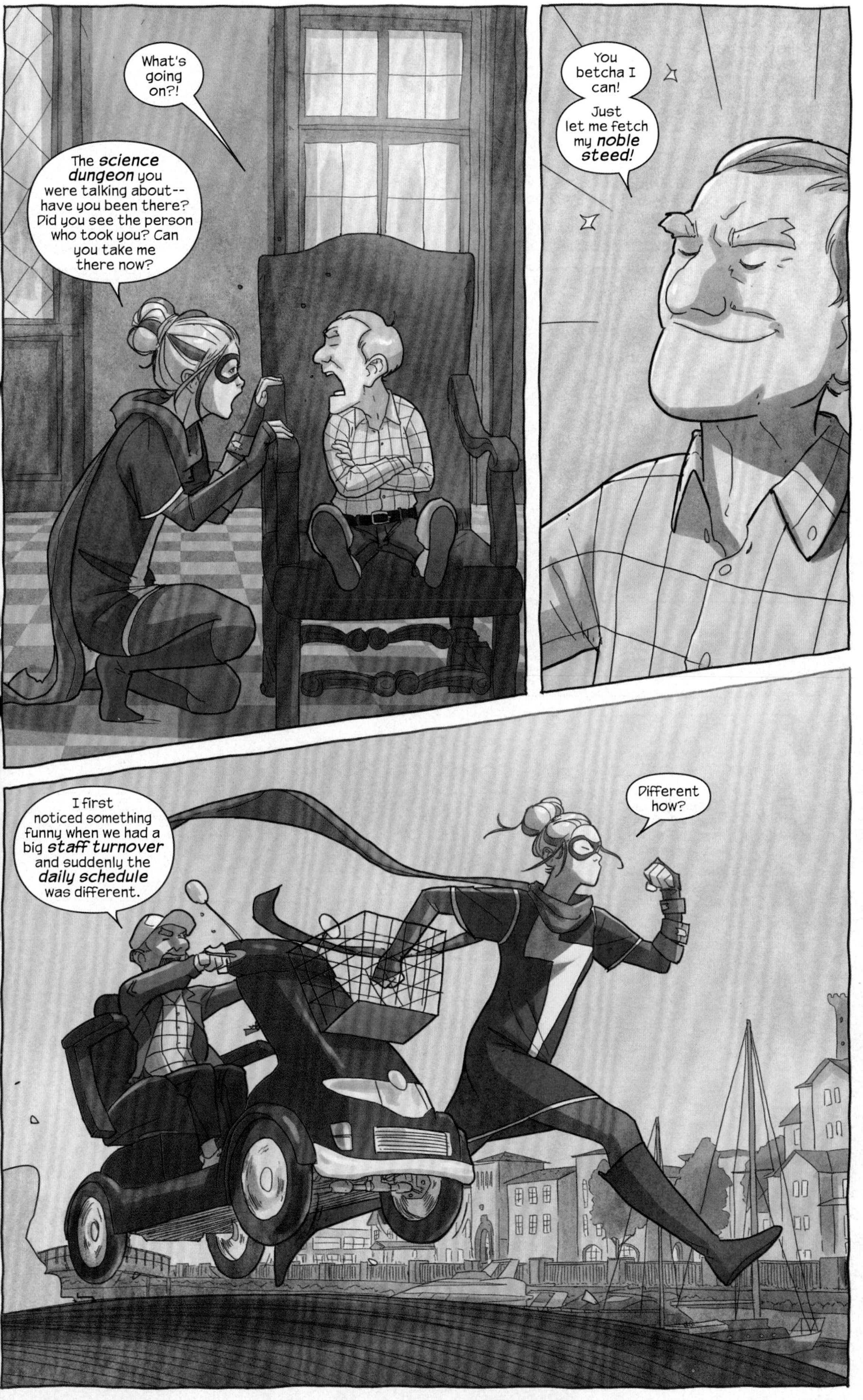
What's going on?!
The science dungeon you were talking about-- have you been there? Did you see the person who took you? Can you take me there now?
You betcha I can!
Just let me fetch my noble steed!
I first noticed something funny when we had a big staff turnover and suddenly the daily schedule was different.
Different how?

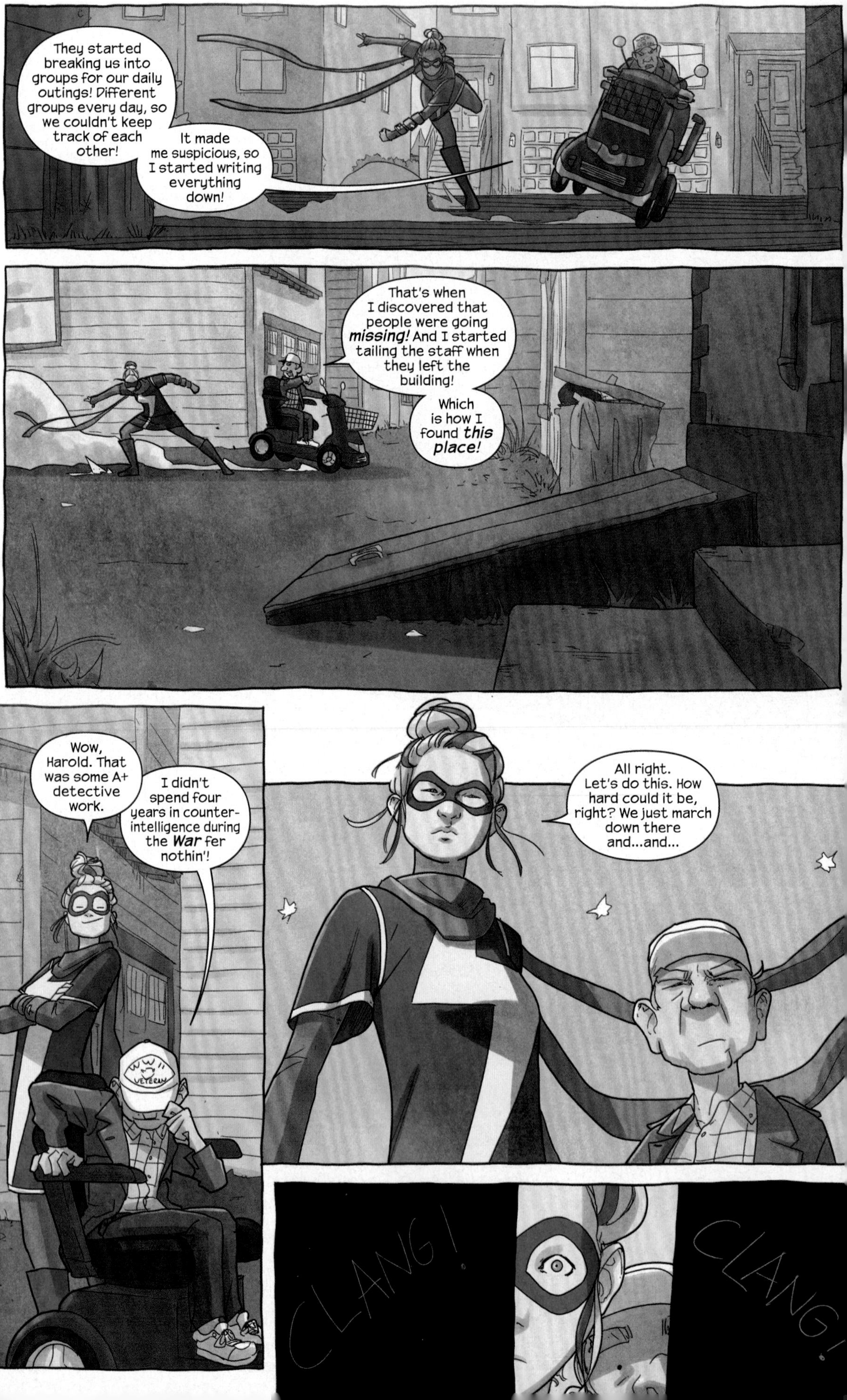
They started breaking us into groups for our daily outings! Different groups every day, so we couldn't keep track of each other!
It made me suspicious, so I started writing everything down!
That's when I discovered that people were going missing! And I started tailing the staff when they left the building!
Which is how I found this place!
Wow, Harold. That was some A+ detective work.
I didn't spend four years in counter-intelligence during the War fer nothin'!
WWII VETERAN
All right. Let's do this. How hard could it be, right? We just march down there and...and...
CLANG!
CLANG!

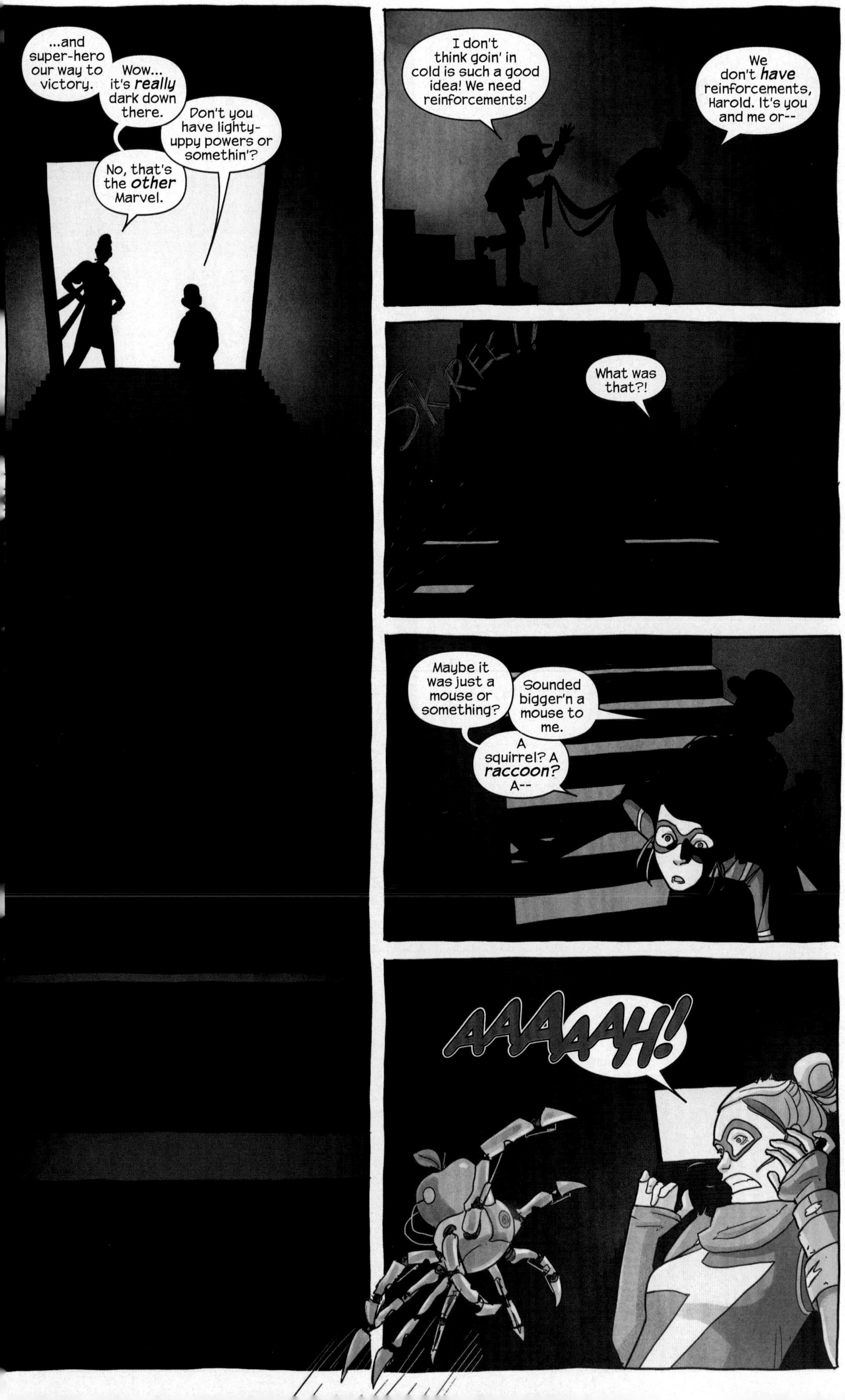
...and super-hero our way to victory.
Wow... it's *really* dark down there.
Don't you have lighty-uppy powers or somethin'?
No, that's the *other* Marvel.
I don't think goin' in cold is such a good idea! We need reinforcements!
We don't *have* reinforcements, Harold. It's you and me or--
SKREE!!
What was that?!
Maybe it was just a mouse or something?
Sounded bigger'n a mouse to me.
A squirrel? A *raccoon?* A--
AAAAAH!

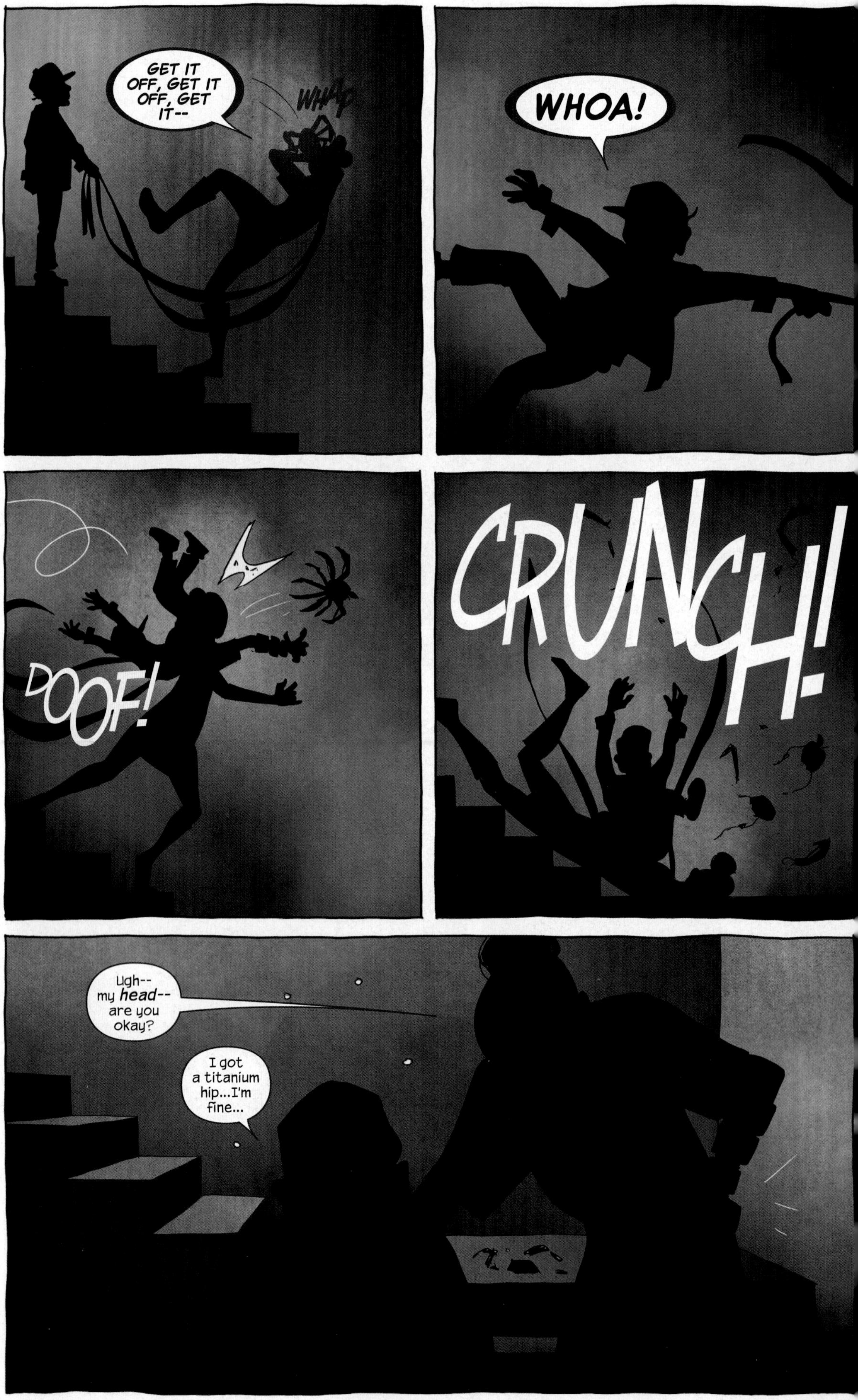
GET IT OFF, GET IT OFF, GET IT--
WHAP
WHOA!
DOOF!
CRUNCH!
Ugh-- my *head*-- are you okay?
I got a titanium hip...I'm fine...

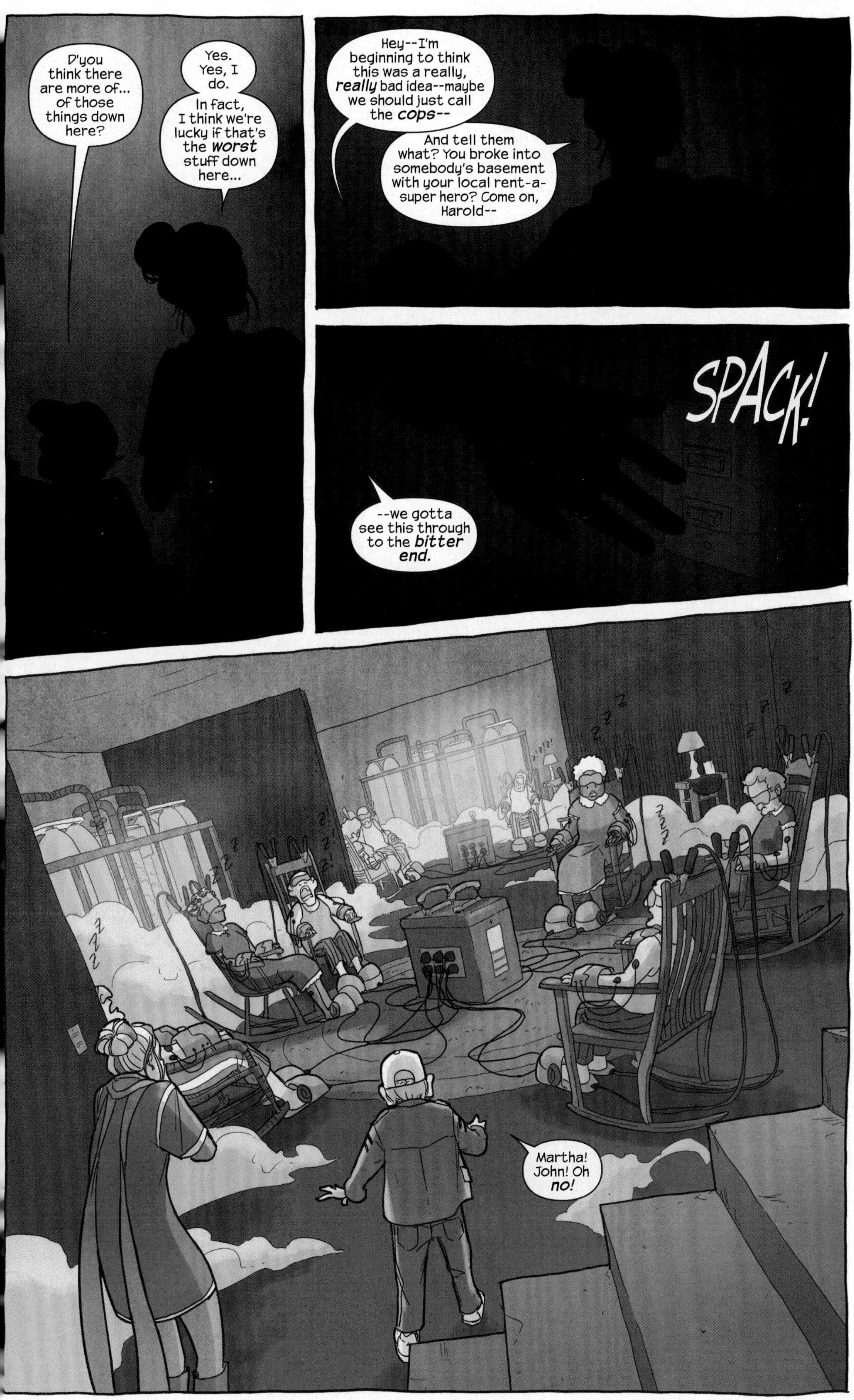
D'you think there are more of... of those things down here?
Yes. Yes, I do.
In fact, I think we're lucky if that's the **worst** stuff down here...
Hey--I'm beginning to think this was a really, ***really*** bad idea--maybe we should just call the ***cops***--
And tell them what? You broke into somebody's basement with your local rent-a-super hero? Come on, Harold--
SPACK!
--we gotta see this through to the ***bitter end.***
Martha! John! Oh ***no!***

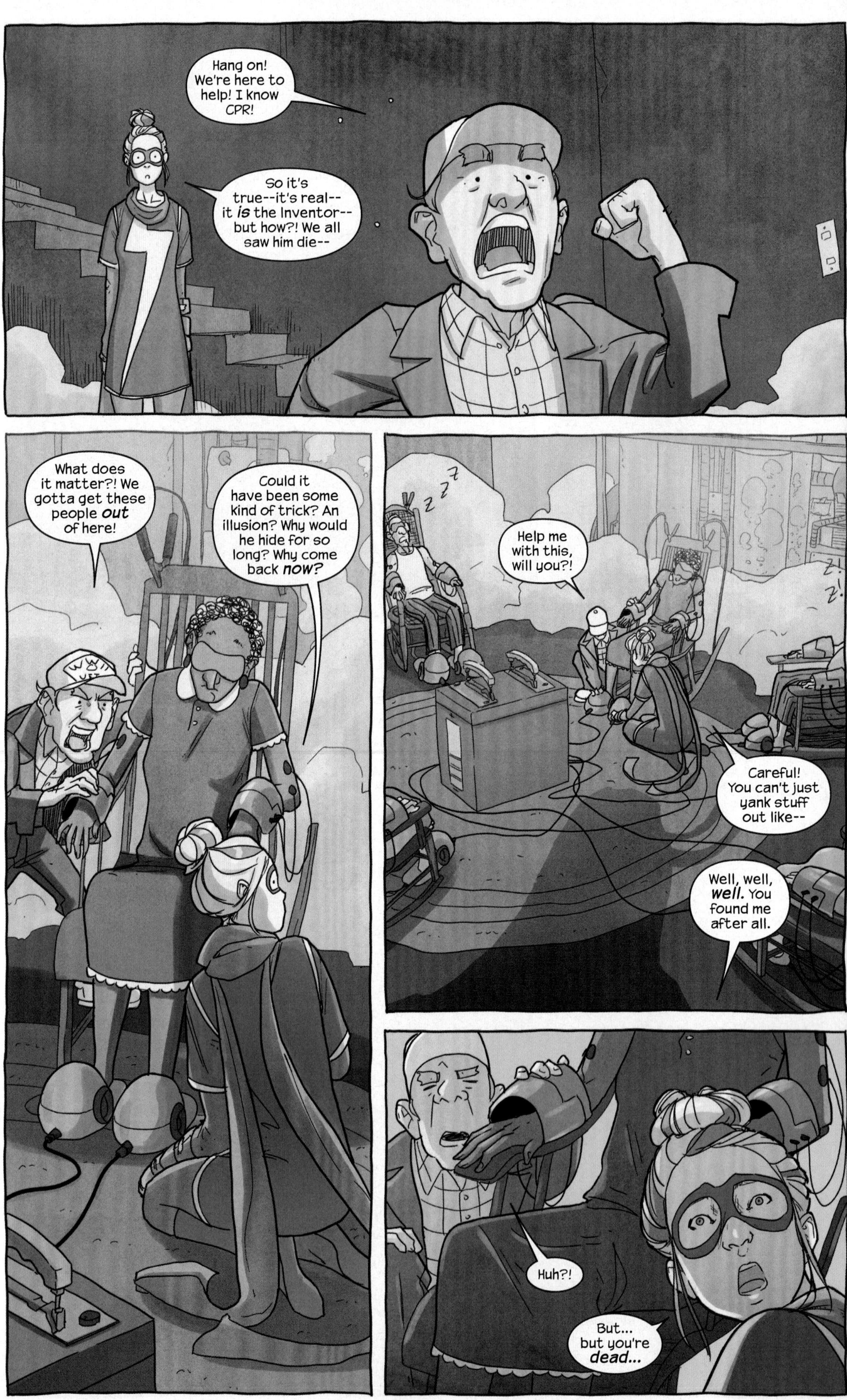
Hang on! We're here to help! I know CPR!
So it's true--it's real--it *is* the Inventor--but how?! We all saw him die--
What does it matter?! We gotta get these people *out* of here!
Could it have been some kind of trick? An illusion? Why would he hide for so long? Why come back *now?*
Z Z Z
Help me with this, will you?!
Z! Z!
Careful! You can't just yank stuff out like--
Well, well, *well.* You found me after all.
Huh?!
But... but you're *dead...*

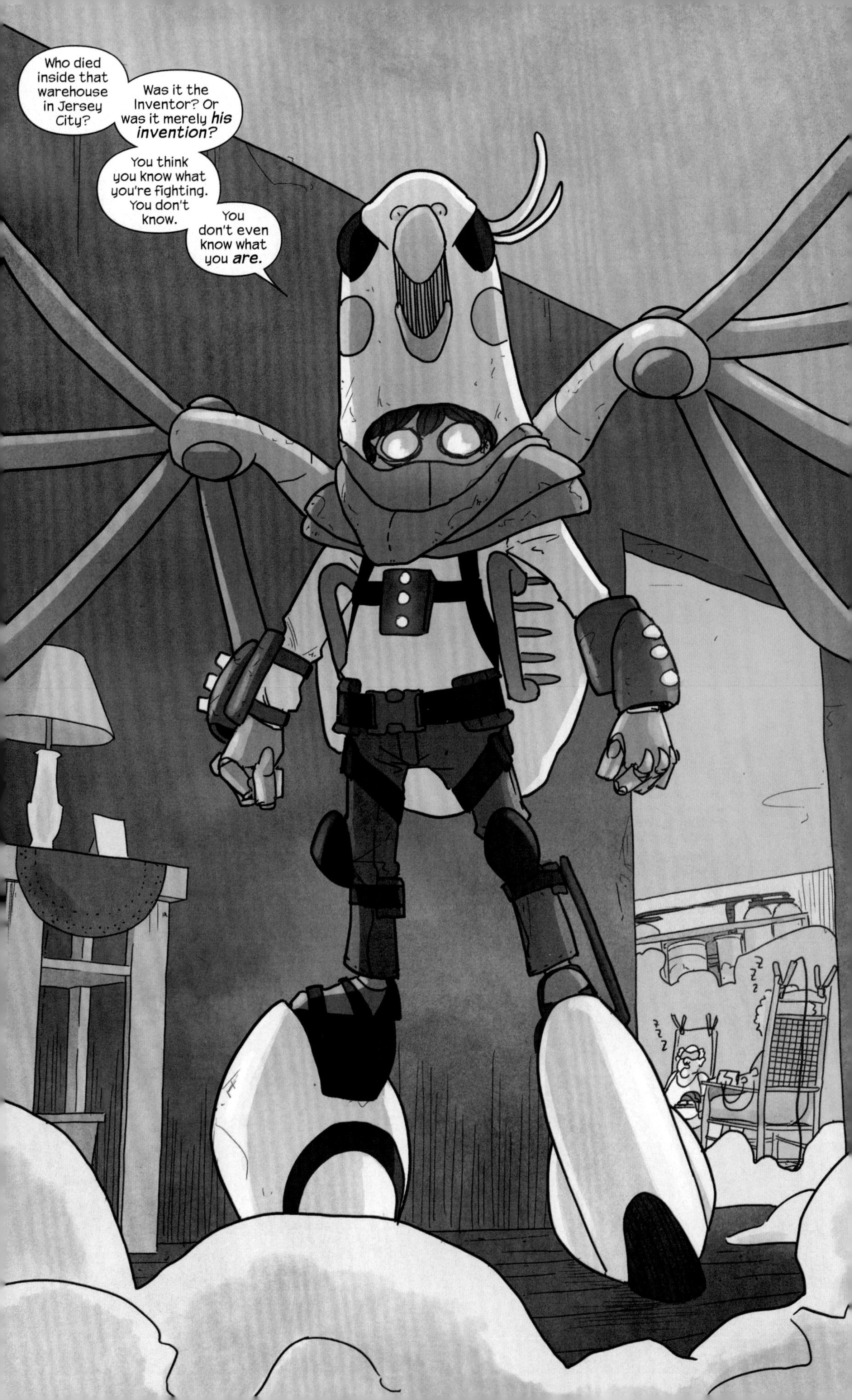
Who died inside that warehouse in Jersey City?
Was it the Inventor? Or was it merely *his invention*?
You think you know what you're fighting. You don't know.
You don't even know what you *are*.

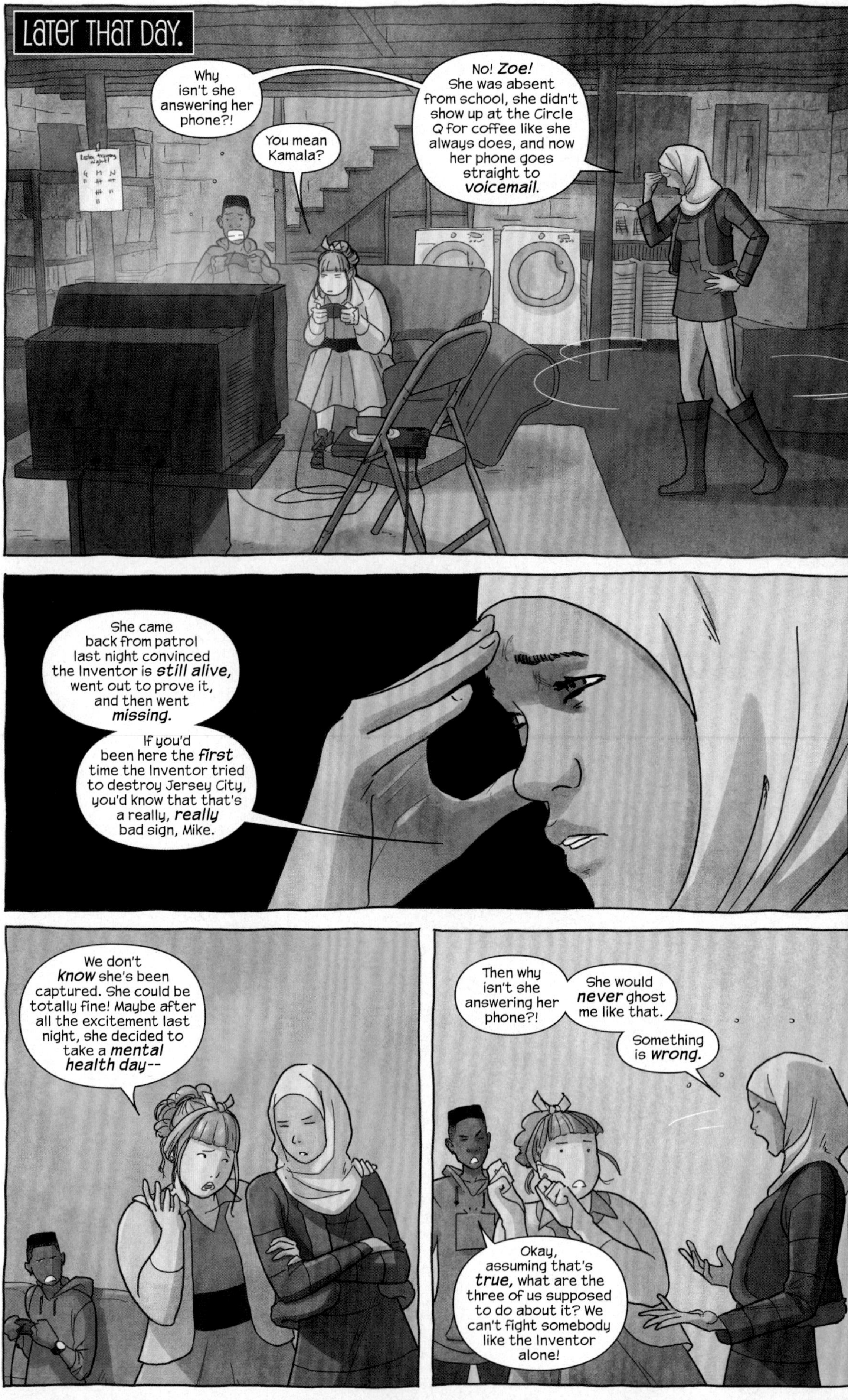
LATER THAT DAY.
Why isn't she answering her phone?!
You mean Kamala?
No! Zoe! She was absent from school, she didn't show up at the Circle Q for coffee like she always does, and now her phone goes straight to voicemail.
She came back from patrol last night convinced the Inventor is still alive, went out to prove it, and then went missing.
If you'd been here the first time the Inventor tried to destroy Jersey City, you'd know that that's a really, really bad sign, Mike.
We don't know she's been captured. She could be totally fine! Maybe after all the excitement last night, she decided to take a mental health day--
Then why isn't she answering her phone?!
She would never ghost me like that.
Something is wrong.
Okay, assuming that's true, what are the three of us supposed to do about it? We can't fight somebody like the Inventor alone!

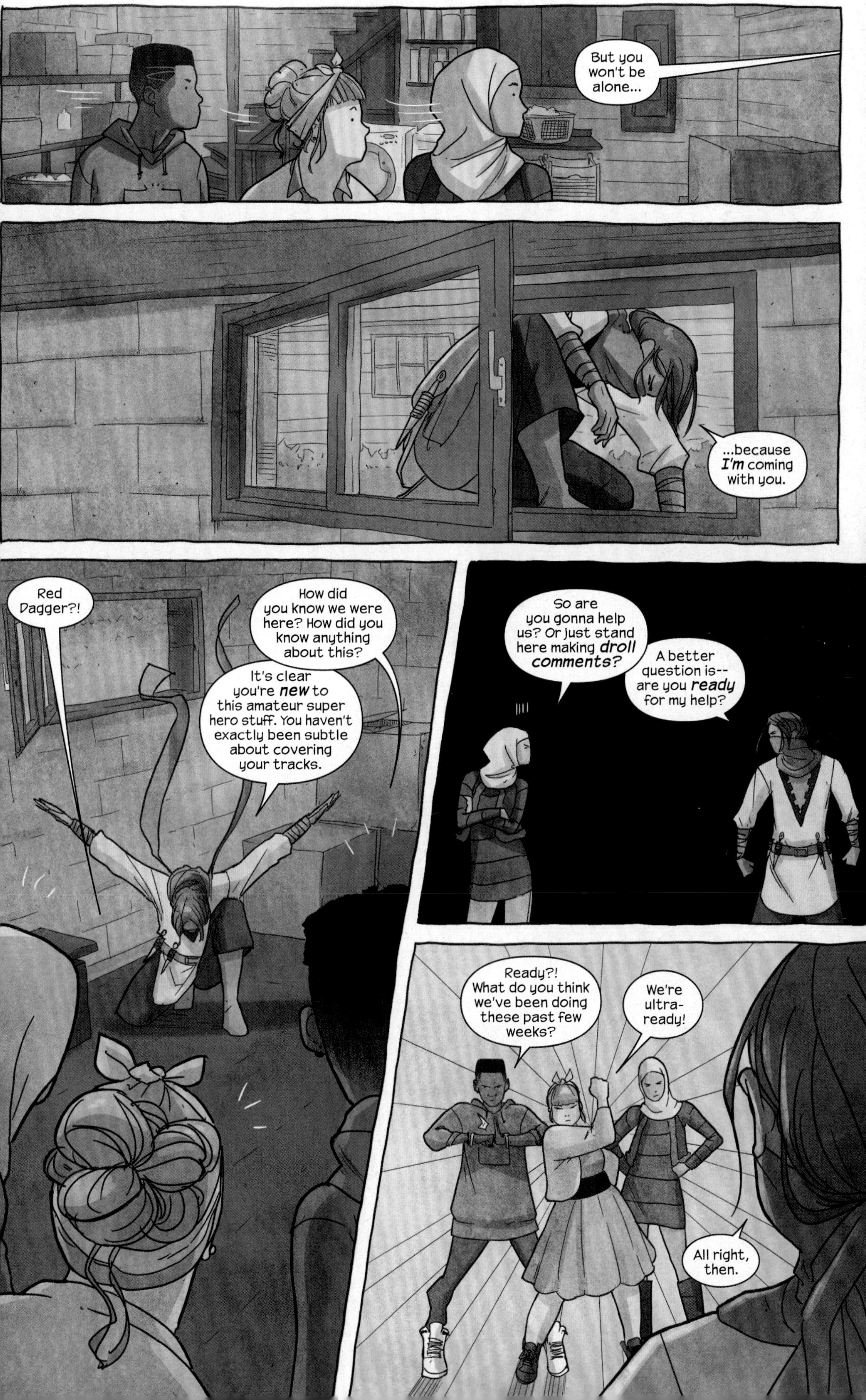
But you won't be alone...
...because I'm coming with you.
Red Dagger?!
How did you know we were here? How did you know anything about this?
It's clear you're new to this amateur super hero stuff. You haven't exactly been subtle about covering your tracks.
So are you gonna help us? Or just stand here making droll comments?
A better question is-- are you ready for my help?
Ready?! What do you think we've been doing these past few weeks?
We're ultra-ready!
All right, then.

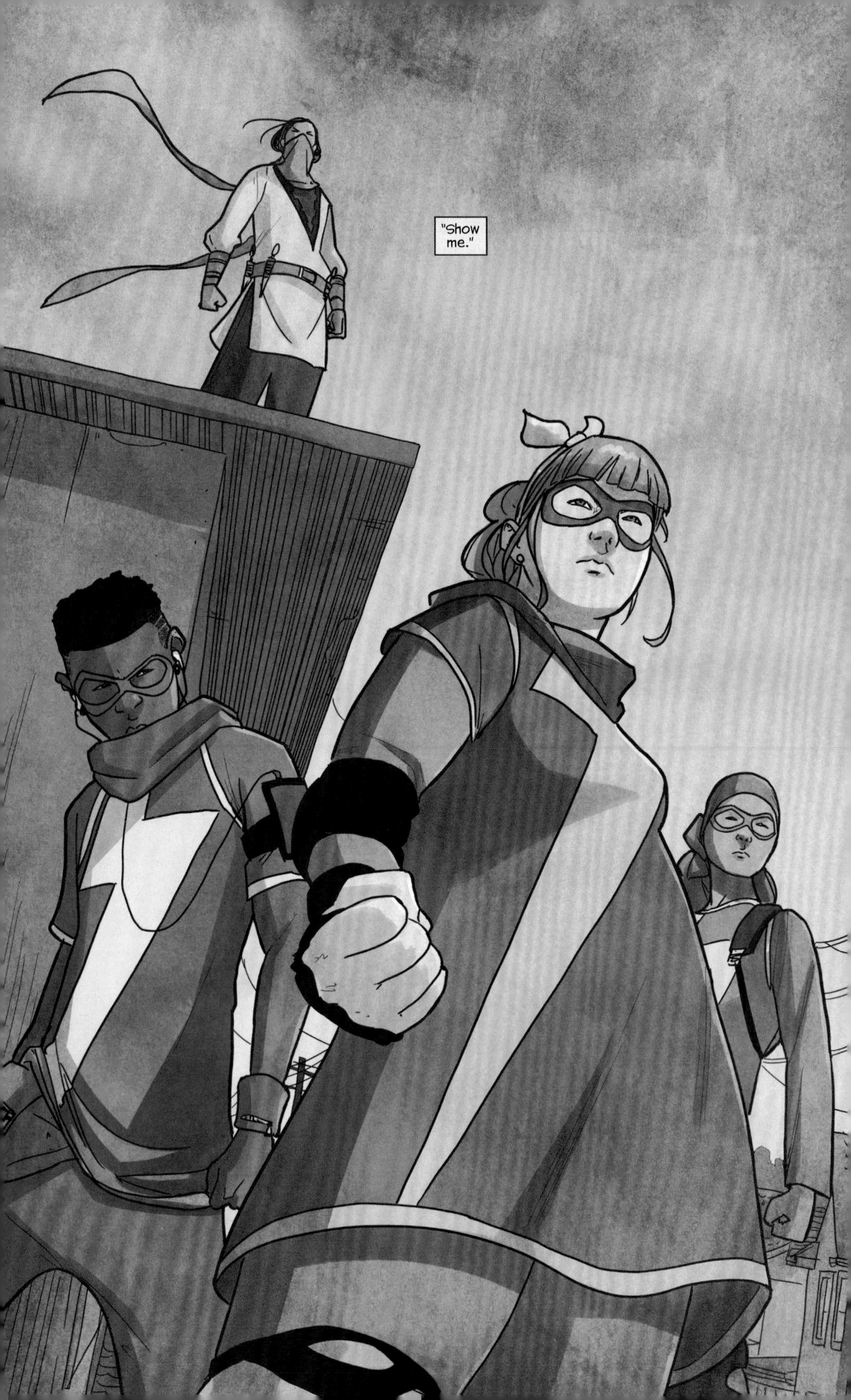
"Show me."

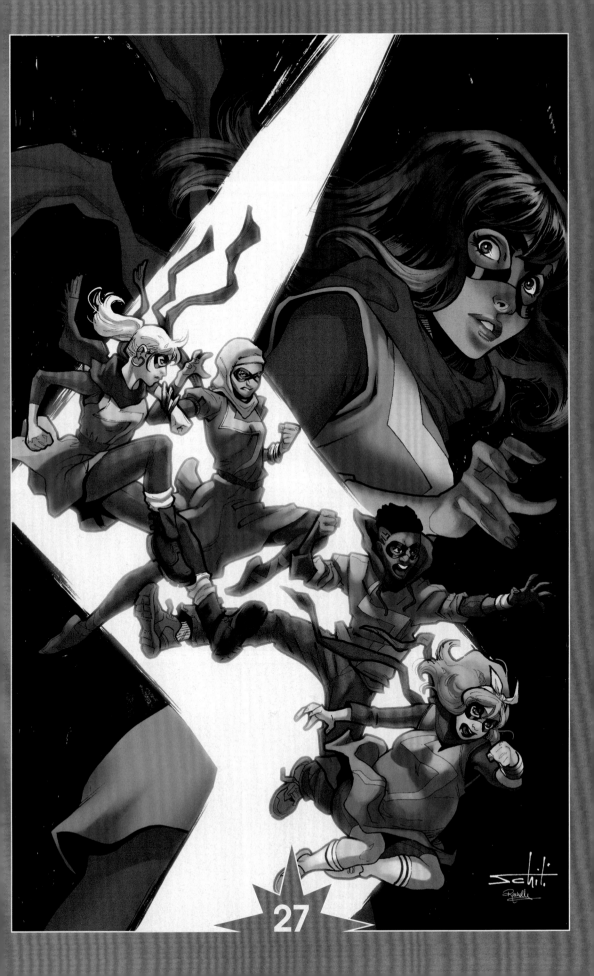

27

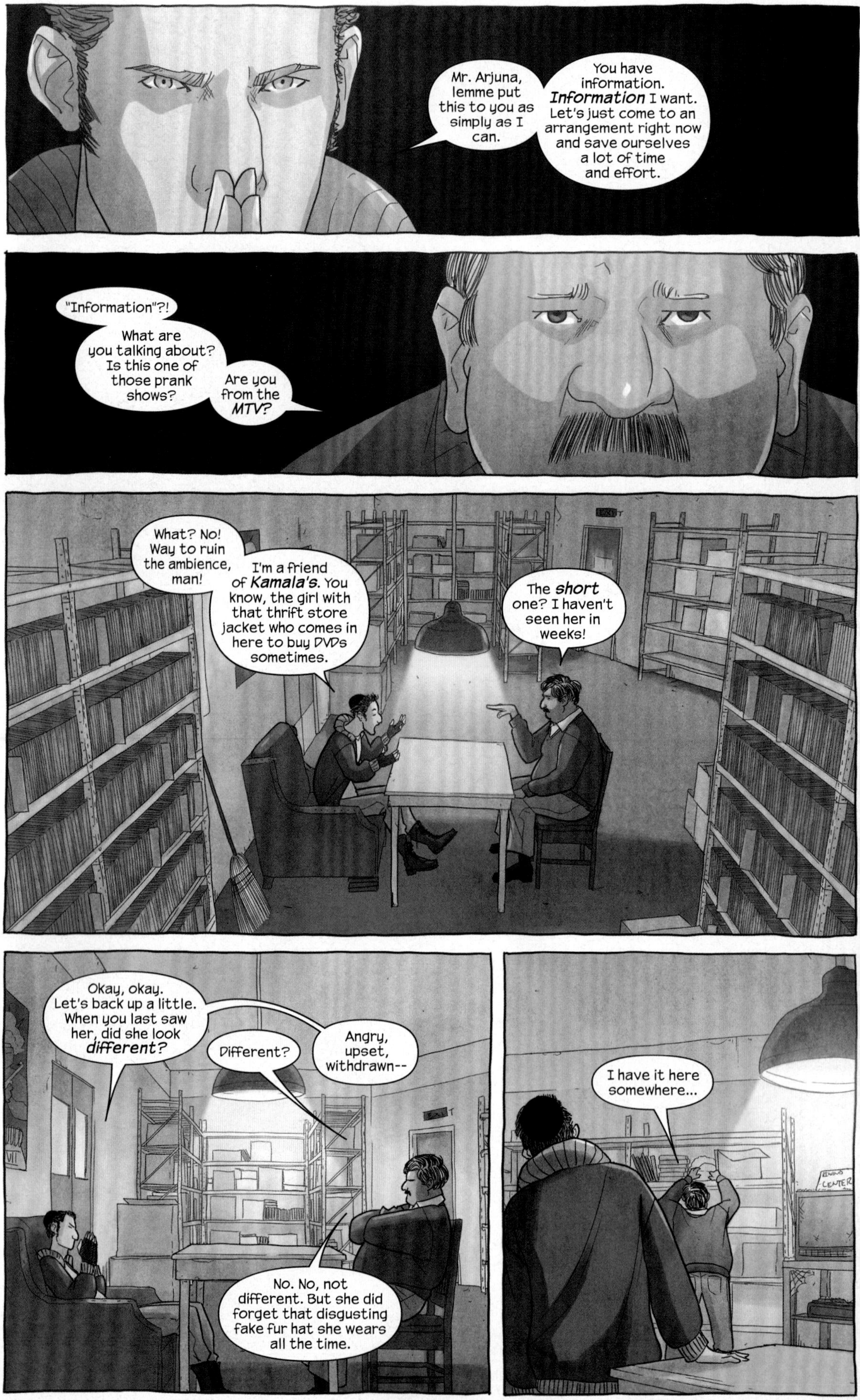
Mr. Arjuna, lemme put this to you as simply as I can.
You have information. Information I want. Let's just come to an arrangement right now and save ourselves a lot of time and effort.
"Information"?!
What are you talking about? Is this one of those prank shows?
Are you from the MTV?
What? No! Way to ruin the ambience, man!
I'm a friend of Kamala's. You know, the girl with that thrift store jacket who comes in here to buy DVDs sometimes.
The short one? I haven't seen her in weeks!
EXIT
Okay, okay. Let's back up a little. When you last saw her, did she look different?
Different?
Angry, upset, withdrawn--
No. No, not different. But she did forget that disgusting fake fur hat she wears all the time.
I have it here somewhere...

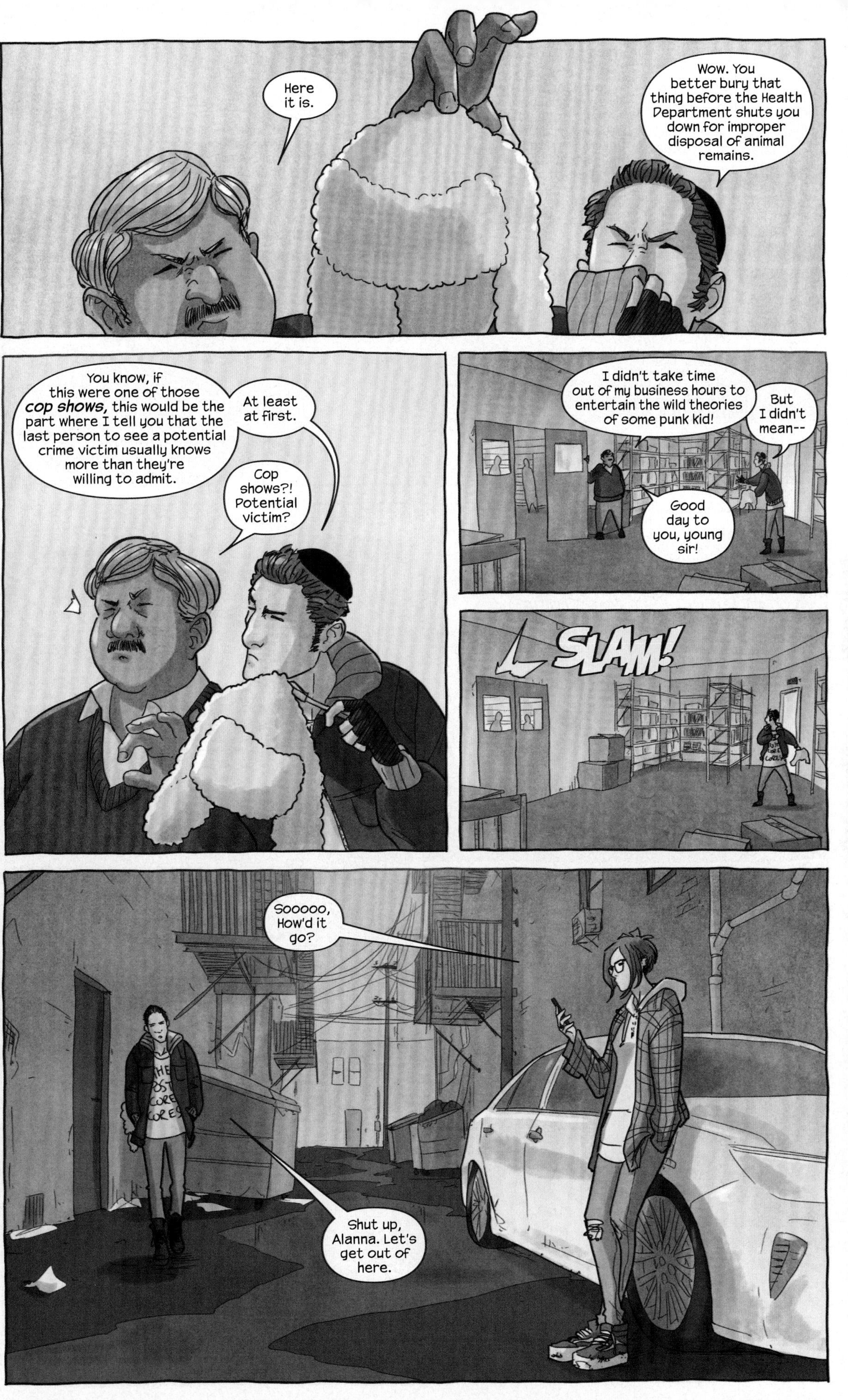
Here it is.
Wow. You better bury that thing before the Health Department shuts you down for improper disposal of animal remains.
You know, if this were one of those **cop shows,** this would be the part where I tell you that the last person to see a potential crime victim usually knows more than they're willing to admit.
At least at first.
Cop shows?! Potential victim?
I didn't take time out of my business hours to entertain the wild theories of some punk kid!
But I didn't mean--
Good day to you, young sir!
SLAM!
Sooooo, How'd it go?
Shut up, Alanna. Let's get out of here.

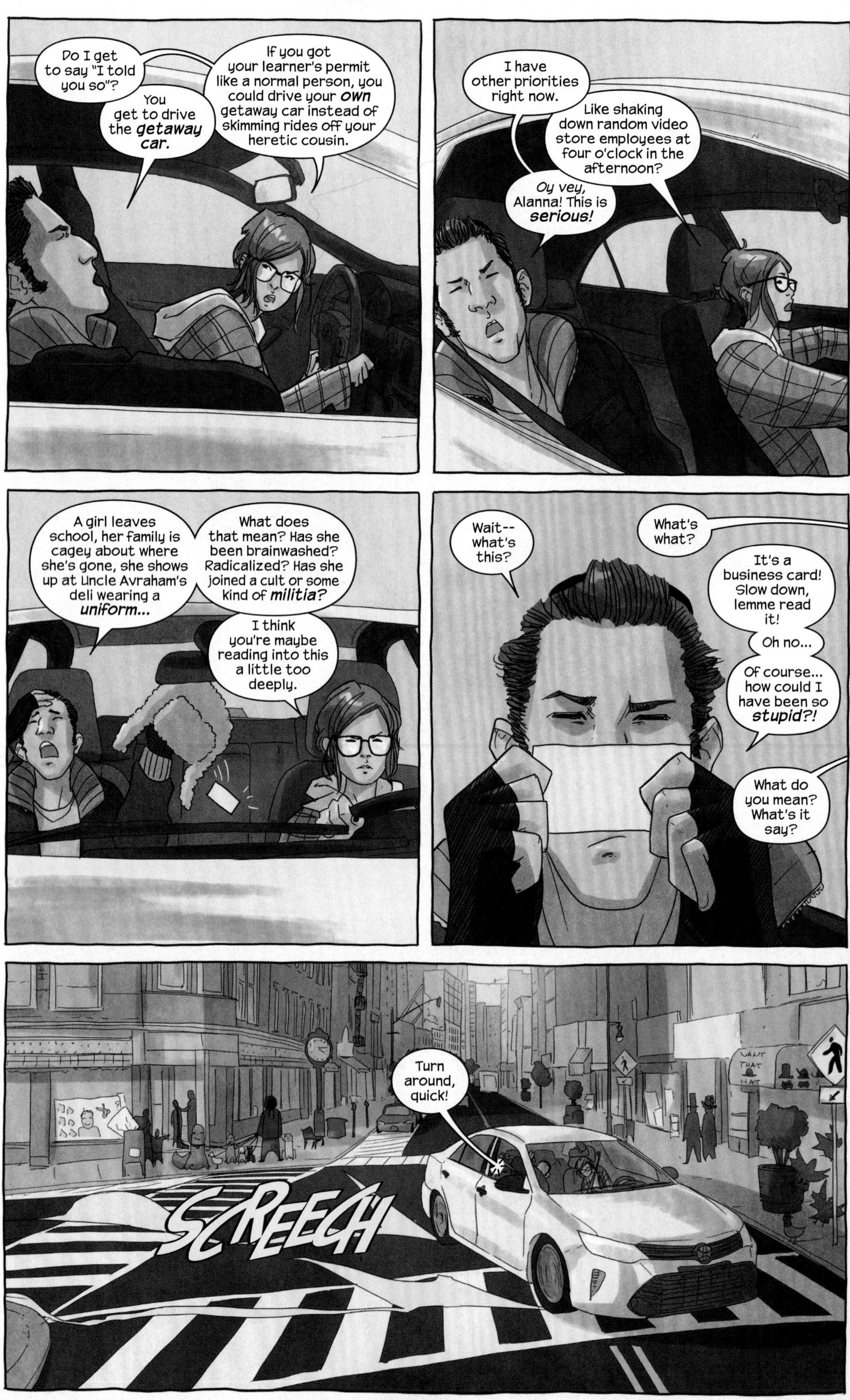
Do I get to say "I told you so"?
You get to drive the *getaway car.*
If you got your learner's permit like a normal person, you could drive your *own* getaway car instead of skimming rides off your heretic cousin.
I have other priorities right now.
Like shaking down random video store employees at four o'clock in the afternoon?
Oy vey, Alanna! This is *serious!*
A girl leaves school, her family is cagey about where she's gone, she shows up at Uncle Avraham's deli wearing a *uniform...*
What does that mean? Has she been brainwashed? Radicalized? Has she joined a cult or some kind of *militia?*
I think you're maybe reading into this a little too deeply.
Wait-- what's this?
What's what?
It's a business card! Slow down, lemme read it!
Oh no...
Of course... how could I have been so *stupid?!*
What do you mean? What's it say?
Turn around, quick!
WANT THAT HAT
SCREECH

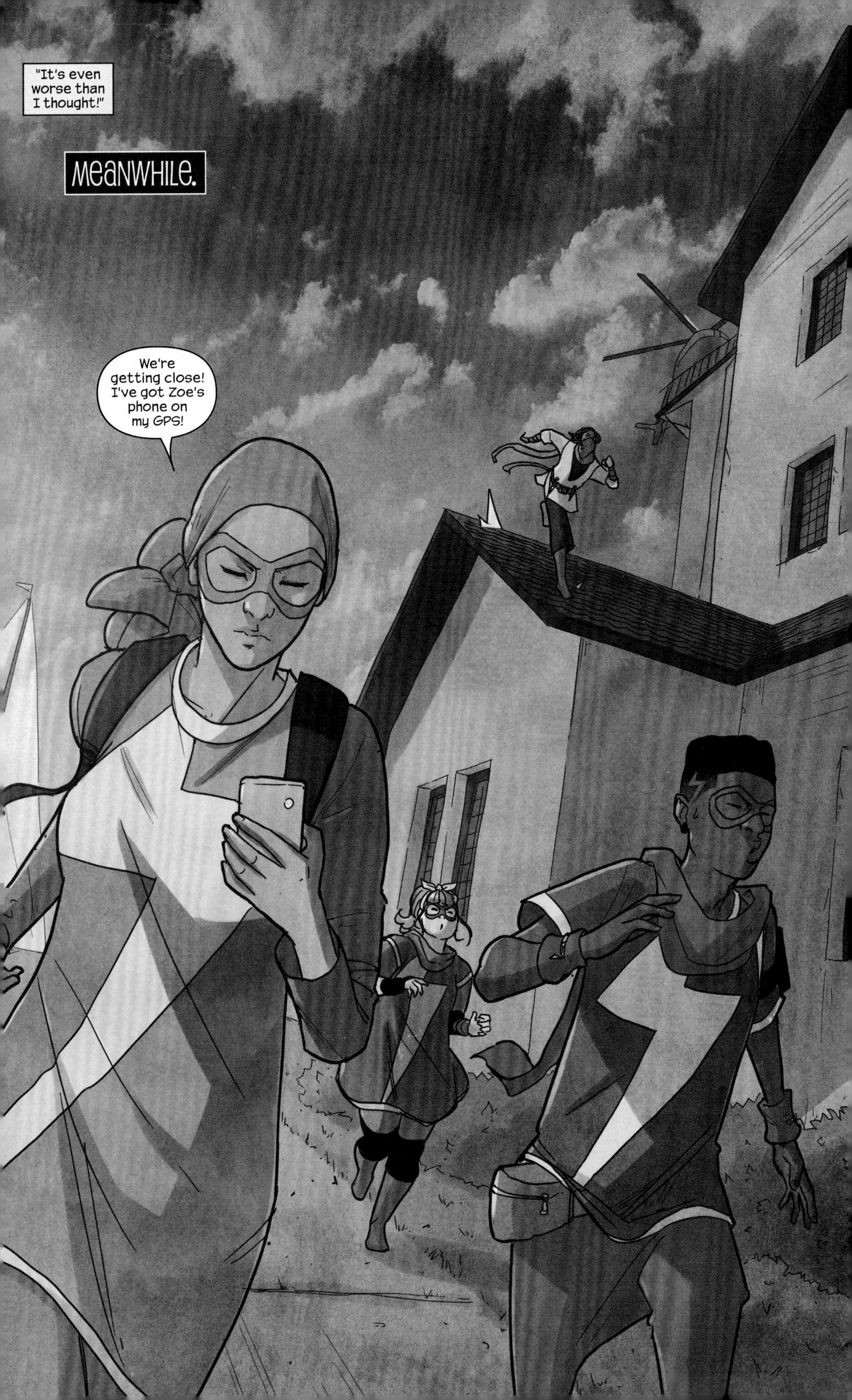
"It's even worse than I thought!"
MEANWHILE.
We're getting close! I've got Zoe's phone on my GPS!

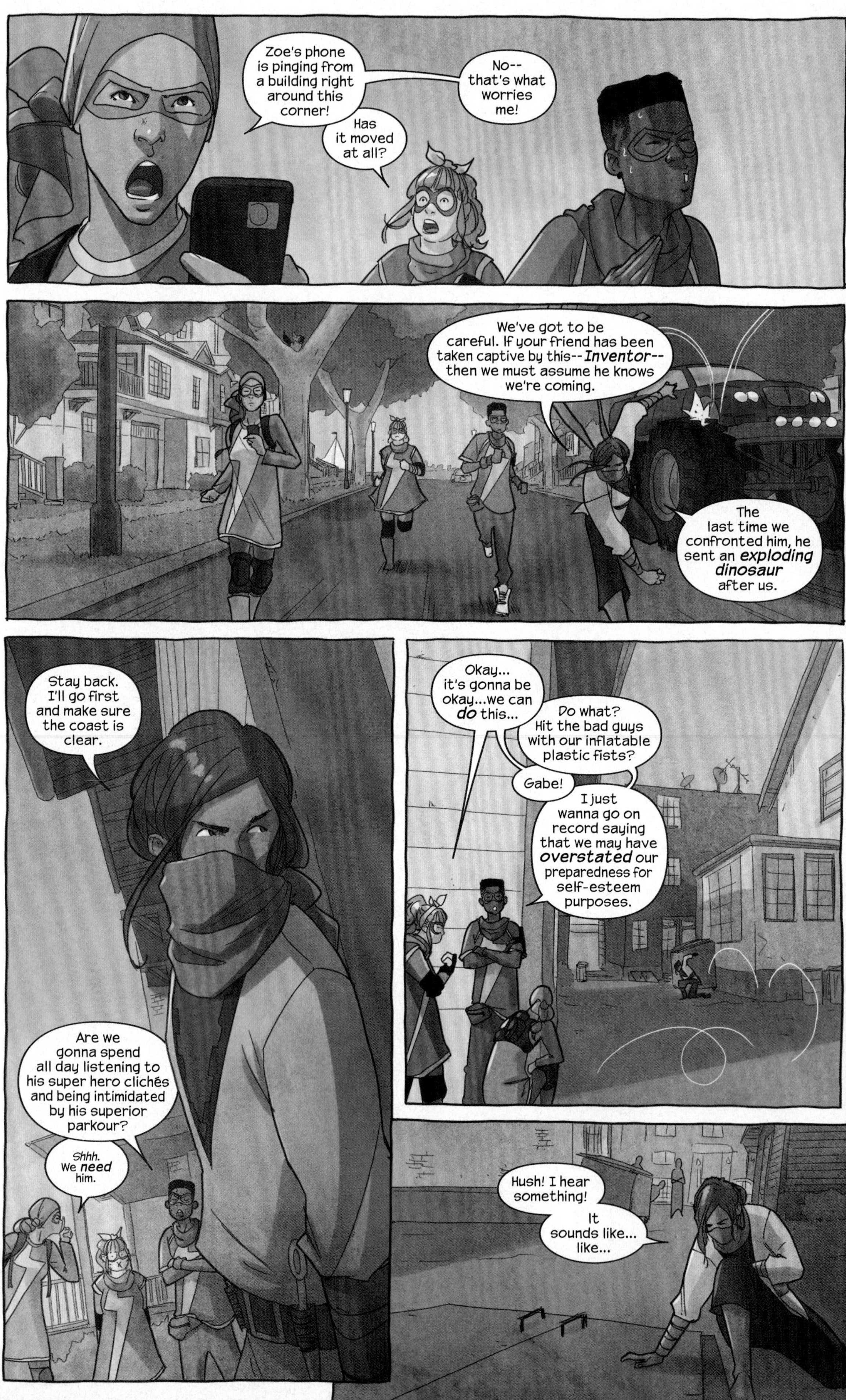
Zoe's phone is pinging from a building right around this corner!
Has it moved at all?
No-- that's what worries me!
We've got to be careful. If your friend has been taken captive by this--Inventor-- then we must assume he knows we're coming.
The last time we confronted him, he sent an exploding dinosaur after us.
Stay back. I'll go first and make sure the coast is clear.
Are we gonna spend all day listening to his super hero clichés and being intimidated by his superior parkour?
Shhh. We need him.
Okay... it's gonna be okay...we can do this...
Do what? Hit the bad guys with our inflatable plastic fists?
Gabe!
I just wanna go on record saying that we may have overstated our preparedness for self-esteem purposes.
Hush! I hear something!
It sounds like... like...

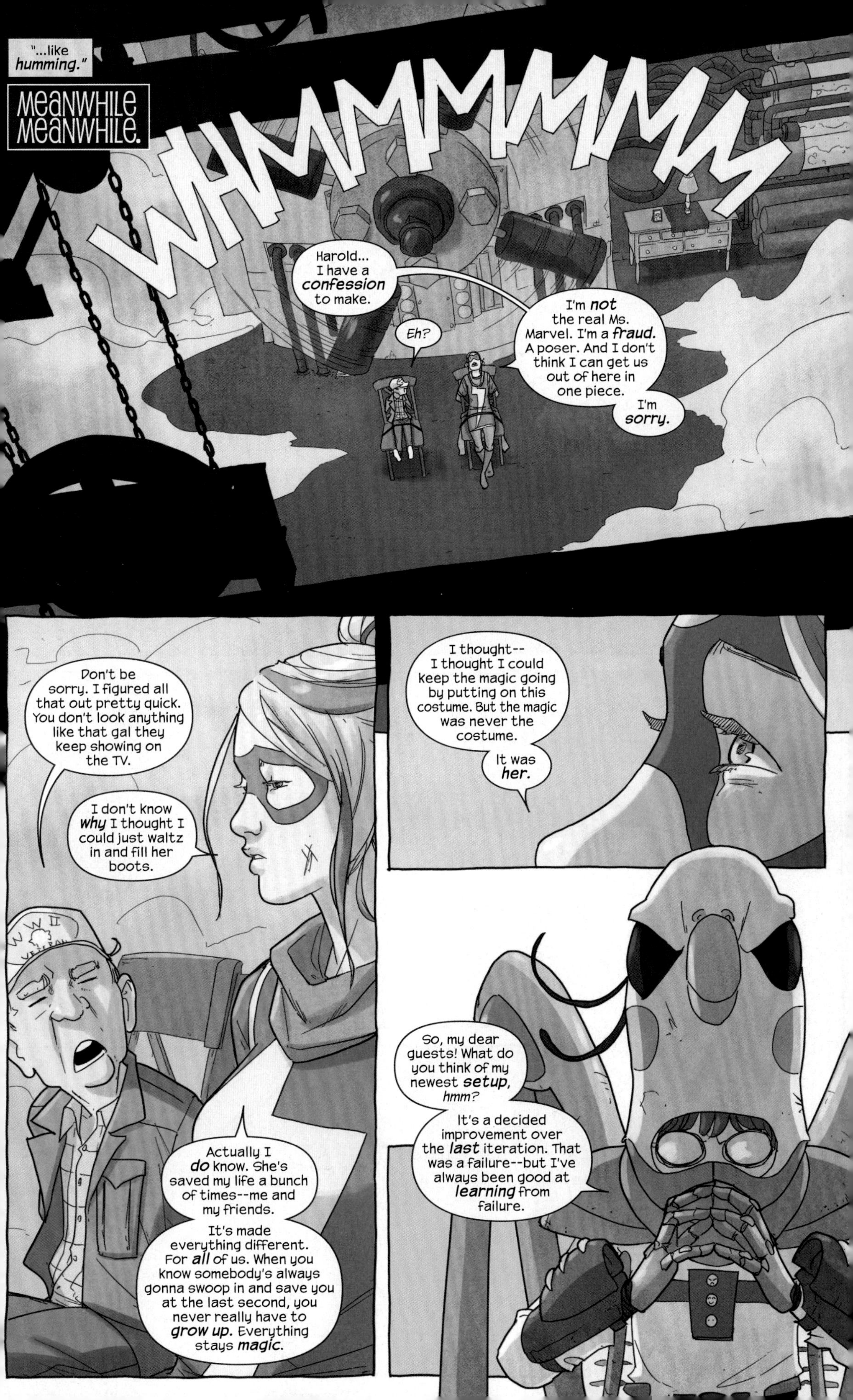
"...like humming."
MEANWHILE MEANWHILE.
WHMMMMMMMM
Harold... I have a confession to make.
Eh?
I'm not the real Ms. Marvel. I'm a fraud. A poser. And I don't think I can get us out of here in one piece.
I'm sorry.
Don't be sorry. I figured all that out pretty quick. You don't look anything like that gal they keep showing on the TV.
I don't know why I thought I could just waltz in and fill her boots.
Actually I do know. She's saved my life a bunch of times--me and my friends.
It's made everything different. For all of us. When you know somebody's always gonna swoop in and save you at the last second, you never really have to grow up. Everything stays magic.
I thought-- I thought I could keep the magic going by putting on this costume. But the magic was never the costume.
It was her.
So, my dear guests! What do you think of my newest setup, hmm?
It's a decided improvement over the last iteration. That was a failure--but I've always been good at learning from failure.
WW II VETERAN

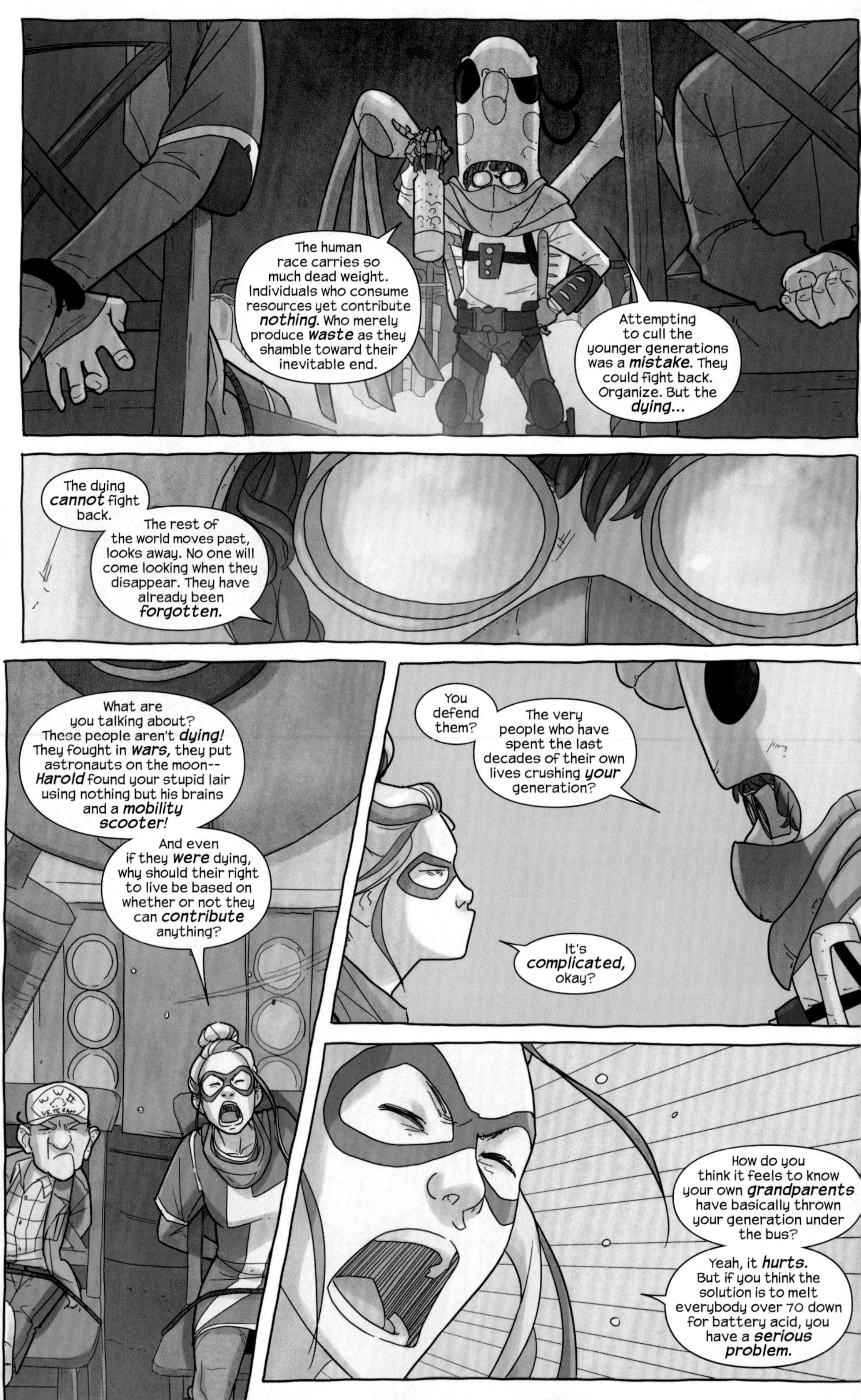
The human race carries so much dead weight. Individuals who consume resources yet contribute nothing. Who merely produce waste as they shamble toward their inevitable end.
Attempting to cull the younger generations was a mistake. They could fight back. Organize. But the dying...
The dying cannot fight back.
The rest of the world moves past, looks away. No one will come looking when they disappear. They have already been forgotten.
What are you talking about? These people aren't dying! They fought in wars, they put astronauts on the moon-- Harold found your stupid lair using nothing but his brains and a mobility scooter!
And even if they were dying, why should their right to live be based on whether or not they can contribute anything?
You defend them?
The very people who have spent the last decades of their own lives crushing your generation?
It's complicated, okay?
How do you think it feels to know your own grandparents have basically thrown your generation under the bus?
Yeah, it hurts. But if you think the solution is to melt everybody over 70 down for battery acid, you have a serious problem.

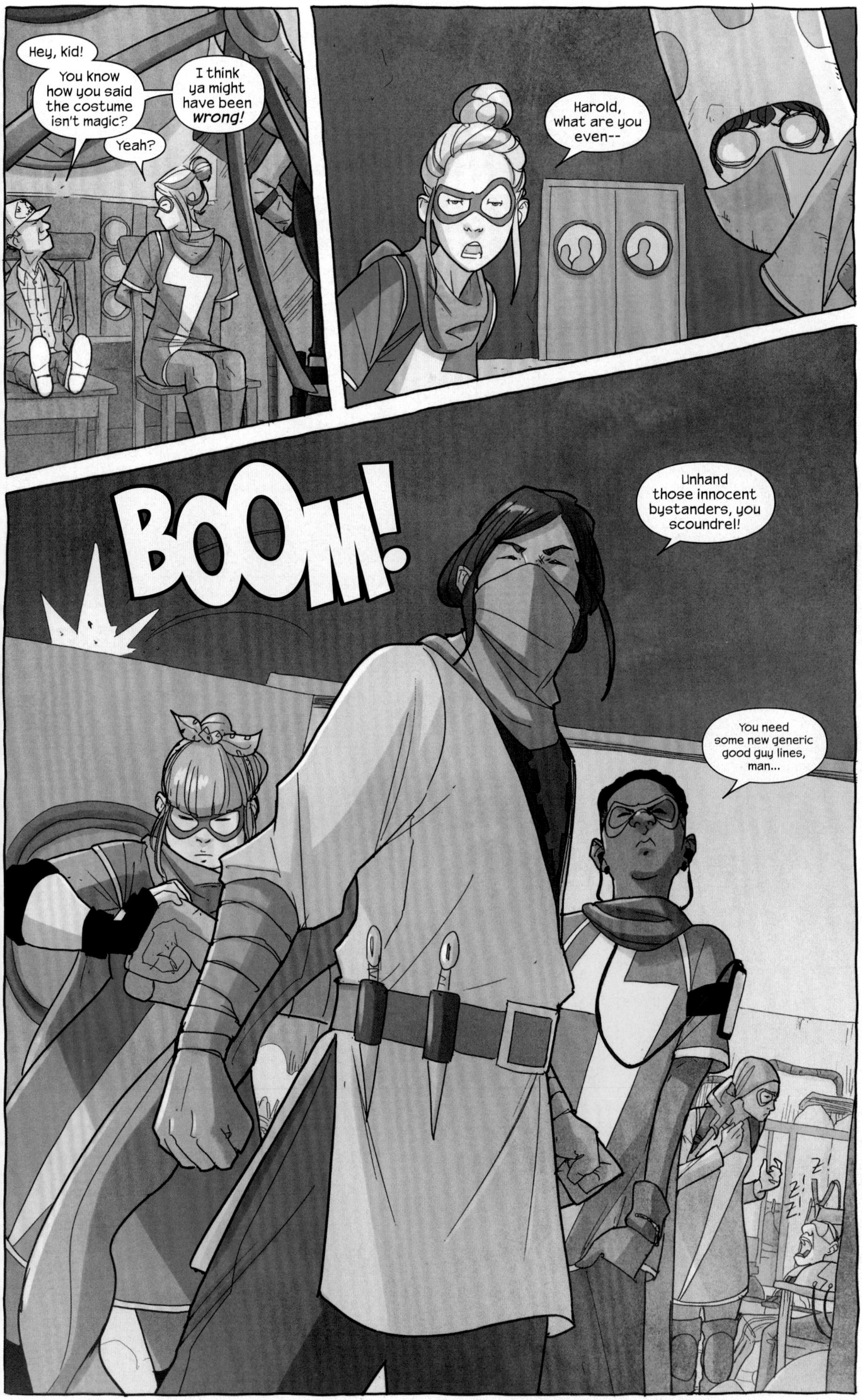

Hey, kid!
You know how you said the costume isn't magic?
Yeah?
I think ya might have been *wrong!*
Harold, what are you even--
BOOM!
Unhand those innocent bystanders, you scoundrel!
You need some new generic good guy lines, man...

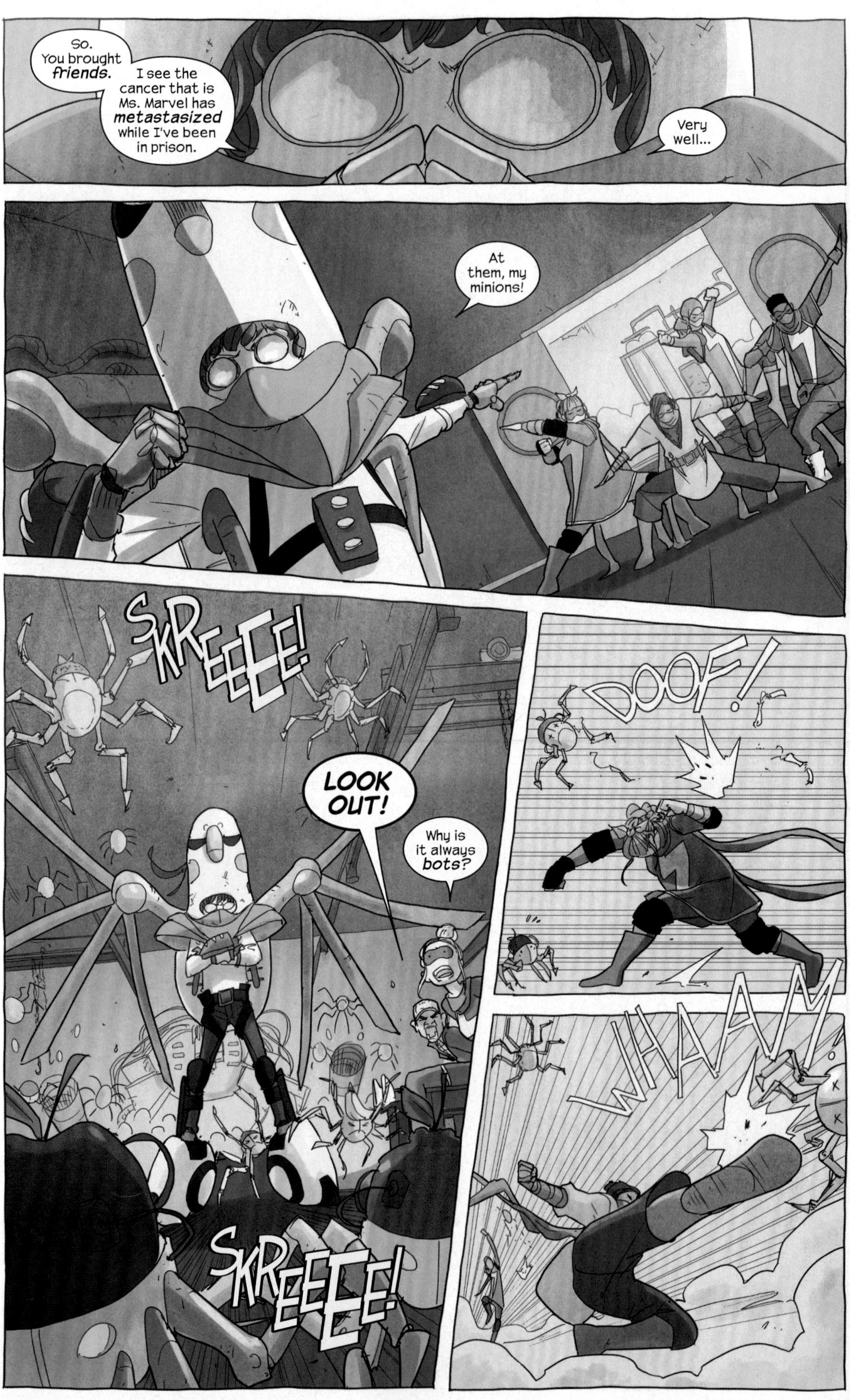
So. You brought *friends.*
I see the cancer that is Ms. Marvel has *metastasized* while I've been in prison.
Very well...
At them, my minions!
SKREEEEE!
LOOK OUT!
Why is it always *bots?*
SKREEEEE!
DOOF!
WHAAM!

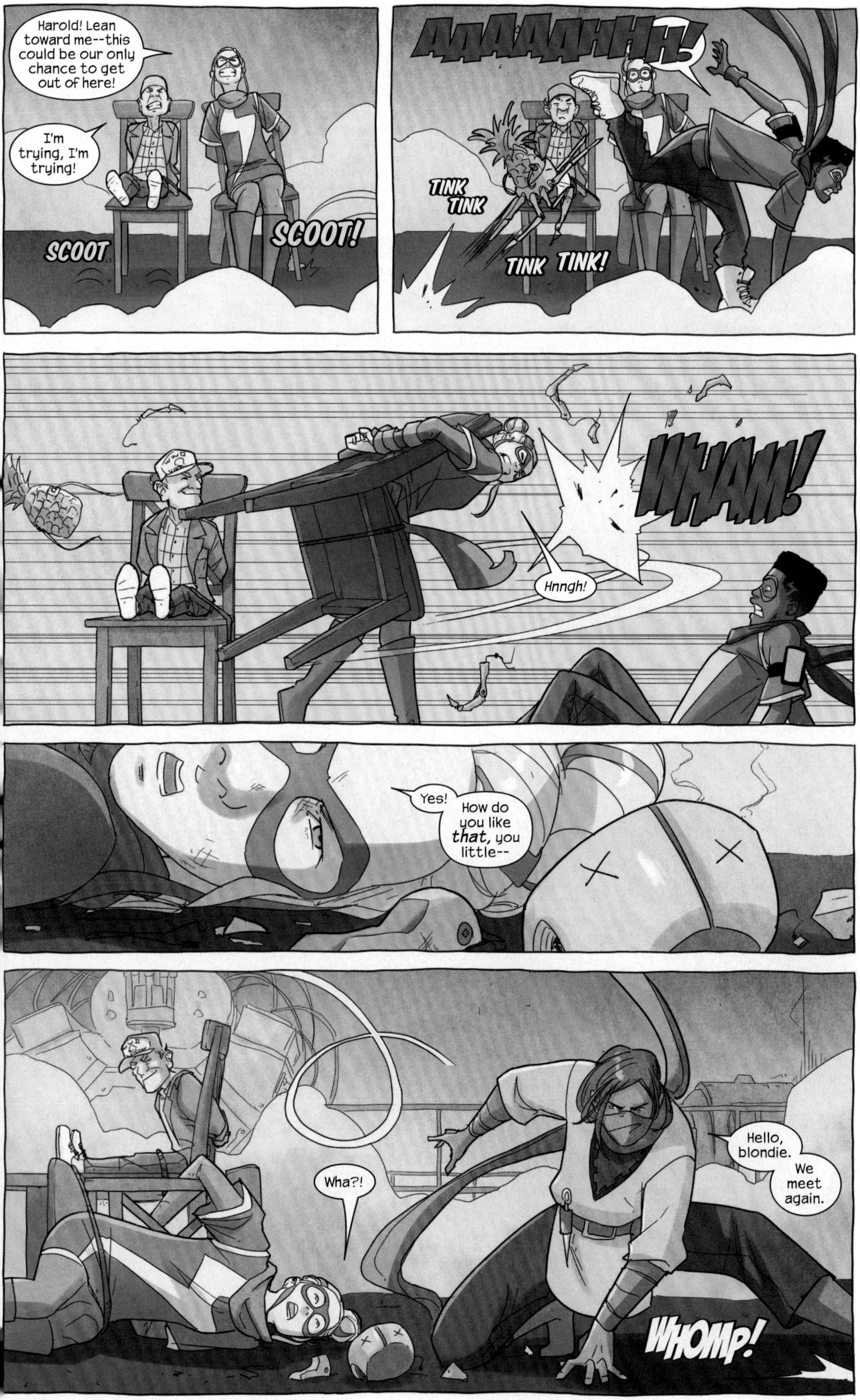
Harold! Lean toward me--this could be our only chance to get out of here!
I'm trying, I'm trying!
SCOOT
SCOOT!
AAAAAHHH!
TINK TINK
TINK TINK!
WHAM!
Hnngh!
Yes!
How do you like *that*, you little--
Wha?!
Hello, blondie.
We meet again.
WHOMP!

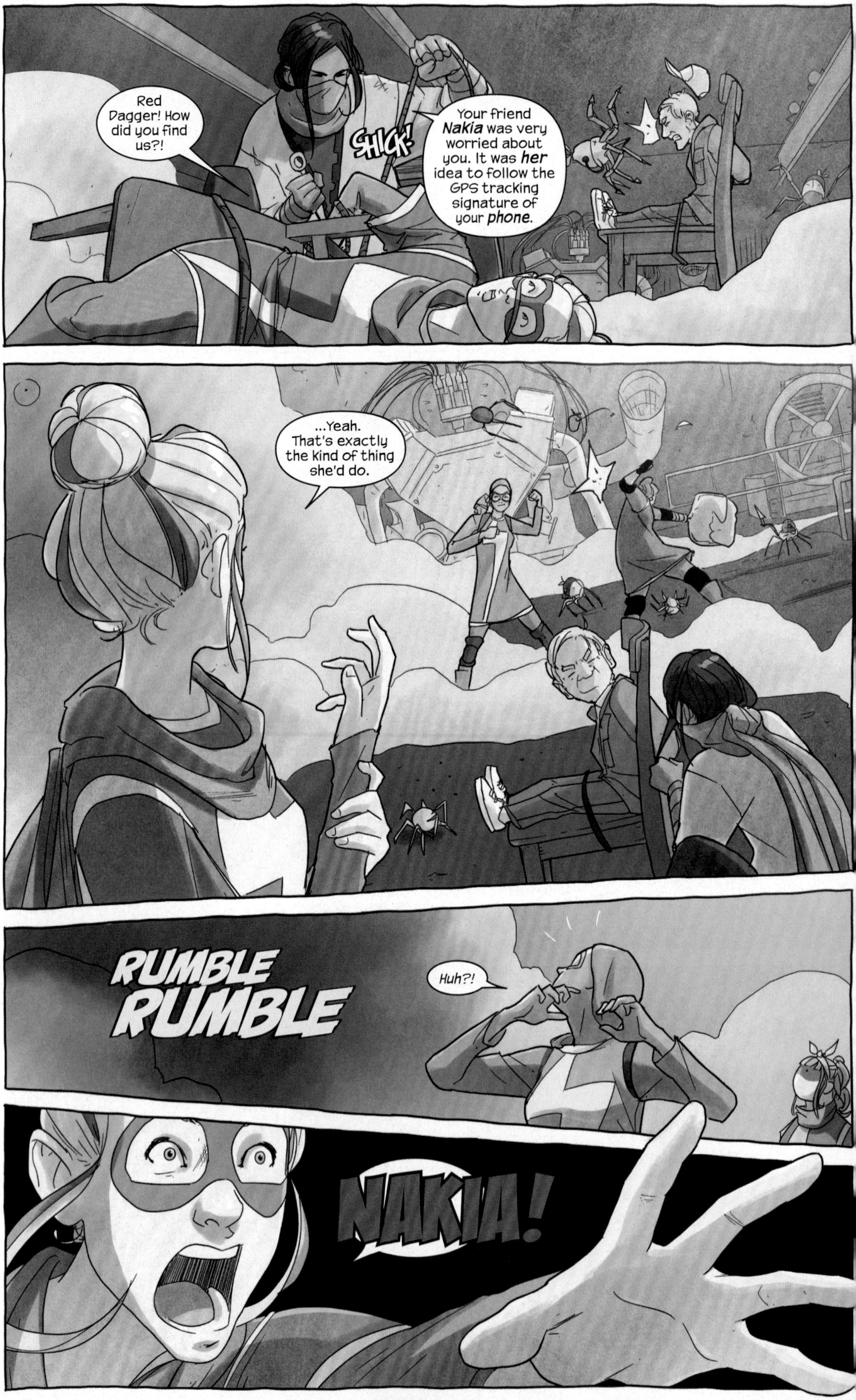

Red Dagger! How did you find us?!
SHICK!
Your friend Nakia was very worried about you. It was her idea to follow the GPS tracking signature of your phone.
...Yeah. That's exactly the kind of thing she'd do.
RUMBLE RUMBLE
Huh?!
NAKIA!

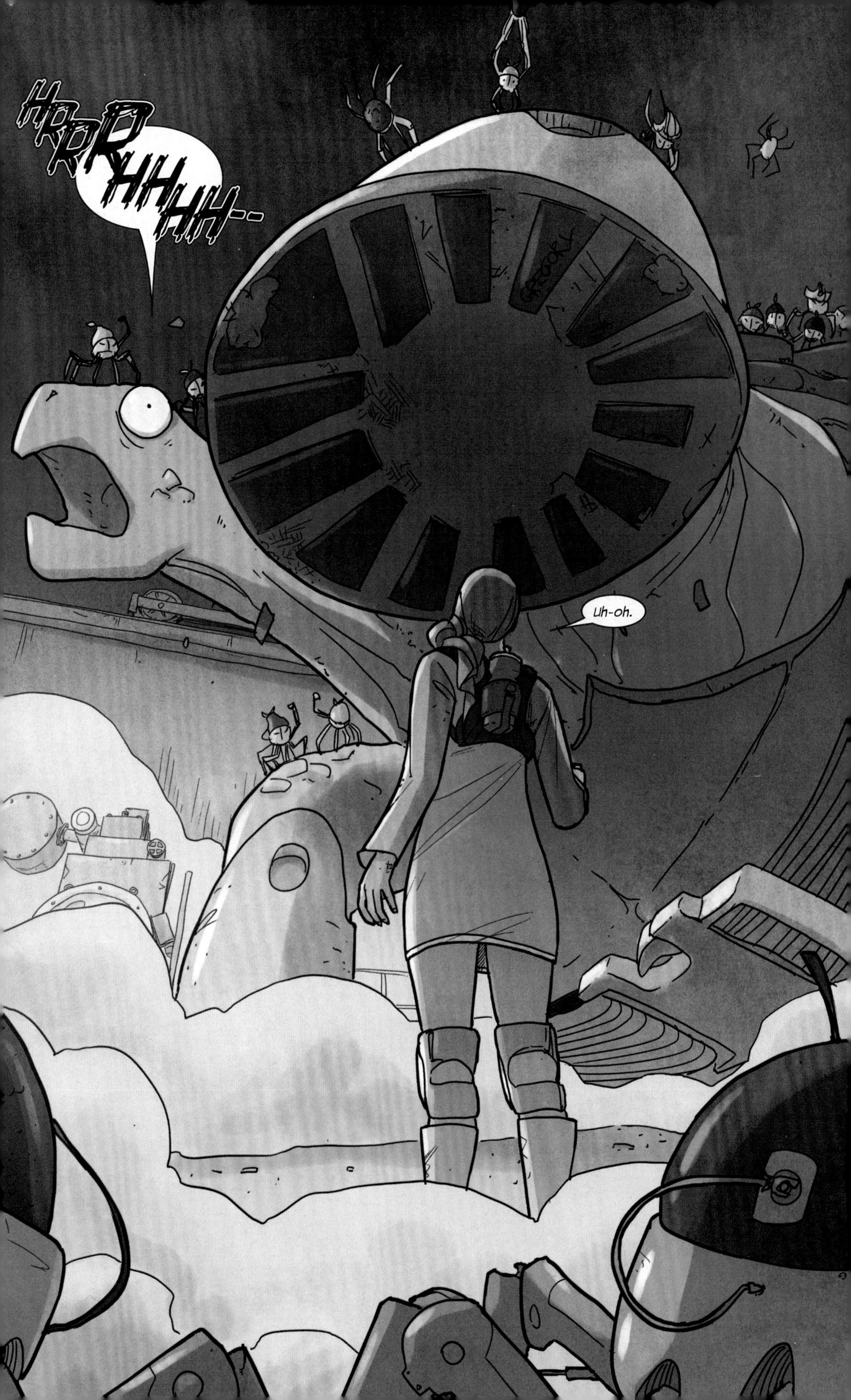
HRRRRHHHHH--
GREGORY
Uh-oh.

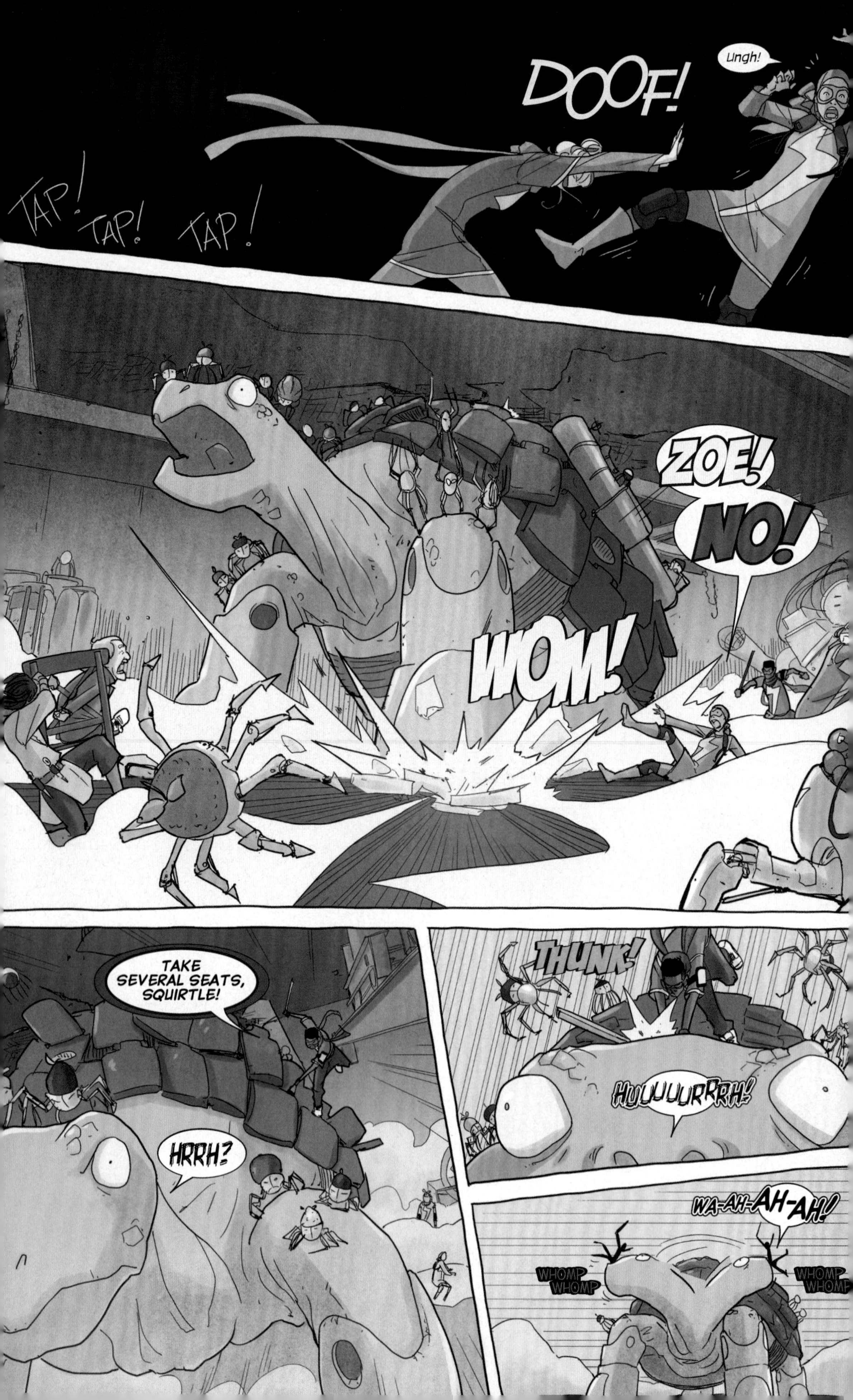
DOOF!
Ungh!
TAP! TAP! TAP!
ZOE!
NO!
WOM!
TAKE SEVERAL SEATS, SQUIRTLE!
HRRH?
THUNK!
HUUUUURRRH!
WA-AH-AH-AH!
WHOMP WHOMP
WHOMP WHOMP

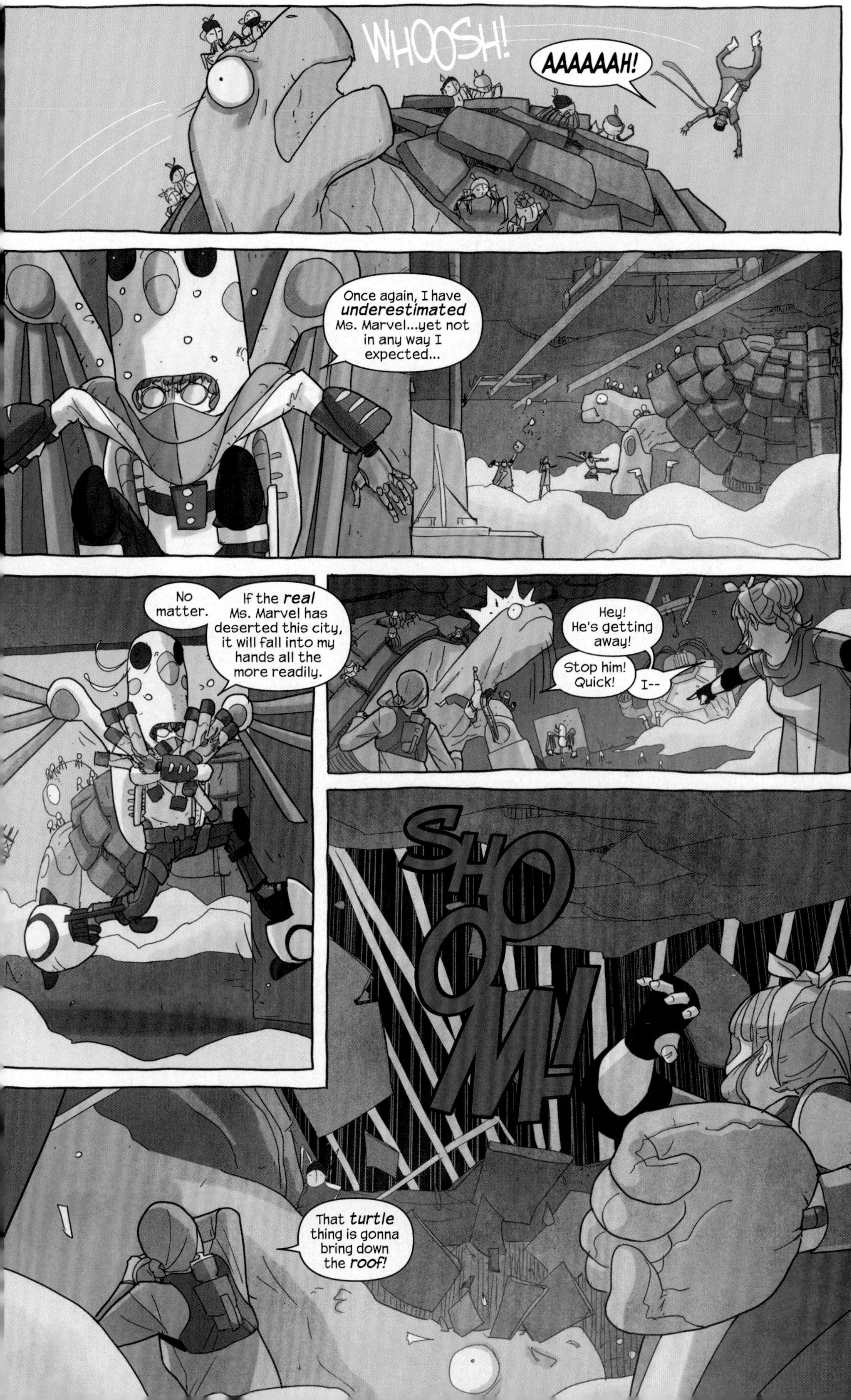
WHOOSH!
AAAAAAH!
Once again, I have *underestimated* Ms. Marvel...yet not in any way I expected...
No matter.
If the *real* Ms. Marvel has deserted this city, it will fall into my hands all the more readily.
Hey! He's getting away!
Stop him! Quick!
I--
SHOOM!
That *turtle* thing is gonna bring down the *roof!*

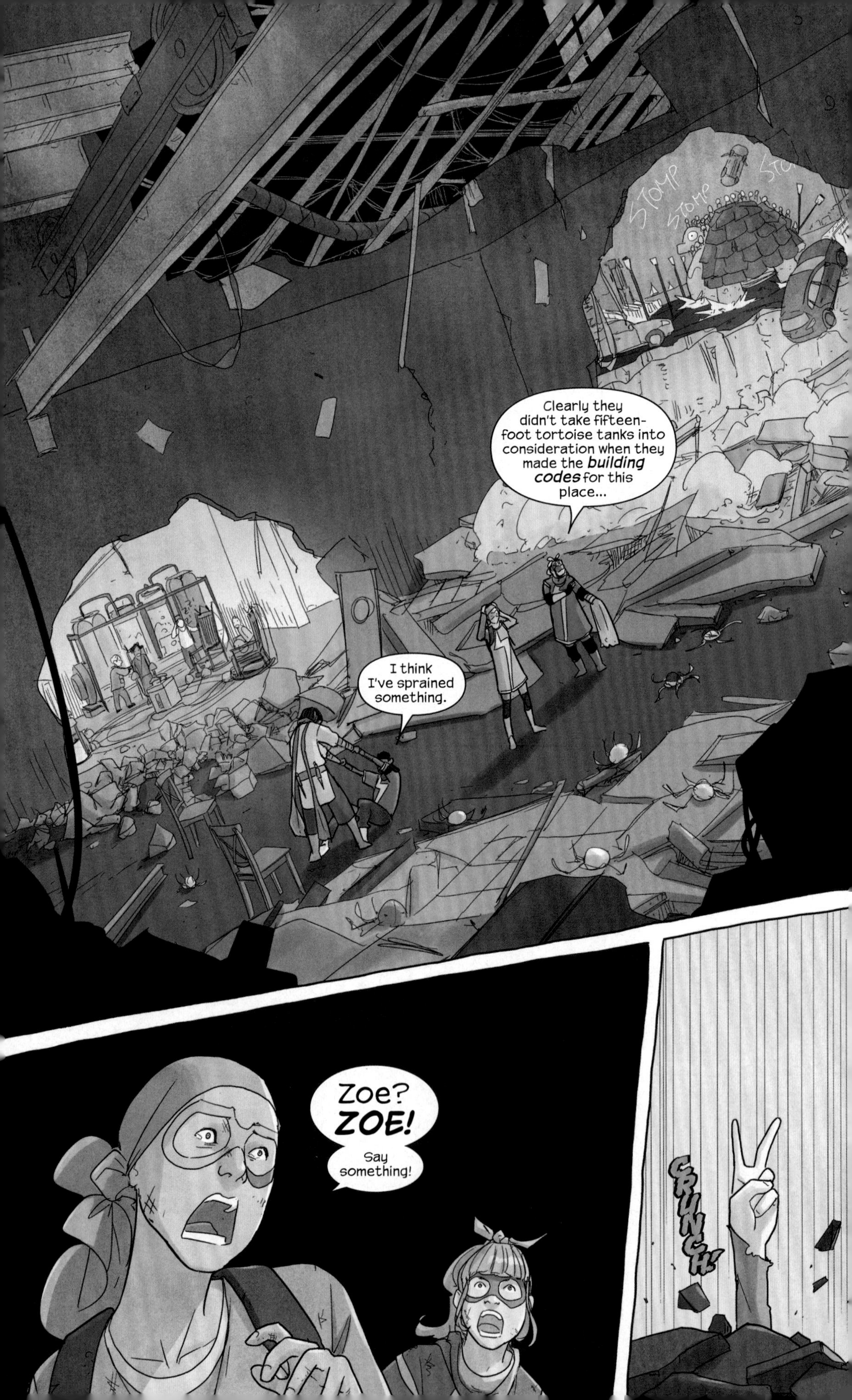
STOMP
STOMP
Clearly they didn't take fifteen-foot tortoise tanks into consideration when they made the *building codes* for this place...
I think I've sprained something.
Zoe? **ZOE!**
Say something!
CRUNCH!

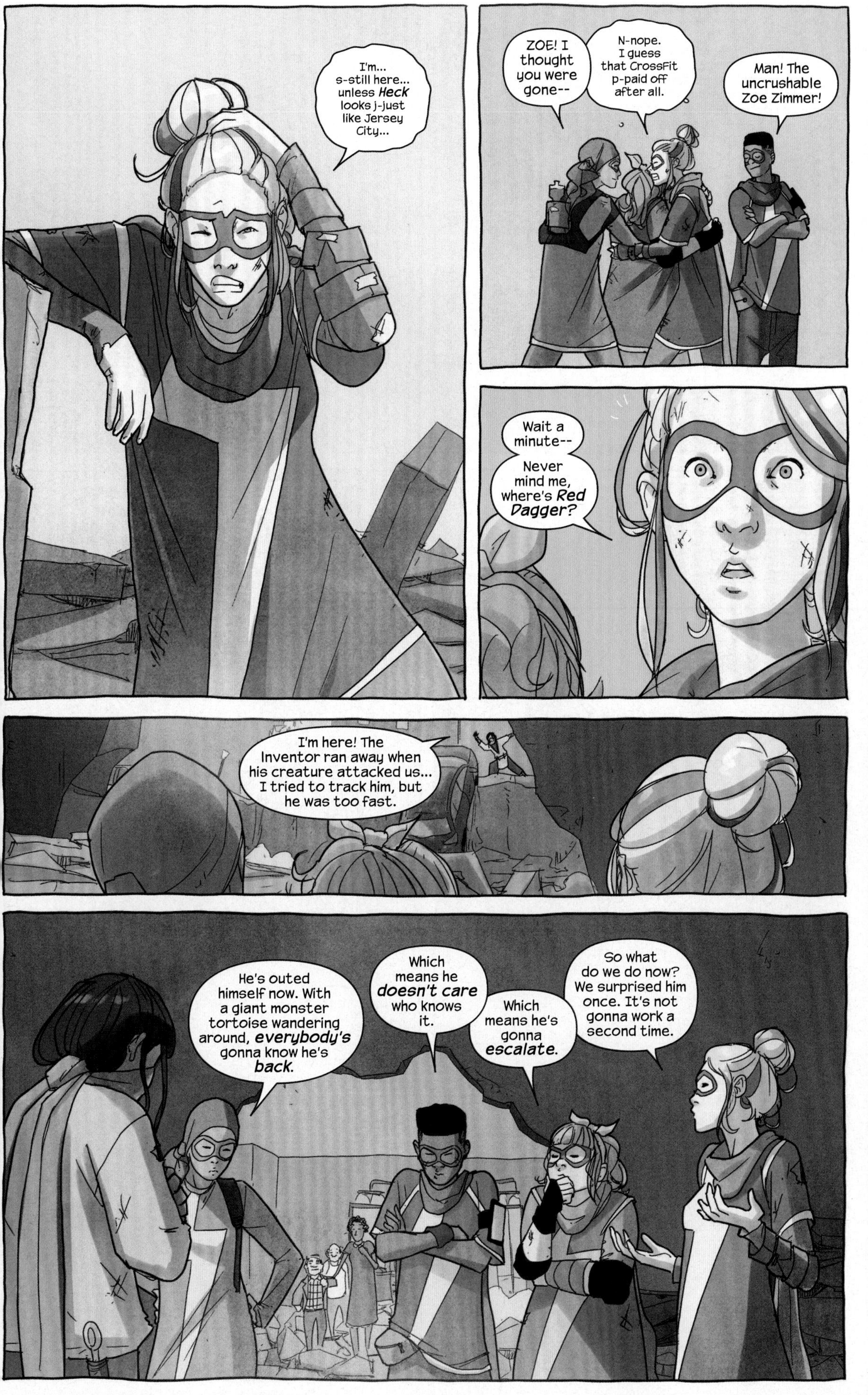

I'm... s-still here... unless *Heck* looks j-just like Jersey City...
ZOE! I thought you were gone--
N-nope. I guess that CrossFit p-paid off after all.
Man! The uncrushable Zoe Zimmer!
Wait a minute--
Never mind me, where's *Red Dagger*?
I'm here! The Inventor ran away when his creature attacked us... I tried to track him, but he was too fast.
He's outed himself now. With a giant monster tortoise wandering around, *everybody's* gonna know he's *back*.
Which means he *doesn't care* who knows it.
Which means he's gonna *escalate*.
So what do we do now? We surprised him once. It's not gonna work a second time.

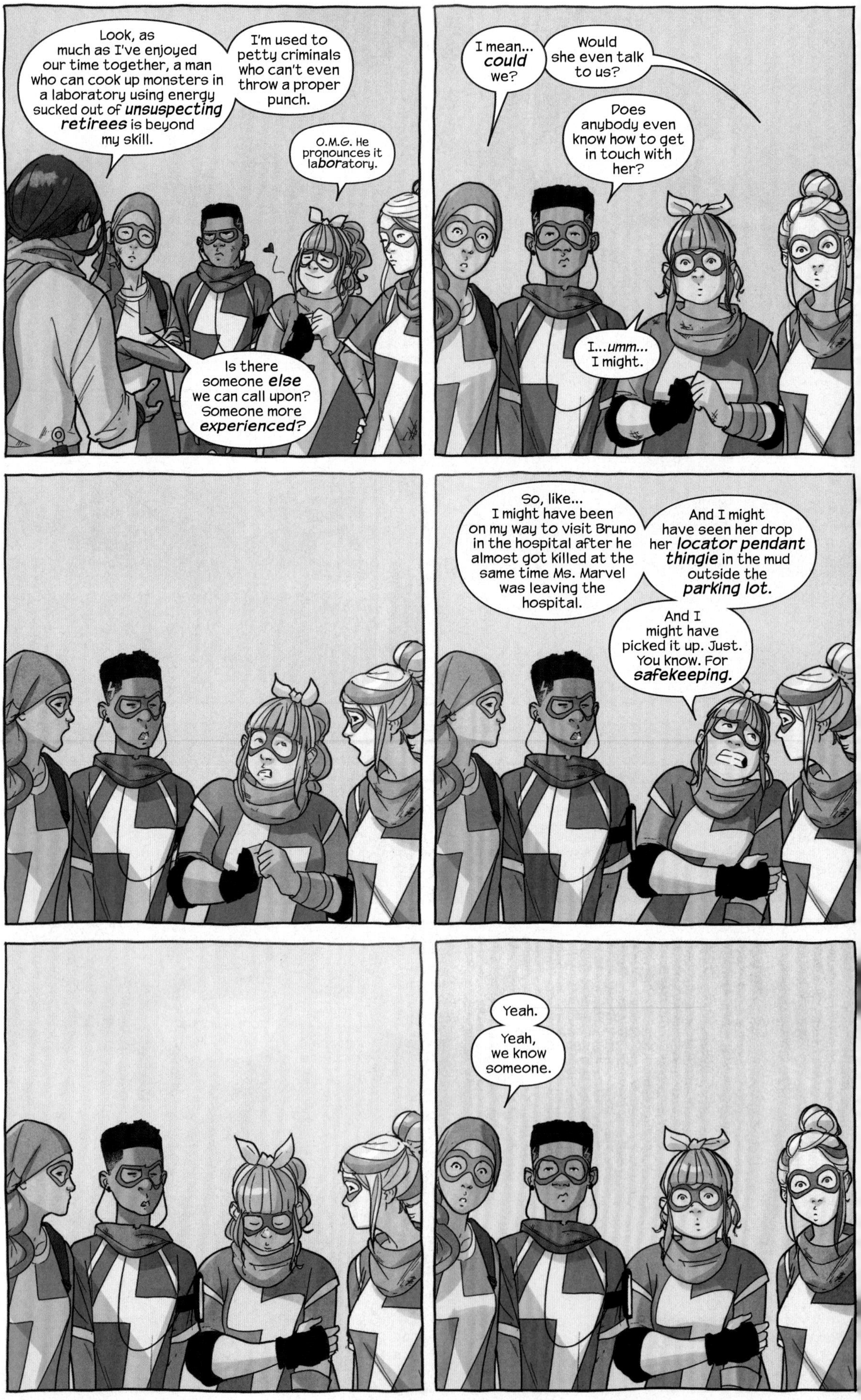
Look, as much as I've enjoyed our time together, a man who can cook up monsters in a laboratory using energy sucked out of *unsuspecting retirees* is beyond my skill.
I'm used to petty criminals who can't even throw a proper punch.
O.M.G. He pronounces it la*bor*atory.
Is there someone *else* we can call upon? Someone more *experienced*?
I mean... *could* we?
Would she even talk to us?
Does anybody even know how to get in touch with her?
I...*umm*... I might.
So, like... I might have been on my way to visit Bruno in the hospital after he almost got killed at the same time Ms. Marvel was leaving the hospital.
And I might have seen her drop her *locator pendant thingie* in the mud outside the *parking lot.*
And I might have picked it up. Just. You know. For *safekeeping.*
Yeah.
Yeah, we know someone.

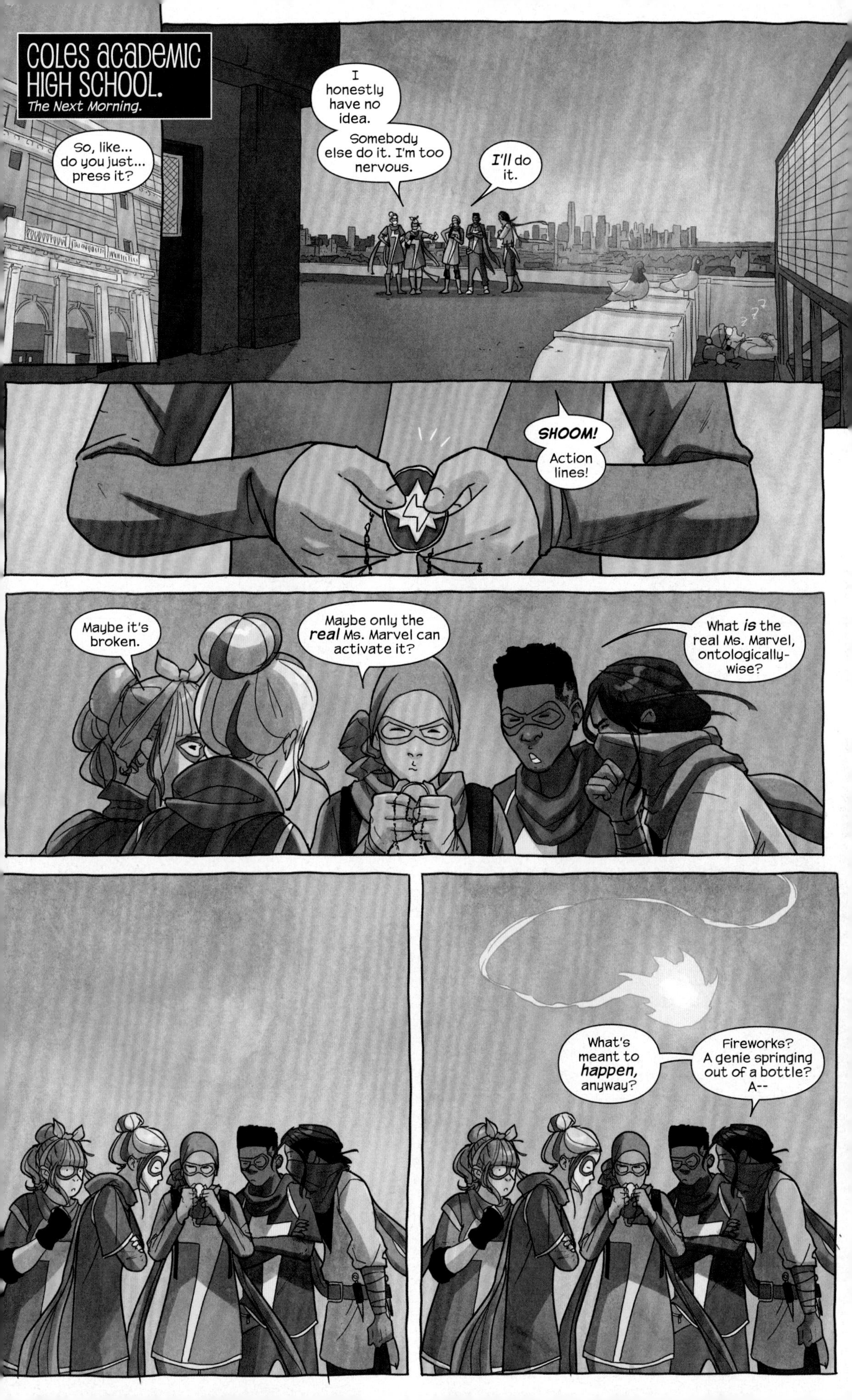

COLES ACADEMIC HIGH SCHOOL.
The Next Morning.
So, like... do you just... press it?
I honestly have no idea.
Somebody else do it. I'm too nervous.
I'll do it.
SHOOM! Action lines!
Maybe it's broken.
Maybe only the real Ms. Marvel can activate it?
What is the real Ms. Marvel, ontologically-wise?
What's meant to happen, anyway?
Fireworks? A genie springing out of a bottle? A--

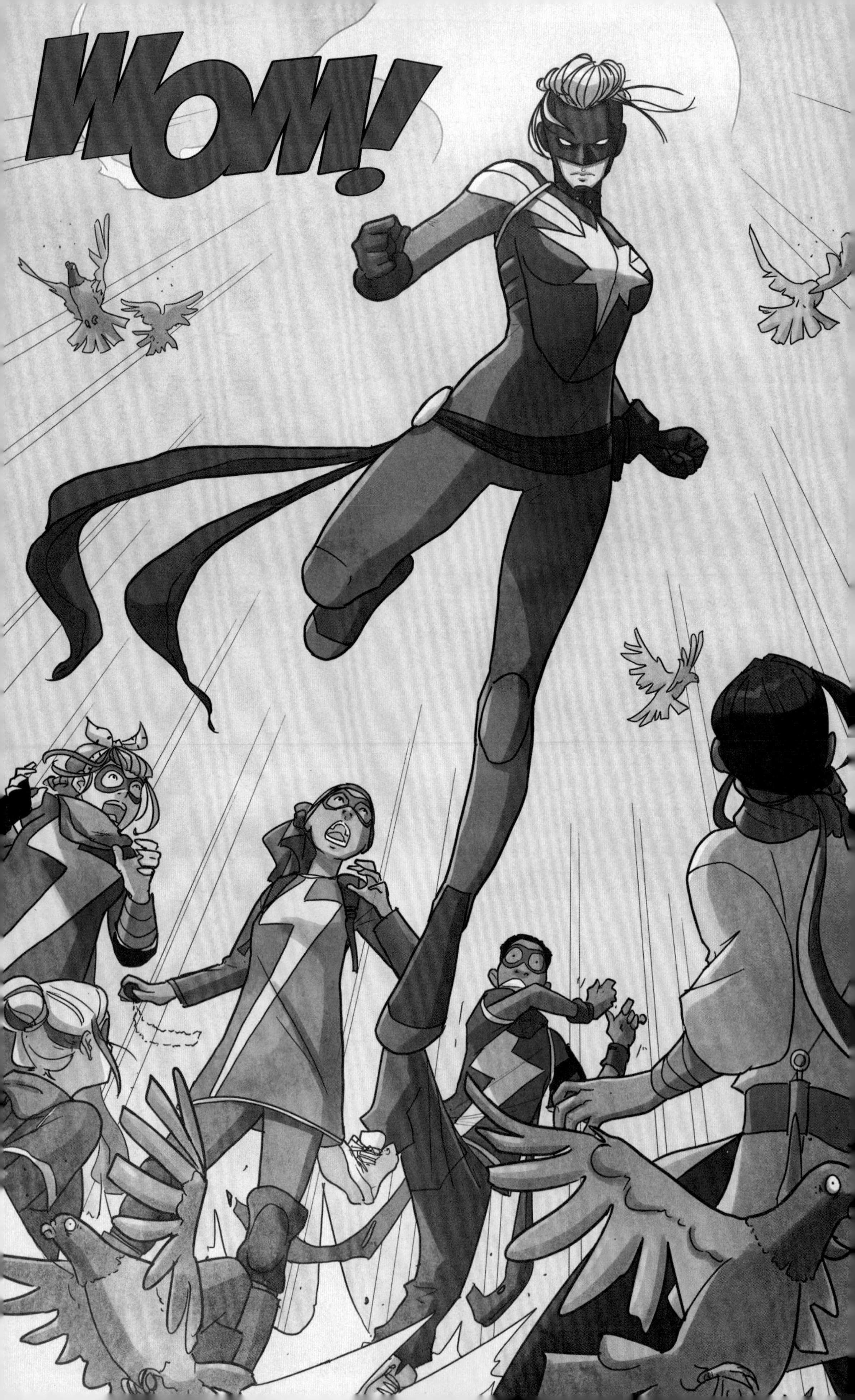
WOM!

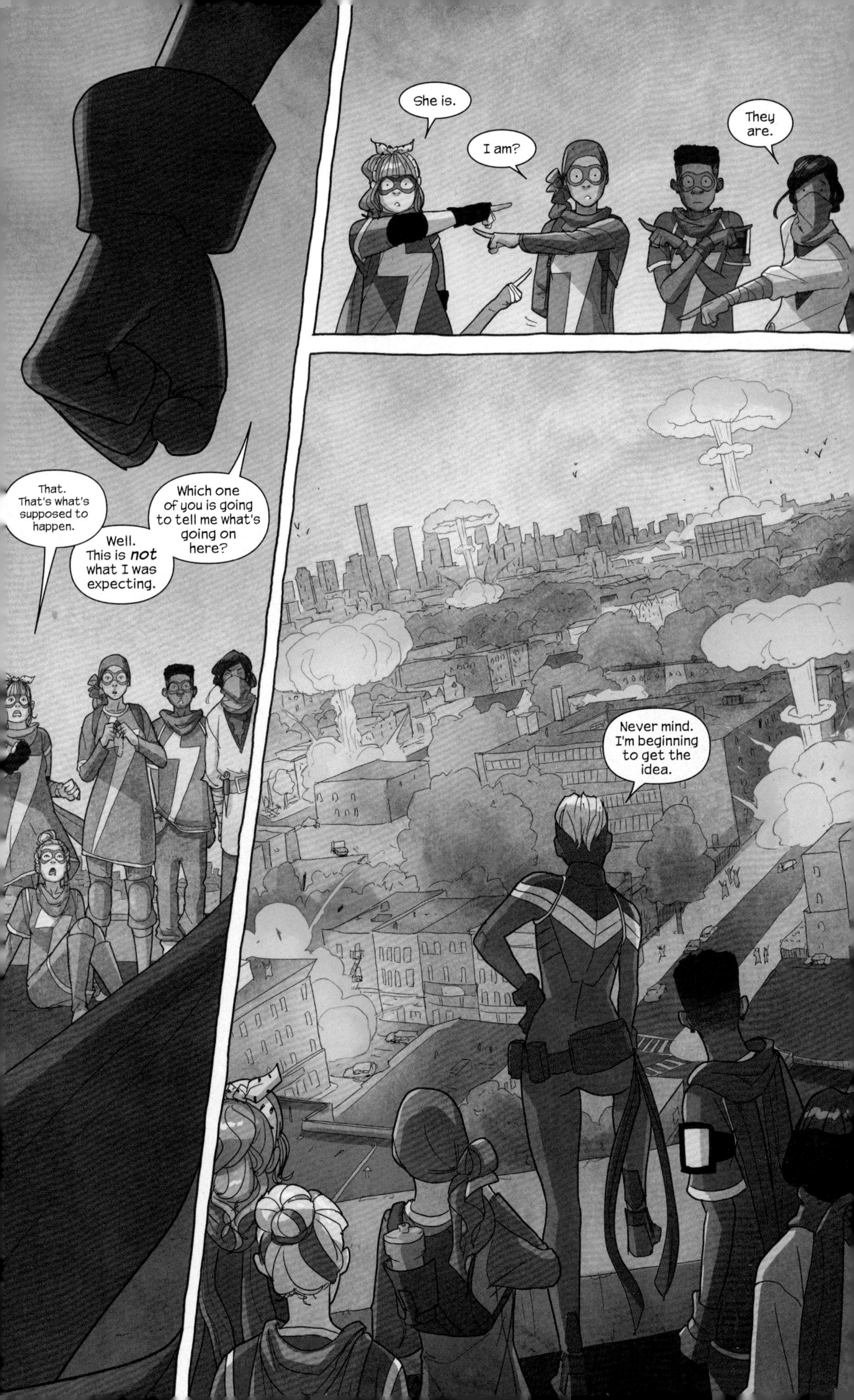
Which one of you is going to tell me what's going on here?
Well. This is *not* what I was expecting.
That. That's what's supposed to happen.
She is.
I am?
They are.
Never mind. I'm beginning to get the idea.

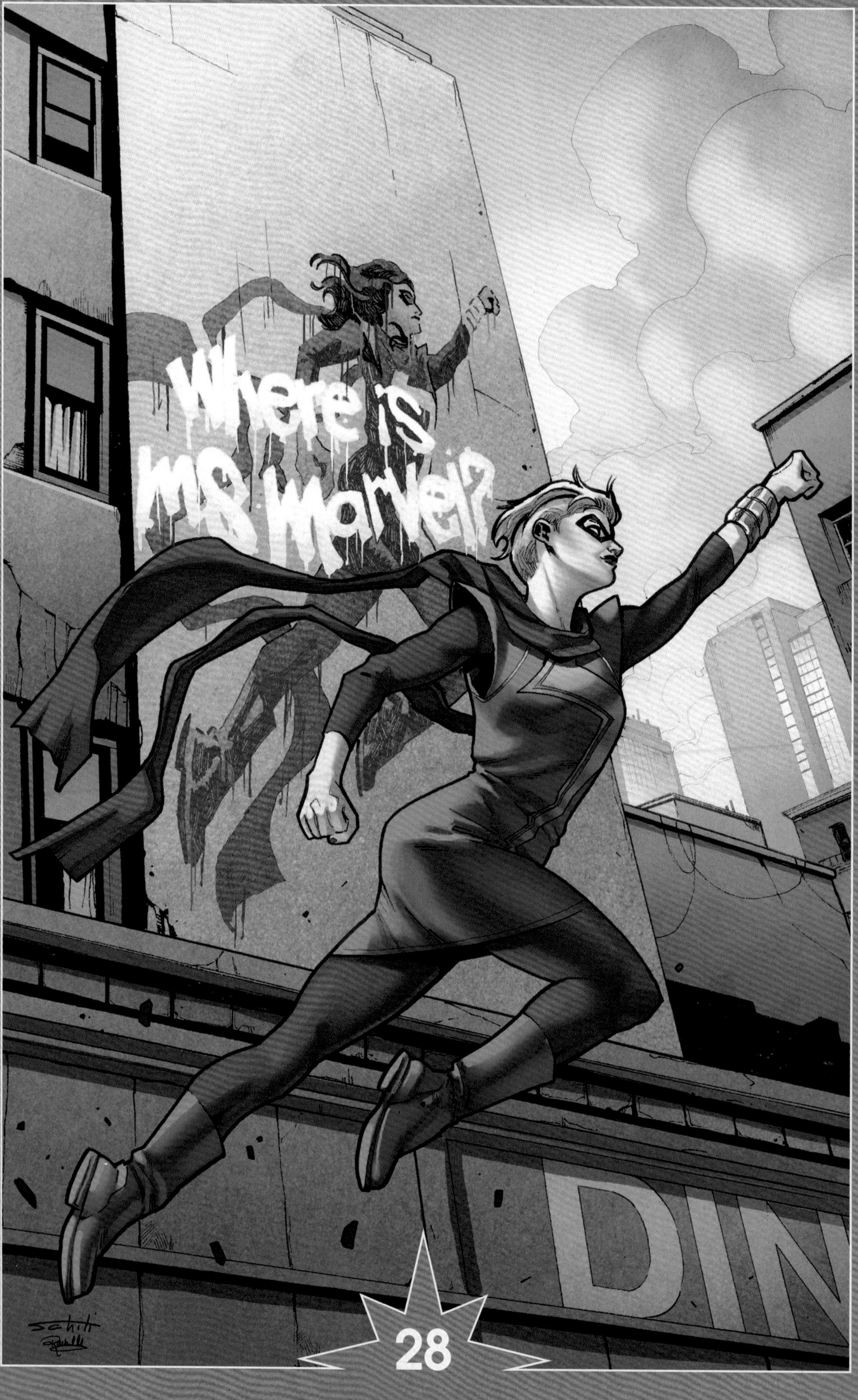
Where is
MS Marvel?
DIN
28

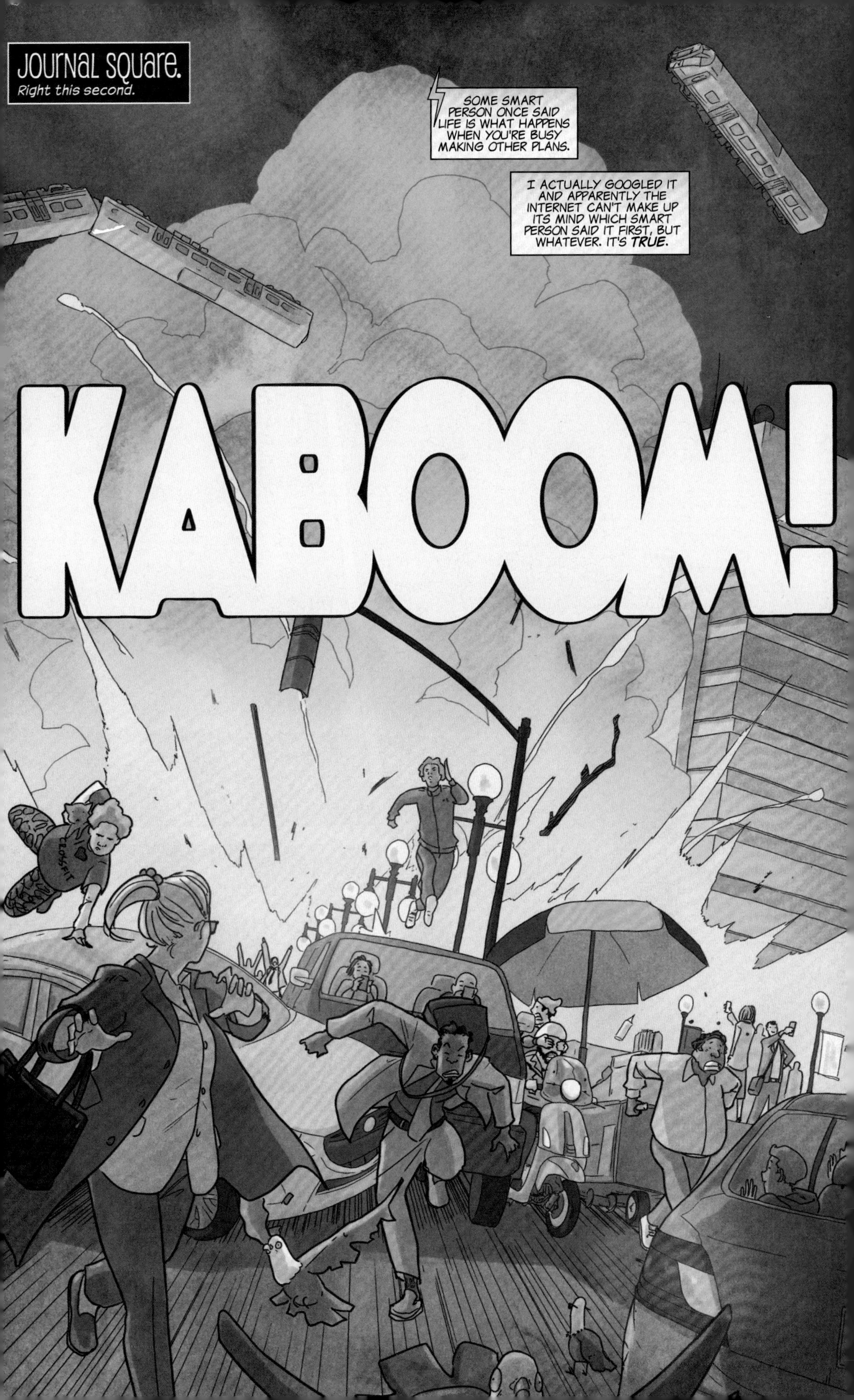
JOURNAL SQUARE.
Right this second.
SOME SMART PERSON ONCE SAID LIFE IS WHAT HAPPENS WHEN YOU'RE BUSY MAKING OTHER PLANS.
I ACTUALLY GOOGLED IT AND APPARENTLY THE INTERNET CAN'T MAKE UP ITS MIND WHICH SMART PERSON SAID IT FIRST, BUT WHATEVER. IT'S TRUE.
KABOOM!
CROSSFIT

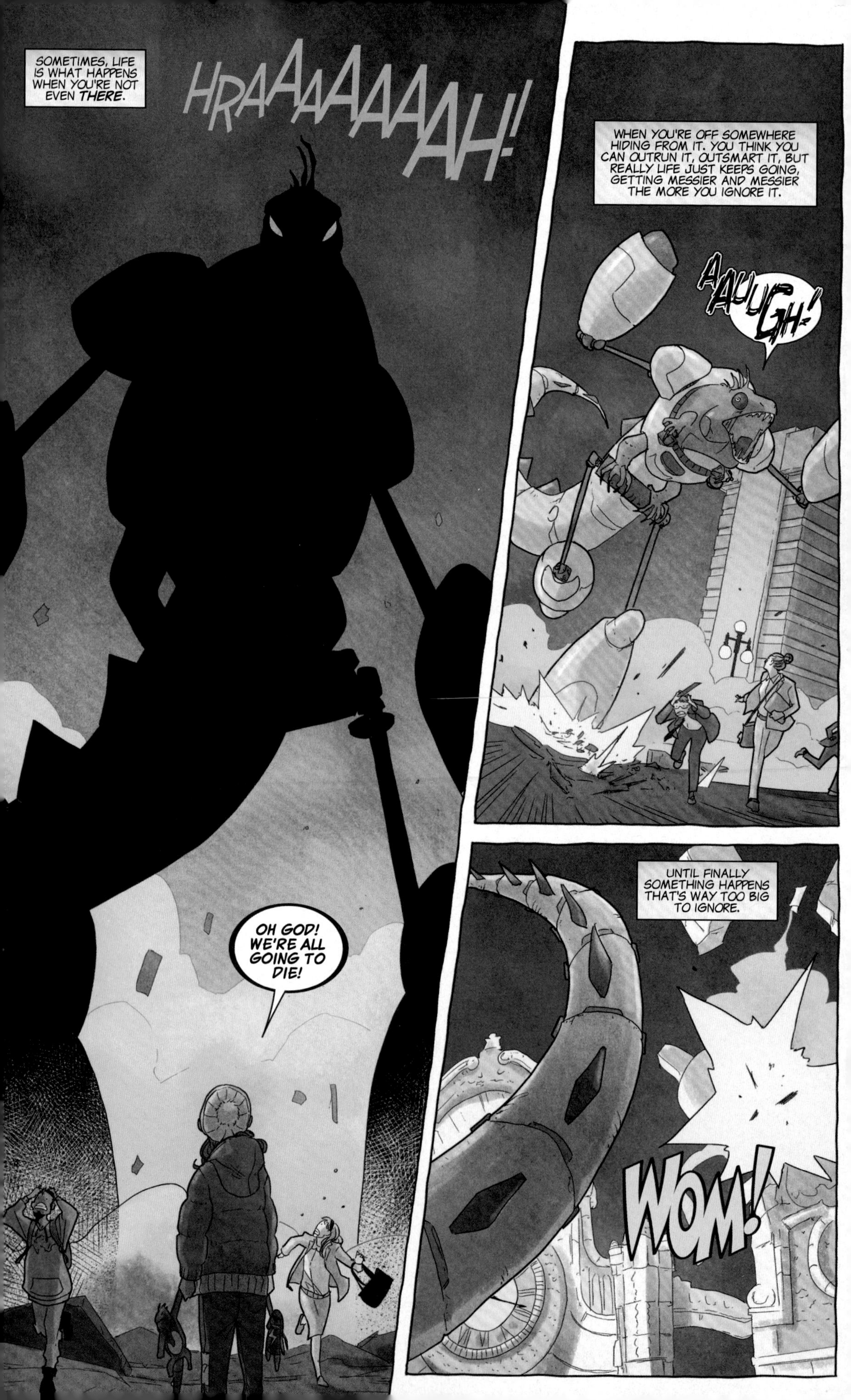
SOMETIMES, LIFE IS WHAT HAPPENS WHEN YOU'RE NOT EVEN THERE.
HRAAAAAAAAH!
OH GOD! WE'RE ALL GOING TO DIE!
WHEN YOU'RE OFF SOMEWHERE HIDING FROM IT. YOU THINK YOU CAN OUTRUN IT, OUTSMART IT, BUT REALLY LIFE JUST KEEPS GOING, GETTING MESSIER AND MESSIER THE MORE YOU IGNORE IT.
AAUUGH!
UNTIL FINALLY SOMETHING HAPPENS THAT'S WAY TOO BIG TO IGNORE.
WOM!

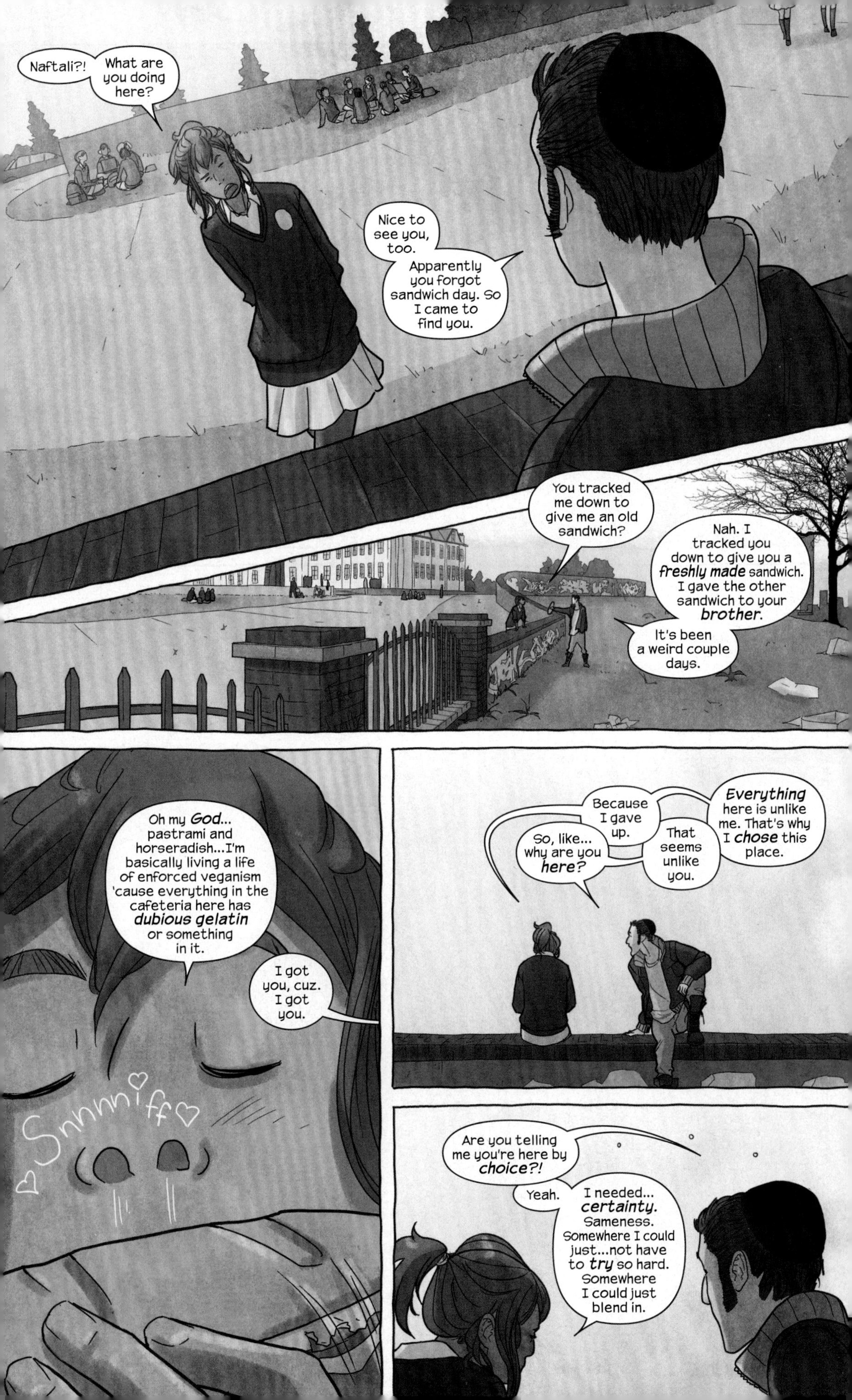

Naftali?!
What are you doing here?
Nice to see you, too.
Apparently you forgot sandwich day. So I came to find you.
You tracked me down to give me an old sandwich?
Nah. I tracked you down to give you a *freshly made* sandwich. I gave the other sandwich to your *brother*.
It's been a weird couple days.
Oh my *God*... pastrami and horseradish...I'm basically living a life of enforced veganism 'cause everything in the cafeteria here has *dubious gelatin* or something in it.
I got you, cuz. I got you.
Snnniff
So, like... why are you *here?*
Because I gave up.
That seems unlike you.
Everything here is unlike me. That's why I *chose* this place.
Are you telling me you're here by *choice?!*
Yeah.
I needed... *certainty.* Sameness. Somewhere I could just...not have to *try* so hard. Somewhere I could just blend in.

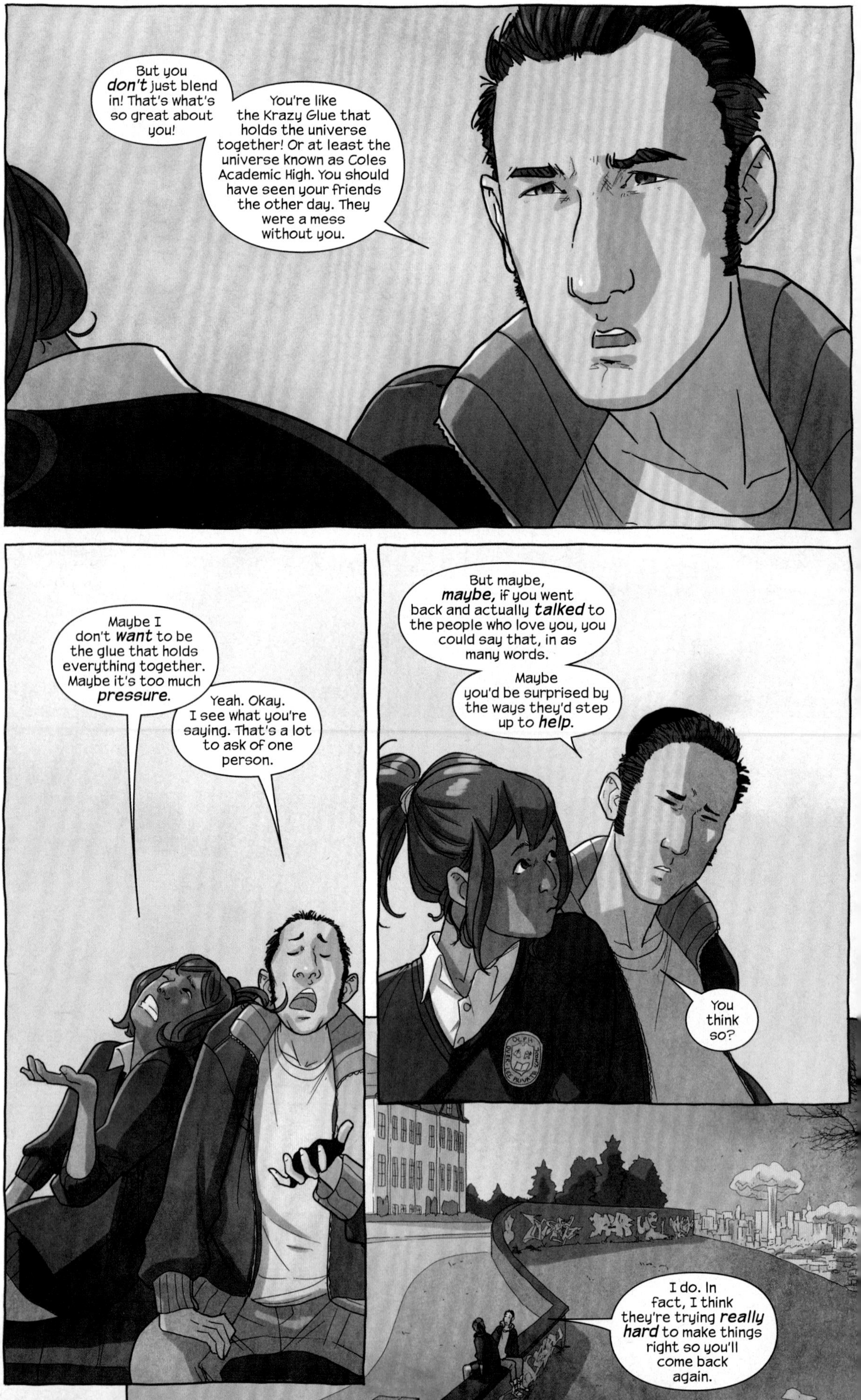
But you *don't* just blend in! That's what's so great about you!
You're like the Krazy Glue that holds the universe together! Or at least the universe known as Coles Academic High. You should have seen your friends the other day. They were a mess without you.
Maybe I don't *want* to be the glue that holds everything together. Maybe it's too much *pressure*.
Yeah. Okay. I see what you're saying. That's a lot to ask of one person.
But maybe, *maybe*, if you went back and actually *talked* to the people who love you, you could say that, in as many words.
Maybe you'd be surprised by the ways they'd step up to *help*.
You think so?
I do. In fact, I think they're trying *really hard* to make things right so you'll come back again.

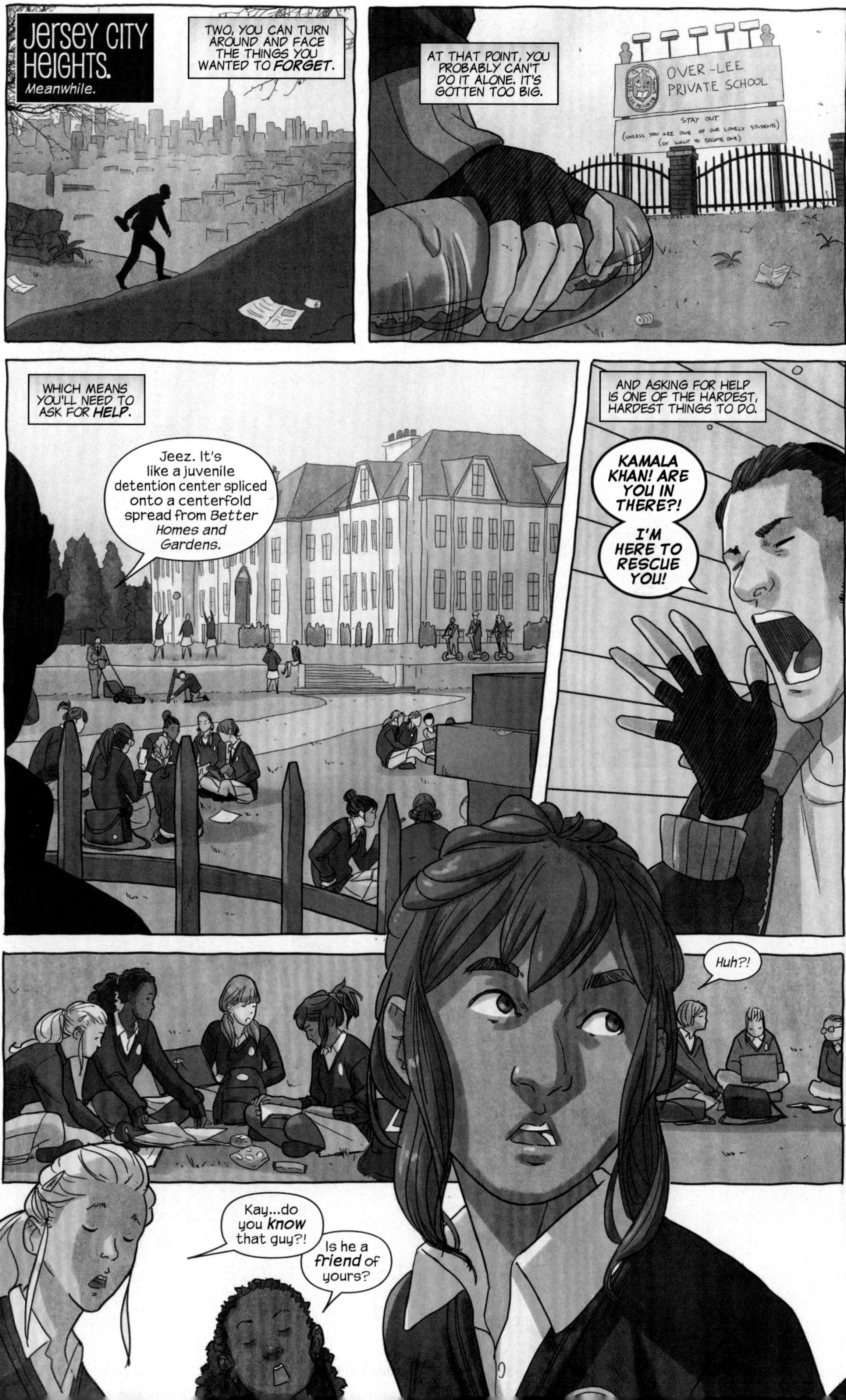

Jersey City Heights.
Meanwhile.
TWO, YOU CAN TURN AROUND AND FACE THE THINGS YOU WANTED TO FORGET.
AT THAT POINT, YOU PROBABLY CAN'T DO IT ALONE. IT'S GOTTEN TOO BIG.
OVER-LEE PRIVATE SCHOOL
STAY OUT
(UNLESS YOU ARE ONE OF OUR LOVELY STUDENTS)
(OR WANT TO BECOME ONE)
WHICH MEANS YOU'LL NEED TO ASK FOR HELP.
Jeez. It's like a juvenile detention center spliced onto a centerfold spread from Better Homes and Gardens.
AND ASKING FOR HELP IS ONE OF THE HARDEST, HARDEST THINGS TO DO.
KAMALA KHAN! ARE YOU IN THERE?!
I'M HERE TO RESCUE YOU!
Huh?!
Kay...do you know that guy?!
Is he a friend of yours?

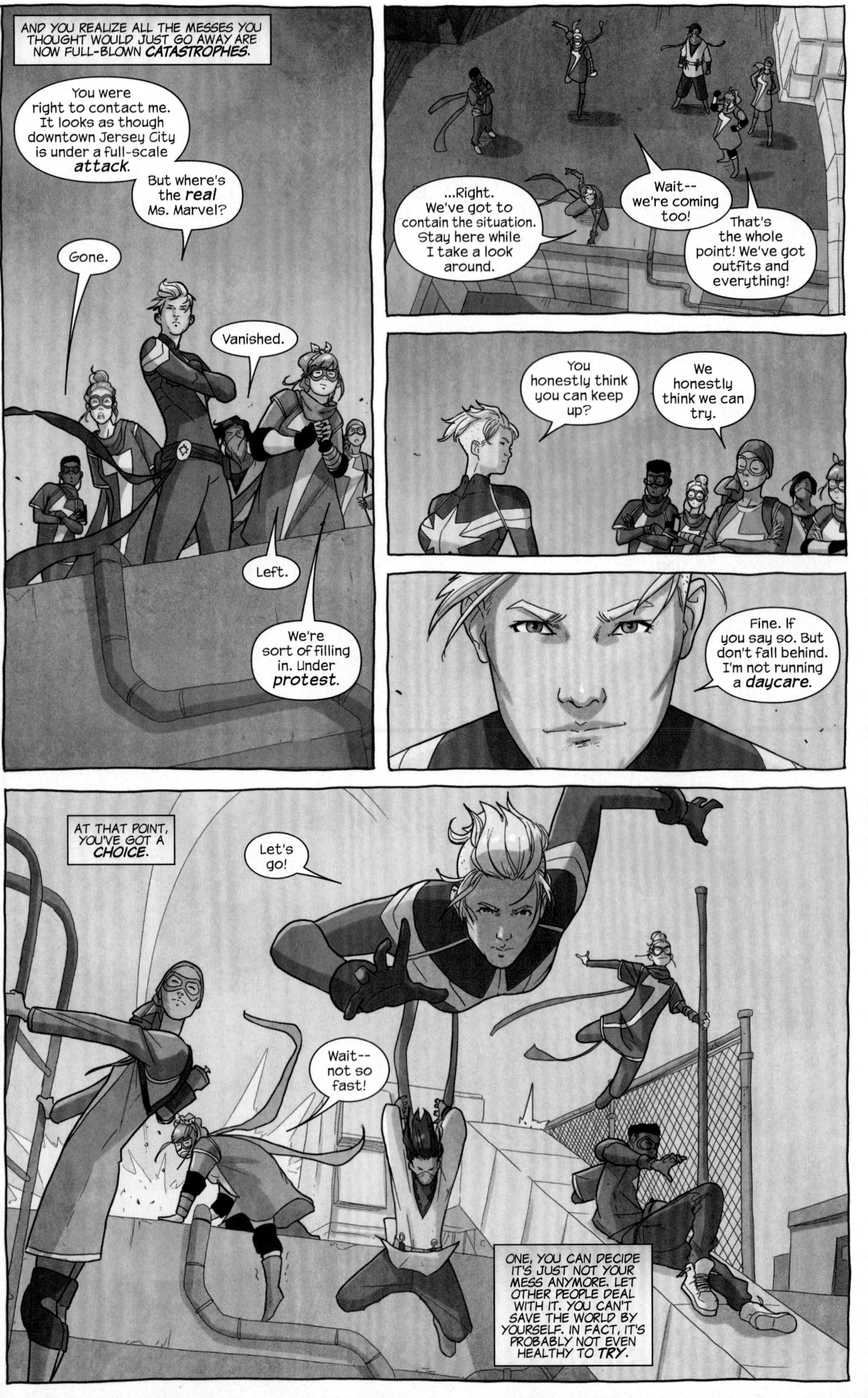
AND YOU REALIZE ALL THE MESSES YOU THOUGHT WOULD JUST GO AWAY ARE NOW FULL-BLOWN CATASTROPHES.
You were right to contact me. It looks as though downtown Jersey City is under a full-scale attack.
But where's the real Ms. Marvel?
Gone.
Vanished.
Left.
We're sort of filling in. Under protest.
...Right. We've got to contain the situation. Stay here while I take a look around.
Wait--we're coming too!
That's the whole point! We've got outfits and everything!
You honestly think you can keep up?
We honestly think we can try.
Fine. If you say so. But don't fall behind. I'm not running a daycare.
AT THAT POINT, YOU'VE GOT A CHOICE.
Let's go!
Wait--not so fast!
ONE, YOU CAN DECIDE IT'S JUST NOT YOUR MESS ANYMORE. LET OTHER PEOPLE DEAL WITH IT. YOU CAN'T SAVE THE WORLD BY YOURSELF. IN FACT, IT'S PROBABLY NOT EVEN HEALTHY TO TRY.

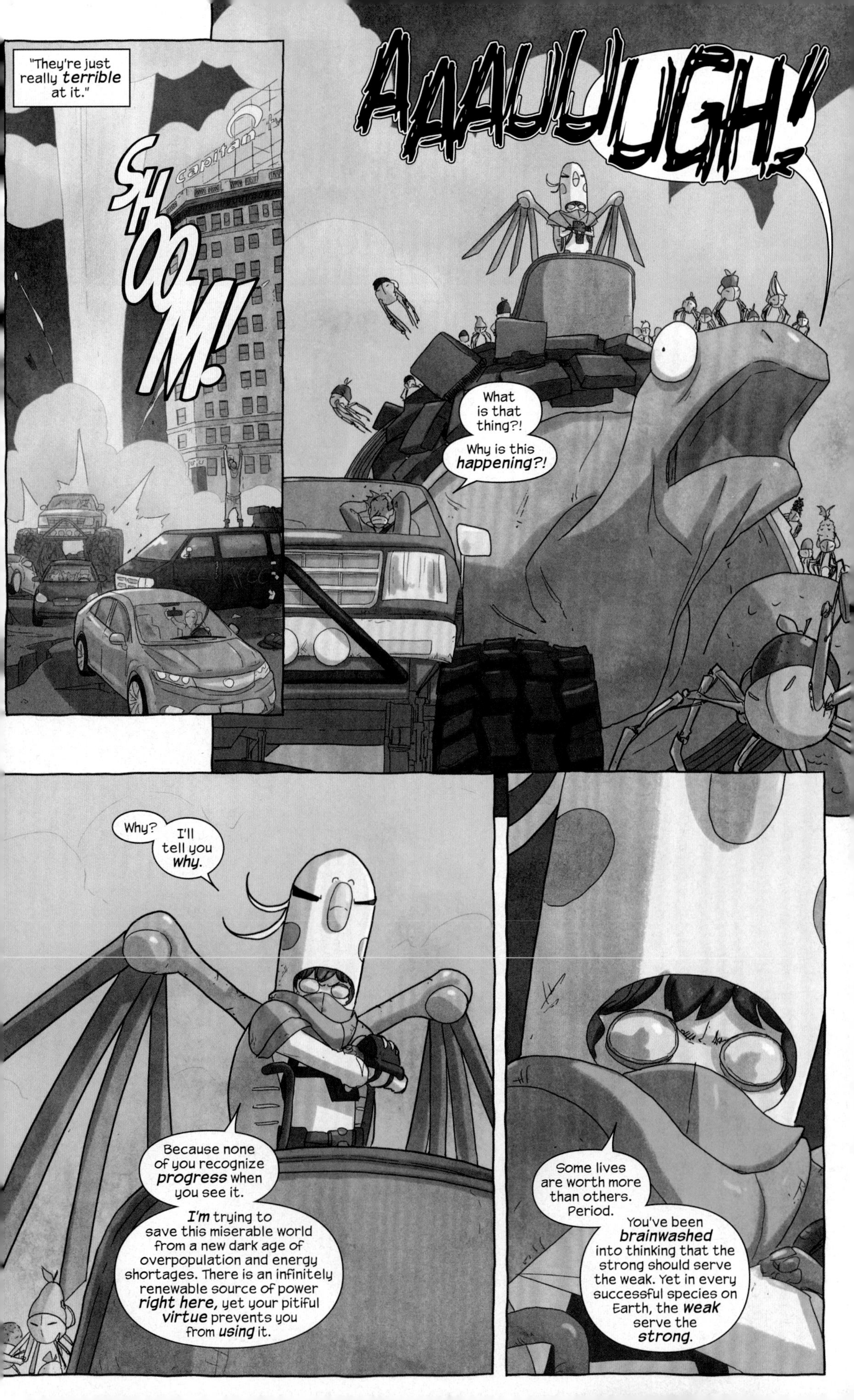
"They're just really *terrible* at it."
SHOOM!
AAAUUUGH!
What is that thing?!
Why is this *happening?!*
Why?
I'll tell you *why*.
Because none of you recognize *progress* when you see it.
I'm trying to save this miserable world from a new dark age of overpopulation and energy shortages. There is an infinitely renewable source of power *right here,* yet your pitiful *virtue* prevents you from *using* it.
Some lives are worth more than others. Period.
You've been *brainwashed* into thinking that the strong should serve the weak. Yet in every successful species on Earth, the *weak* serve the *strong*.

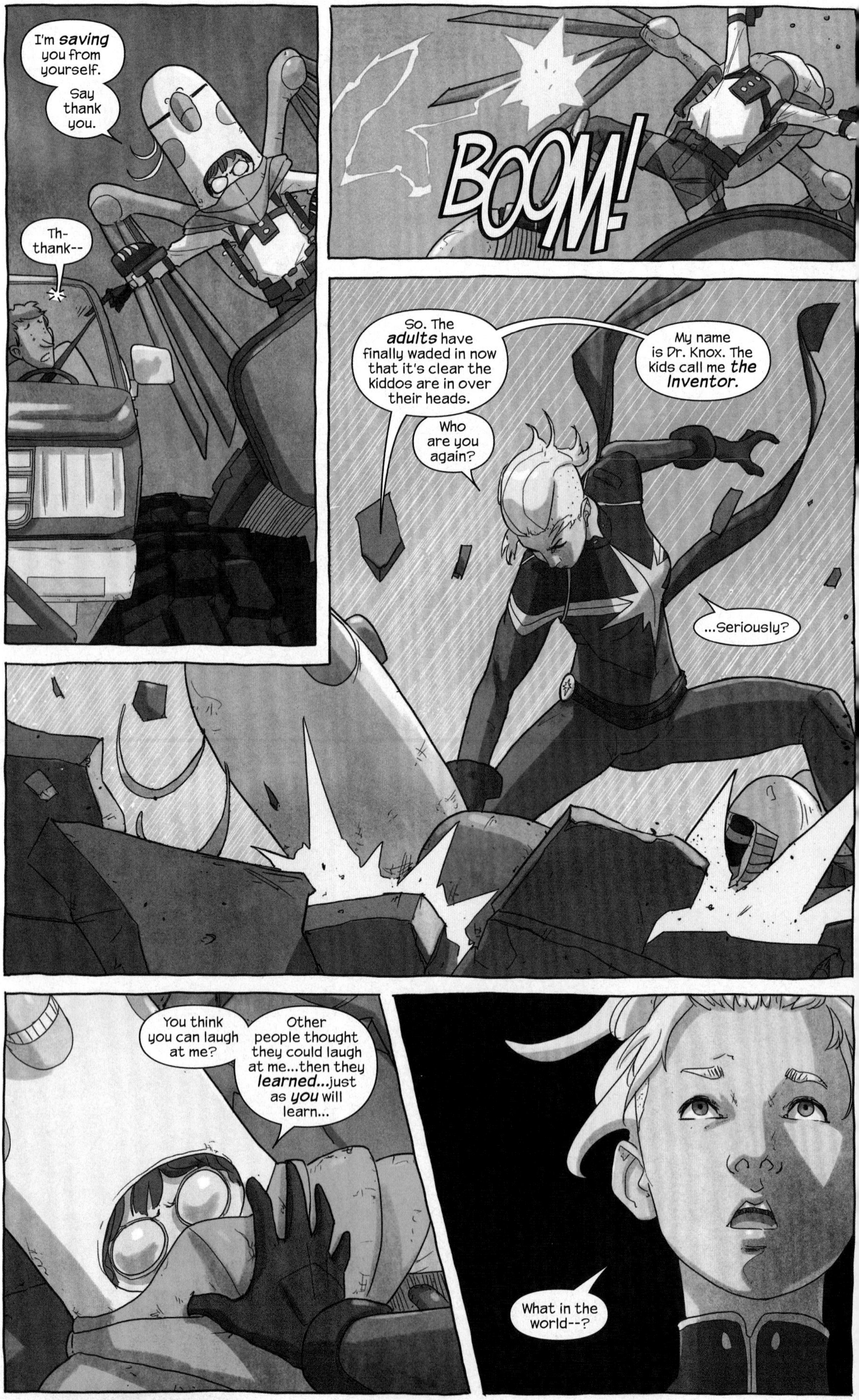
I'm *saving* you from yourself.
Say thank you.
Th- thank--
BOOM!
So. The *adults* have finally waded in now that it's clear the kiddos are in over their heads.
Who are you again?
My name is Dr. Knox. The kids call me *the Inventor.*
...Seriously?
You think you can laugh at me?
Other people thought they could laugh at me...then they *learned...*just as *you* will learn...
What in the world--?

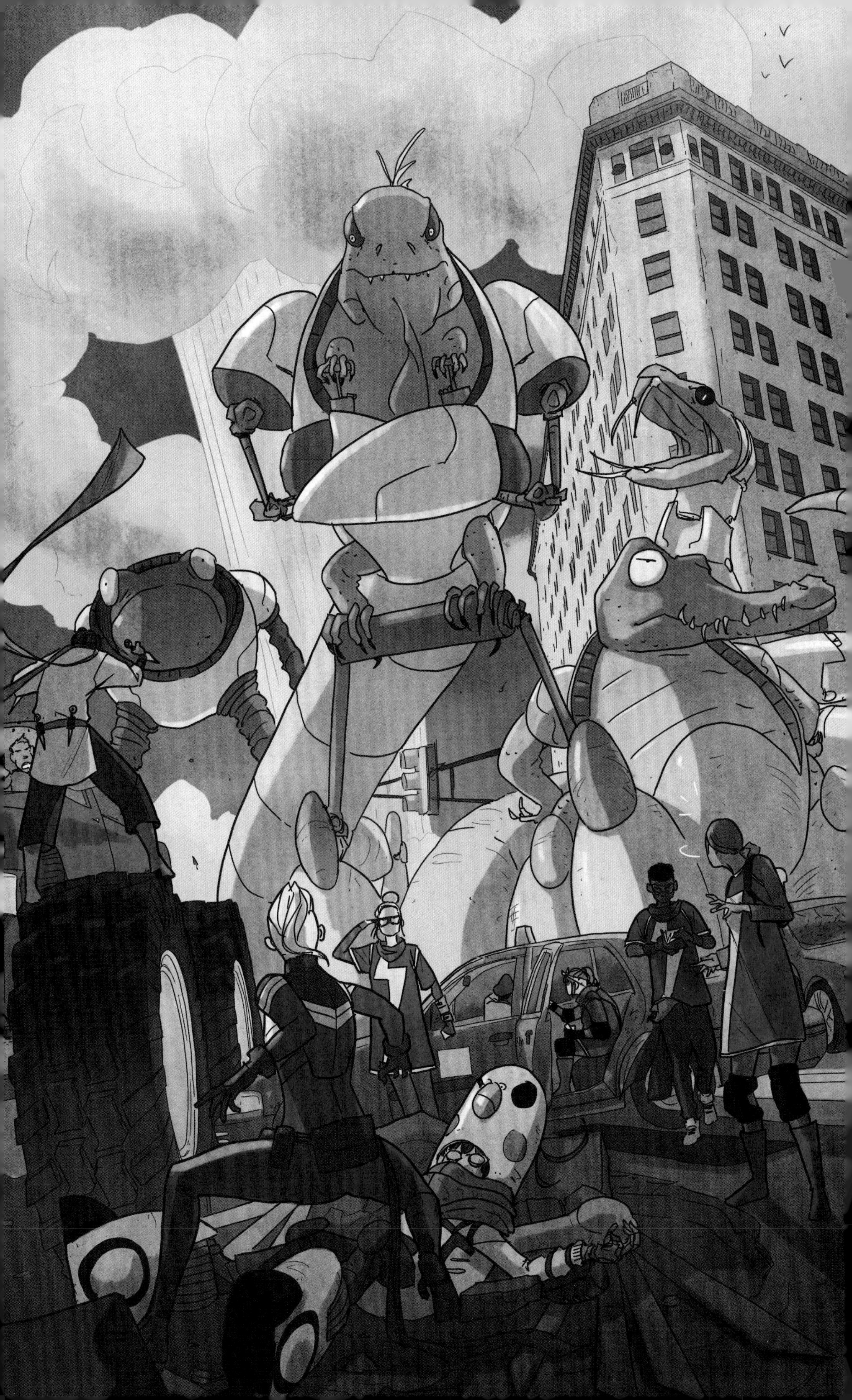

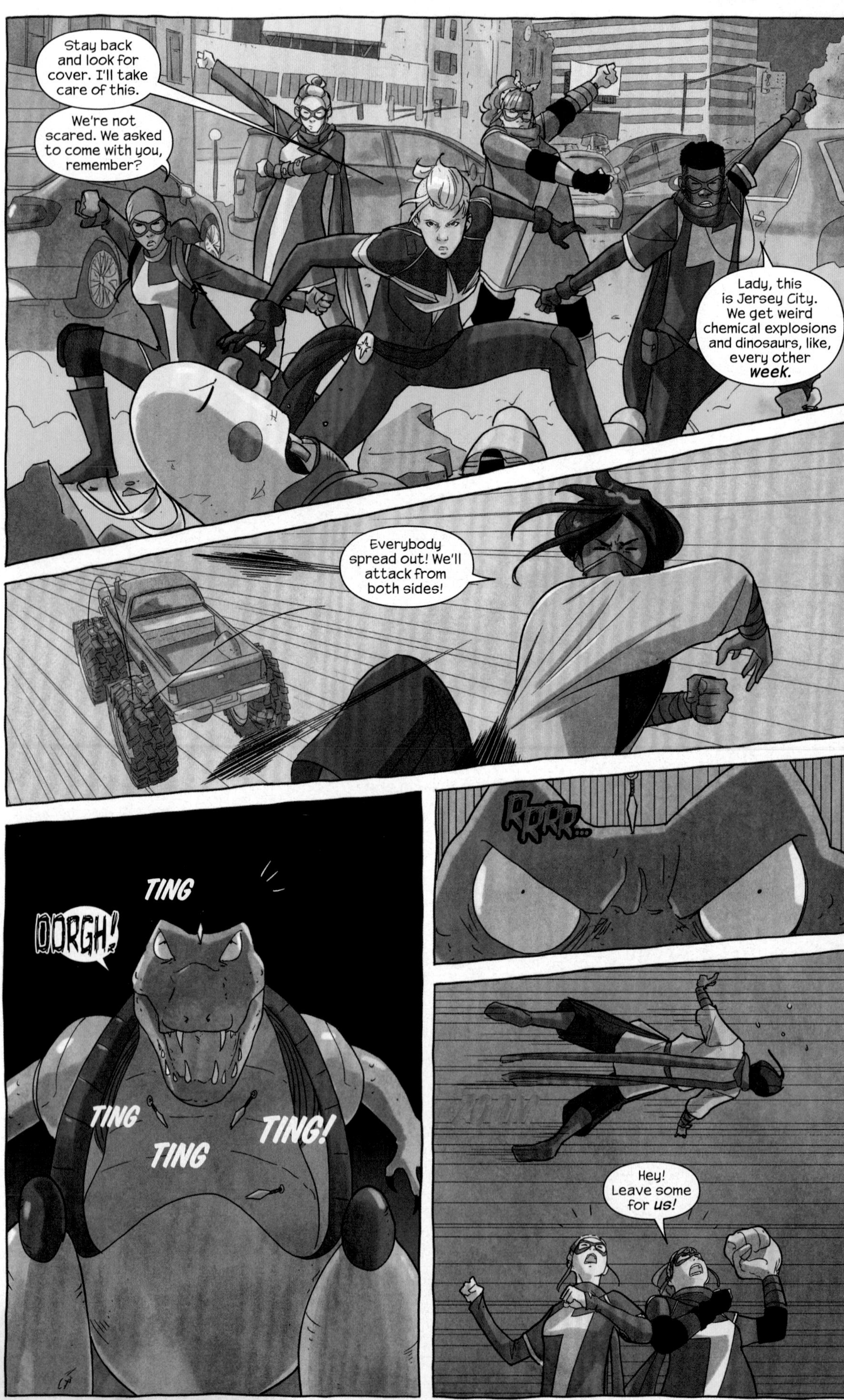
Stay back and look for cover. I'll take care of this.
We're not scared. We asked to come with you, remember?
Lady, this is Jersey City. We get weird chemical explosions and dinosaurs, like, every other **week.**
Everybody spread out! We'll attack from both sides!
TING
OORGH!
TING
TING
TING!
RRRR...
Hey! Leave some for **us!**

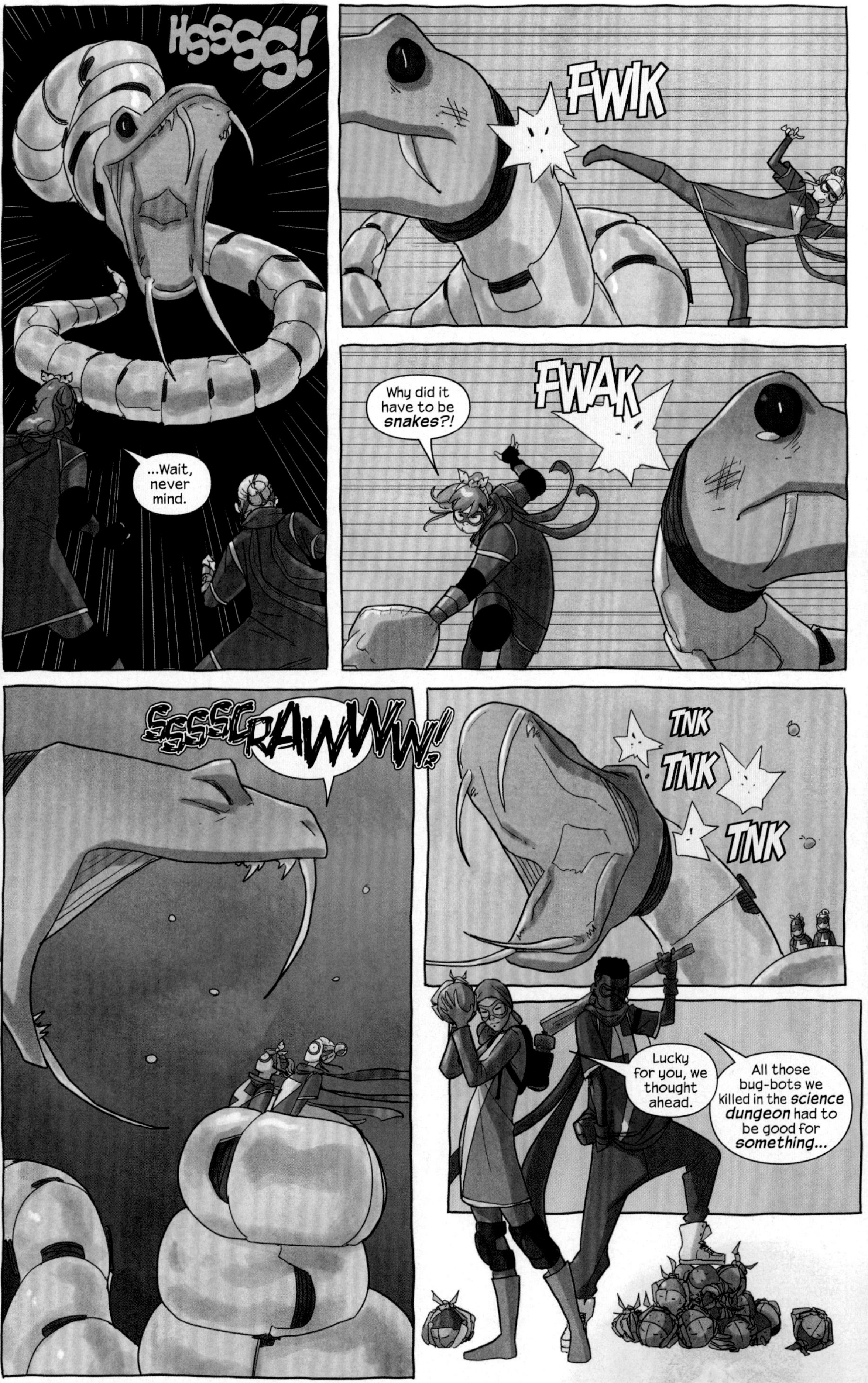
HSSSSS!
...Wait, never mind.
FWIK
FWAK
Why did it have to be snakes?!
SSSSCRAWWW!
TNK
TNK
TNK
Lucky for you, we thought ahead.
All those bug-bots we killed in the science dungeon had to be good for something...

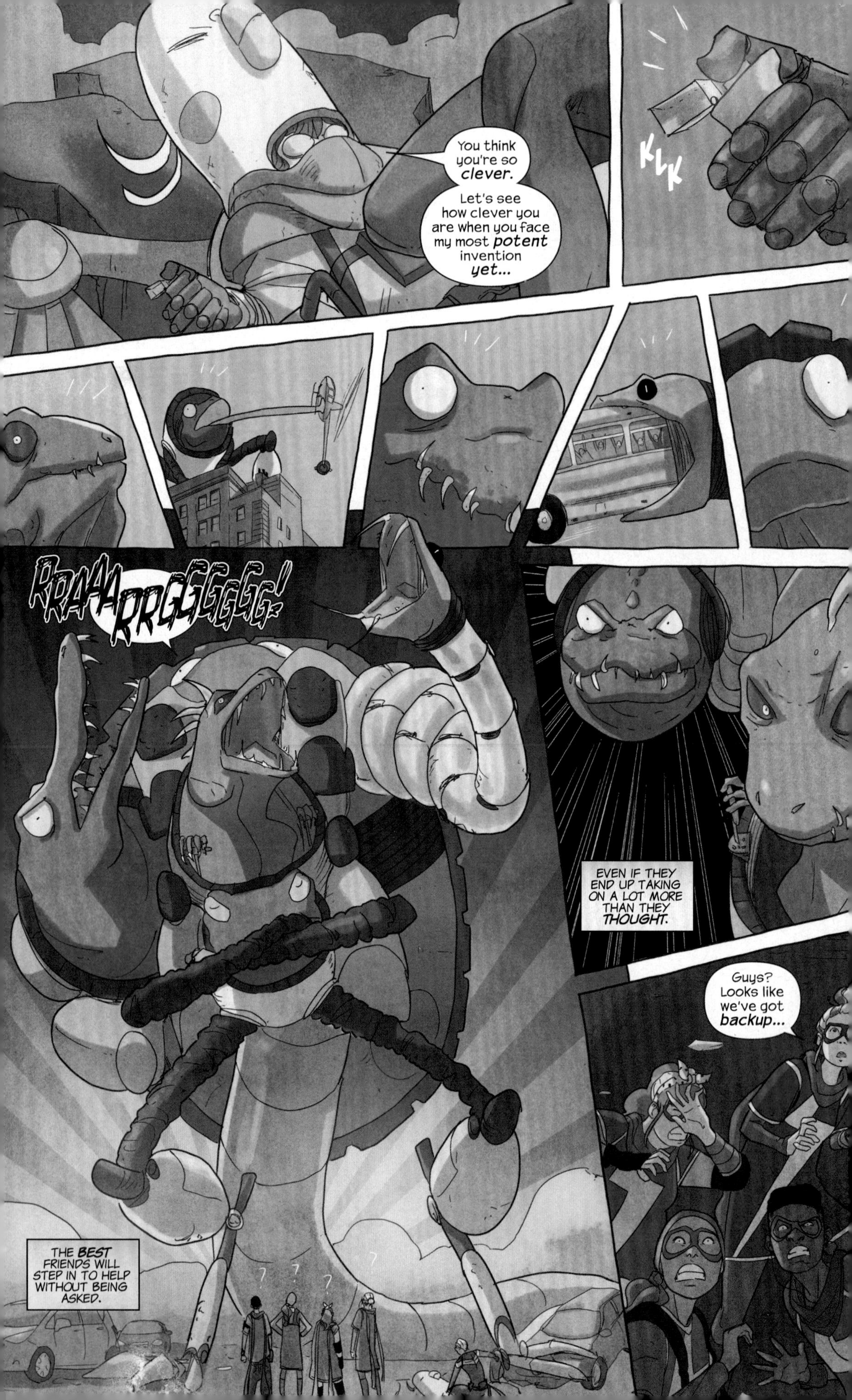
You think you're so *clever.*
Let's see how clever you are when you face my most *potent* invention *yet...*
KLIK
RRAAAARRGGGGGG!
EVEN IF THEY END UP TAKING ON A LOT MORE THAN THEY *THOUGHT.*
THE *BEST* FRIENDS WILL STEP IN TO HELP WITHOUT BEING ASKED.
Guys? Looks like we've got *backup...*

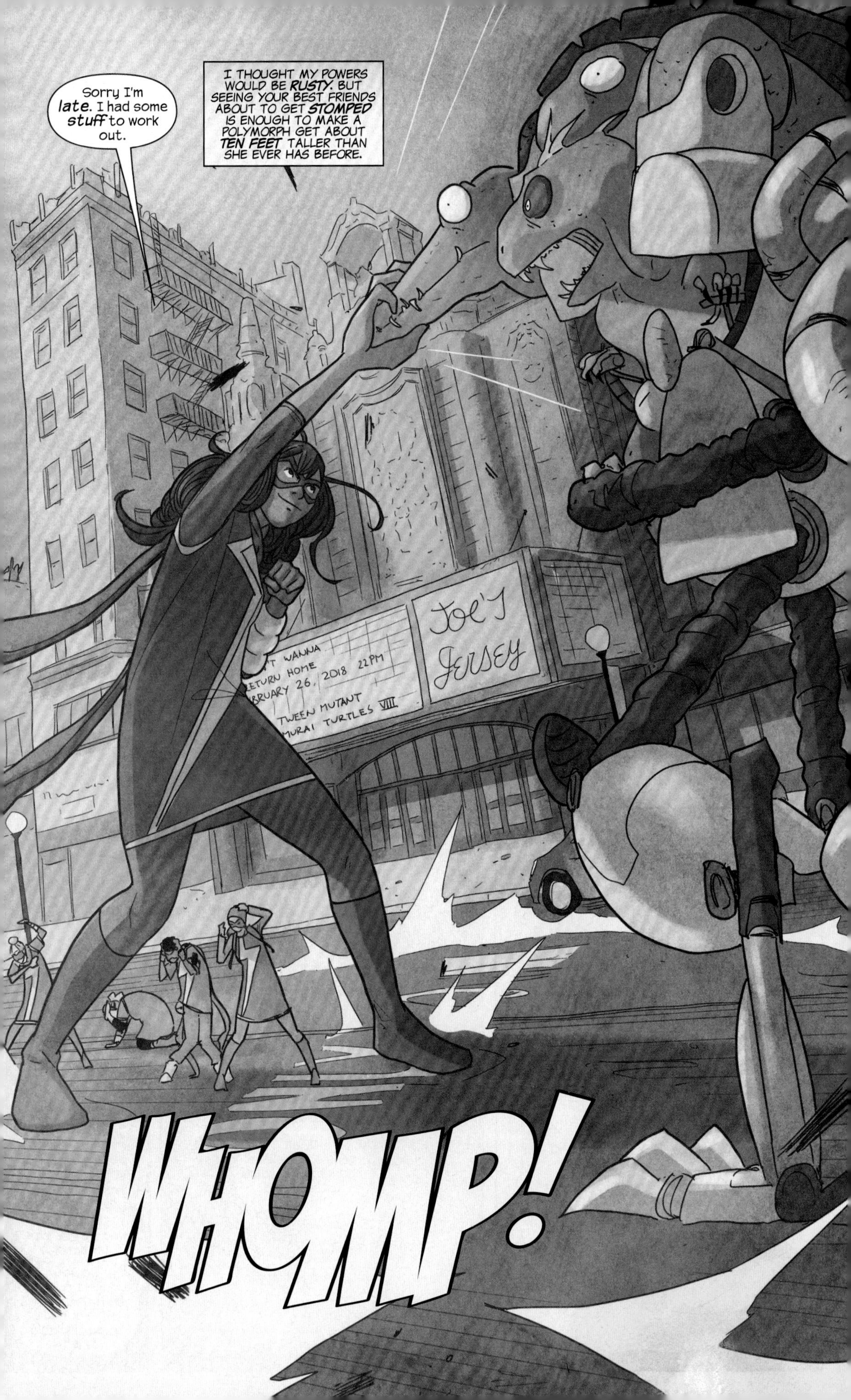

Sorry I'm late. I had some stuff to work out.
I THOUGHT MY POWERS WOULD BE RUSTY. BUT SEEING YOUR BEST FRIENDS ABOUT TO GET STOMPED IS ENOUGH TO MAKE A POLYMORPH GET ABOUT TEN FEET TALLER THAN SHE EVER HAS BEFORE.
'T WANNA RETURN HOME
BRUARY 26, 2018 22PM
TWEEN MUTANT
MURAI TURTLES VIII
Joe's Jersey
WHOMP!

She's **back!**

Of course she's back. She's the real deal.

It's **her!**

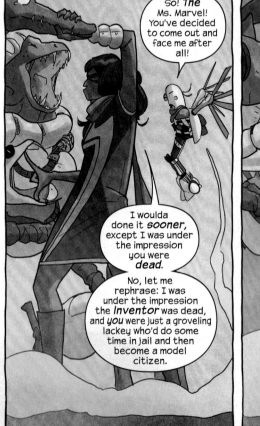

AARGH!

Why you little--

So! **The** Ms. Marvel! You've decided to come out and face me after all!

I woulda done it **sooner**, except I was under the impression you were **dead**.

No, let me rephrase: I was under the impression the **Inventor** was dead, and **you** were just a groveling lackey who'd do some time in jail and then become a model citizen.

Lackey?! I'm disappointed.

Of all people, I would've thought you would understand the **joke**.

That **bird** was **never** the Inventor.

Do you think he cooked **himself** up in a lab? Huh? Who d'you think did **that**?

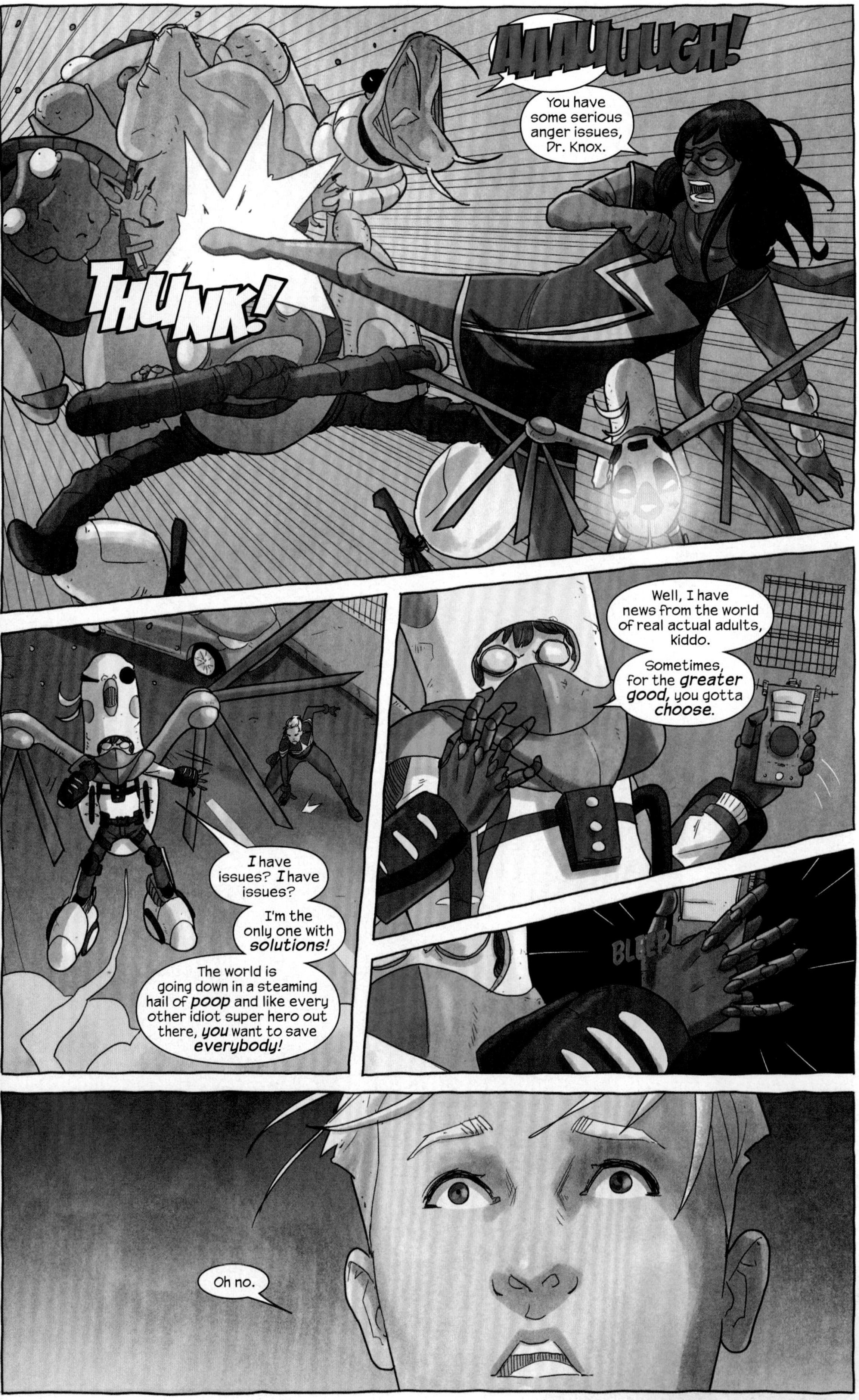
AAAUUUGH!
You have some serious anger issues, Dr. Knox.
THUNK!
I have issues? I have issues?
I'm the only one with solutions!
The world is going down in a steaming hail of poop and like every other idiot super hero out there, you want to save everybody!
Well, I have news from the world of real actual adults, kiddo.
Sometimes, for the greater good, you gotta choose.
BLEEP
Oh no.

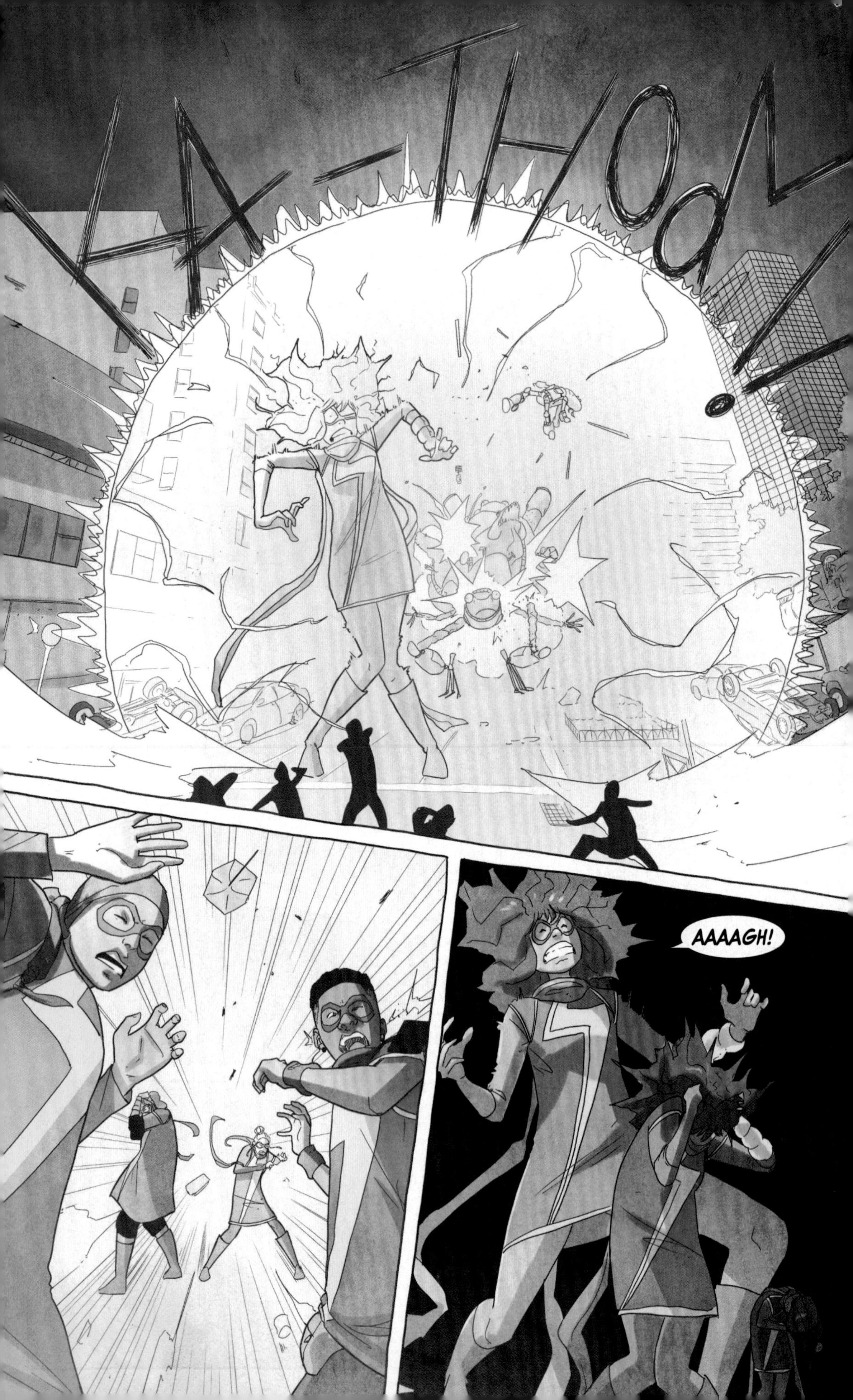
KA-THOOM!
AAAAGH!

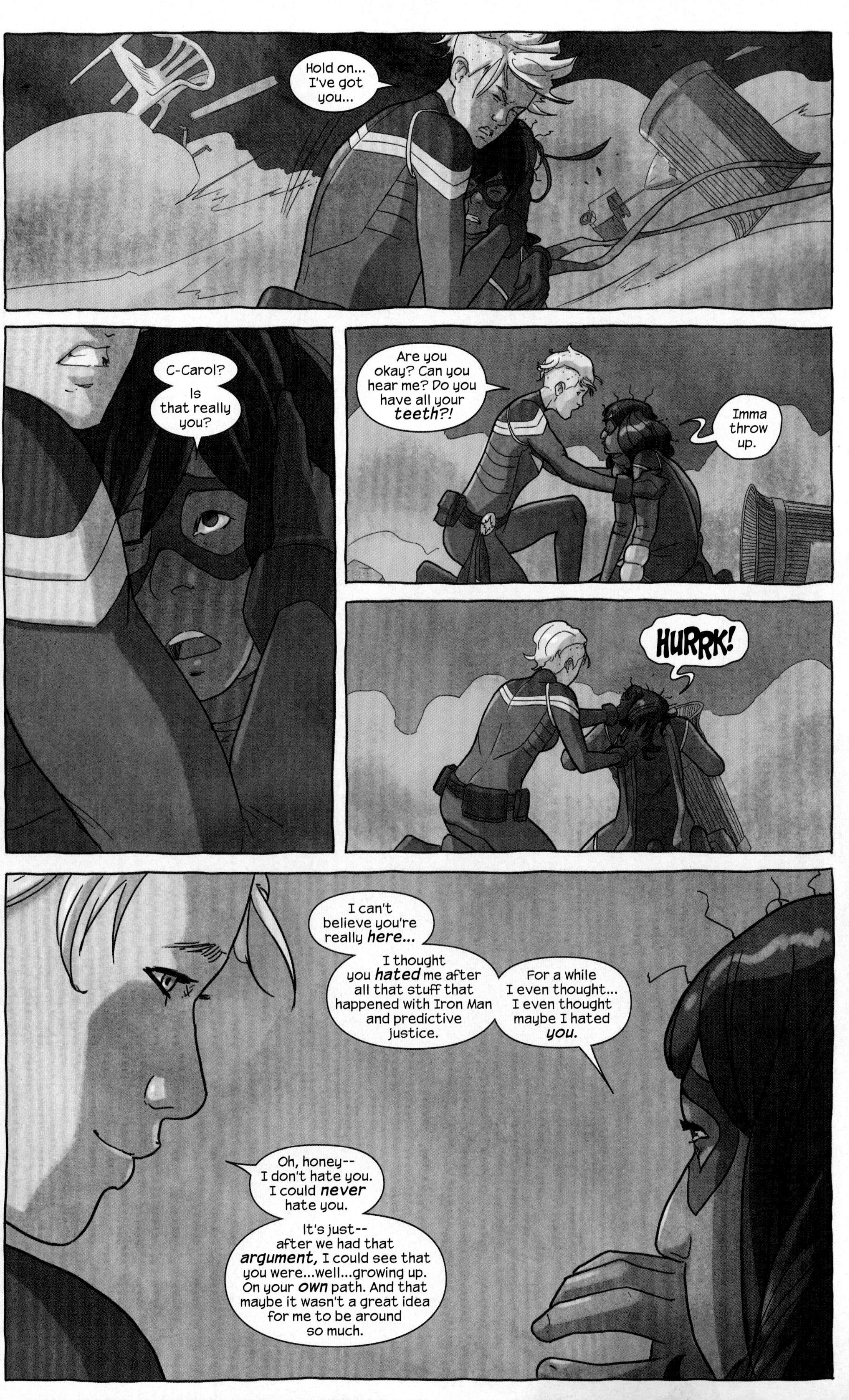
Hold on... I've got you...
C-Carol? Is that really you?
Are you okay? Can you hear me? Do you have all your teeth?!
Imma throw up.
HURRK!
I can't believe you're really here...
I thought you hated me after all that stuff that happened with Iron Man and predictive justice.
For a while I even thought... I even thought maybe I hated you.
Oh, honey-- I don't hate you. I could never hate you.
It's just-- after we had that argument, I could see that you were...well...growing up. On your own path. And that maybe it wasn't a great idea for me to be around so much.

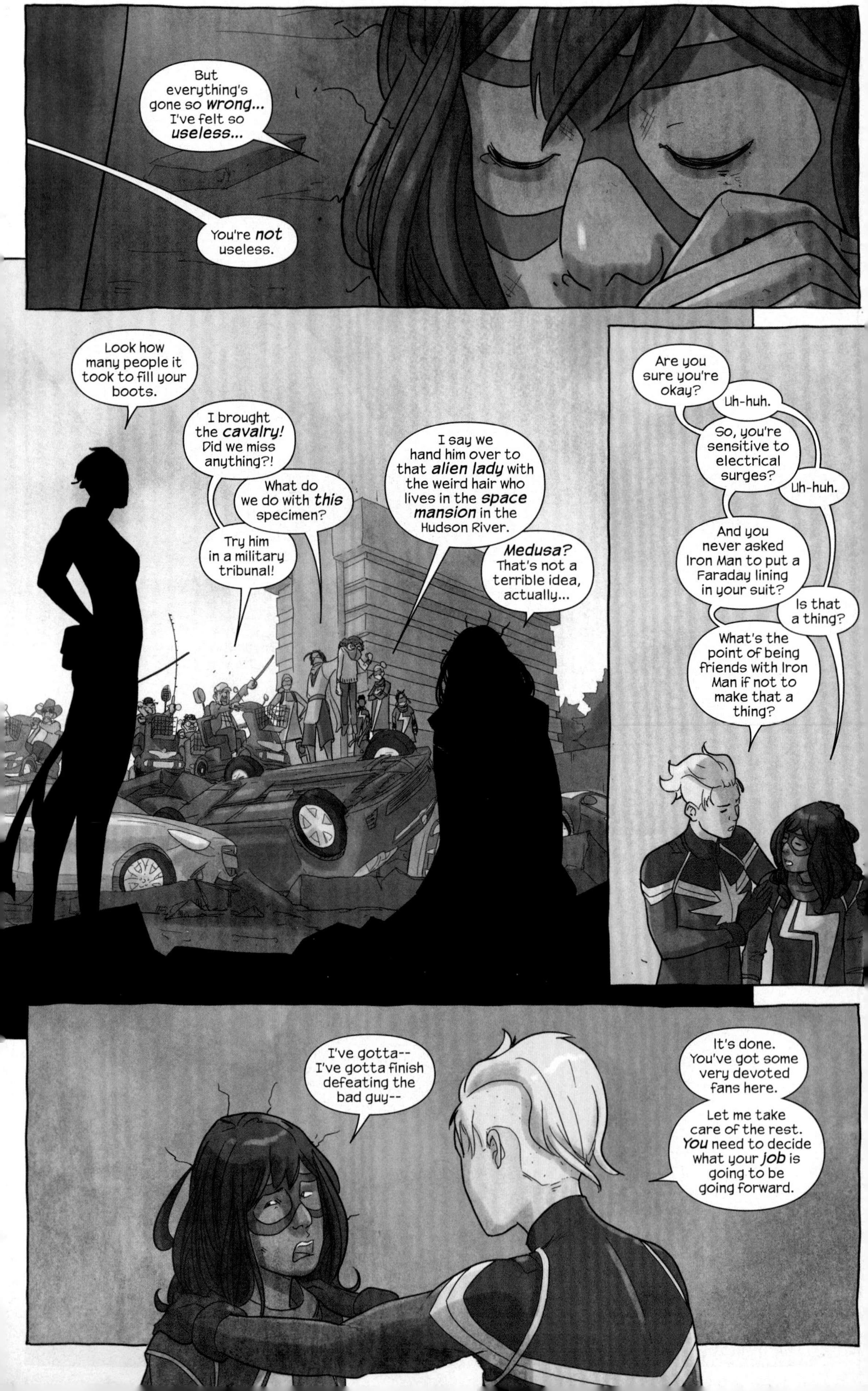
But everything's gone so wrong... I've felt so useless...
You're not useless.
Look how many people it took to fill your boots.
I brought the cavalry! Did we miss anything?!
What do we do with this specimen?
Try him in a military tribunal!
I say we hand him over to that alien lady with the weird hair who lives in the space mansion in the Hudson River.
Medusa? That's not a terrible idea, actually...
Are you sure you're okay?
Uh-huh.
So, you're sensitive to electrical surges?
Uh-huh.
And you never asked Iron Man to put a Faraday lining in your suit?
Is that a thing?
What's the point of being friends with Iron Man if not to make that a thing?
I've gotta-- I've gotta finish defeating the bad guy--
It's done. You've got some very devoted fans here.
Let me take care of the rest. You need to decide what your job is going to be going forward.

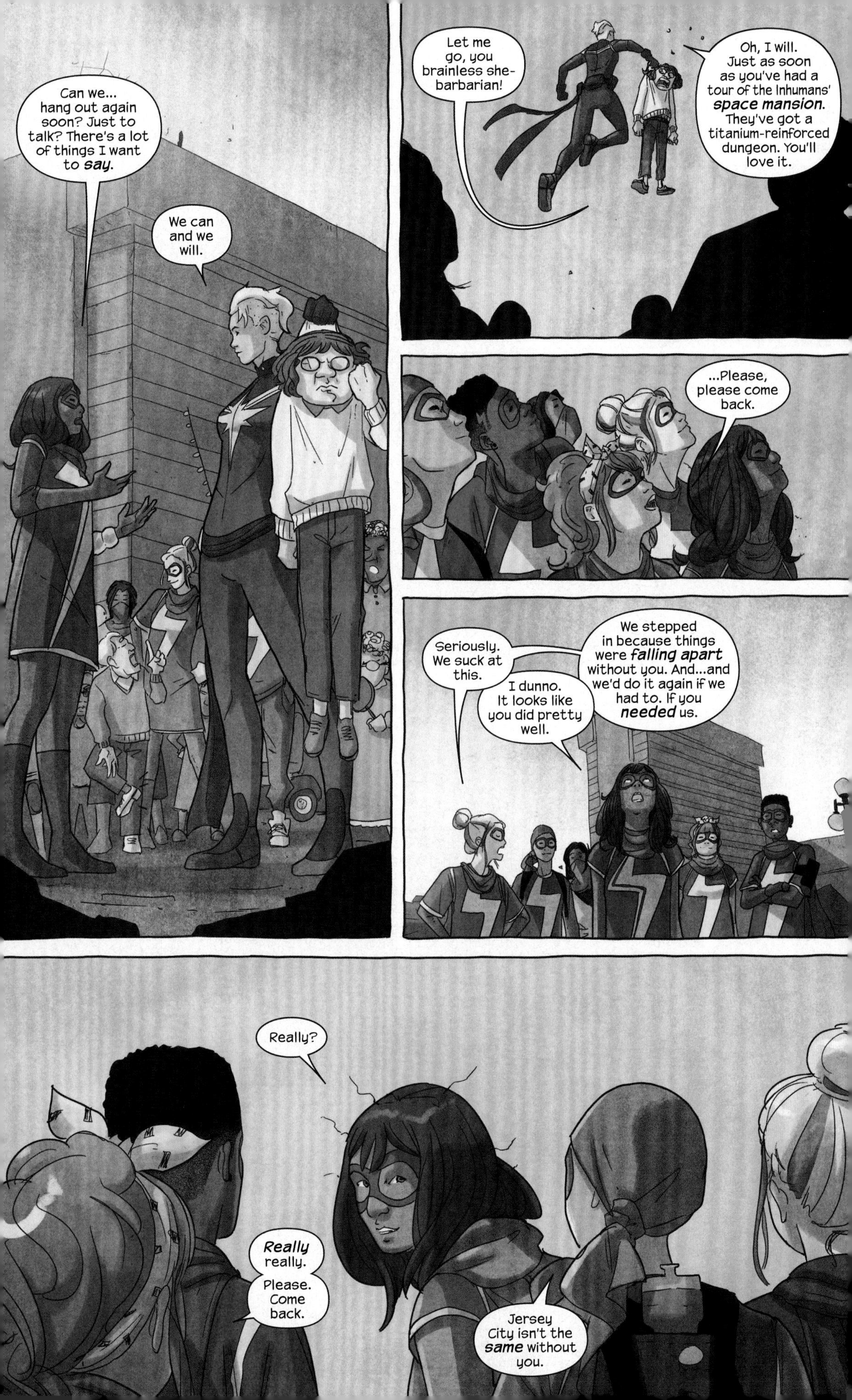
Can we... hang out again soon? Just to talk? There's a lot of things I want to *say*.
We can and we will.
Let me go, you brainless she-barbarian!
Oh, I will. Just as soon as you've had a tour of the Inhumans' *space mansion*. They've got a titanium-reinforced dungeon. You'll love it.
...Please, please come back.
Seriously. We suck at this.
We stepped in because things were *falling apart* without you. And...and we'd do it again if we had to. If you *needed* us.
I dunno. It looks like you did pretty well.
Really?
Really really.
Please. Come back.
Jersey City isn't the *same* without you.

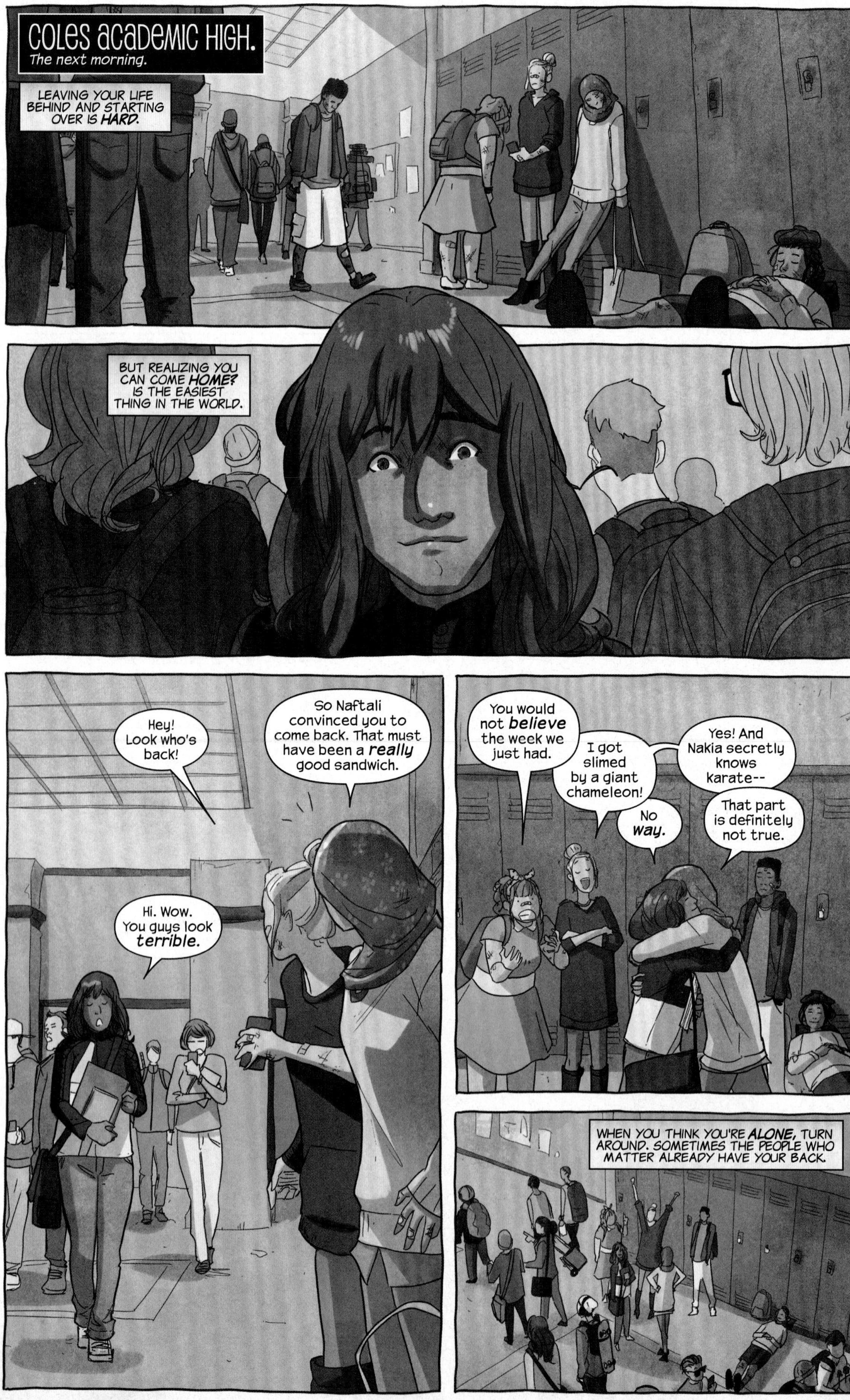
COLES ACADEMIC HIGH.
The next morning.
LEAVING YOUR LIFE BEHIND AND STARTING OVER IS HARD.
BUT REALIZING YOU CAN COME HOME? IS THE EASIEST THING IN THE WORLD.
Hey! Look who's back!
So Naftali convinced you to come back. That must have been a really good sandwich.
Hi. Wow. You guys look terrible.
You would not believe the week we just had.
I got slimed by a giant chameleon!
No way.
Yes! And Nakia secretly knows karate--
That part is definitely not true.
WHEN YOU THINK YOU'RE ALONE, TURN AROUND. SOMETIMES THE PEOPLE WHO MATTER ALREADY HAVE YOUR BACK.

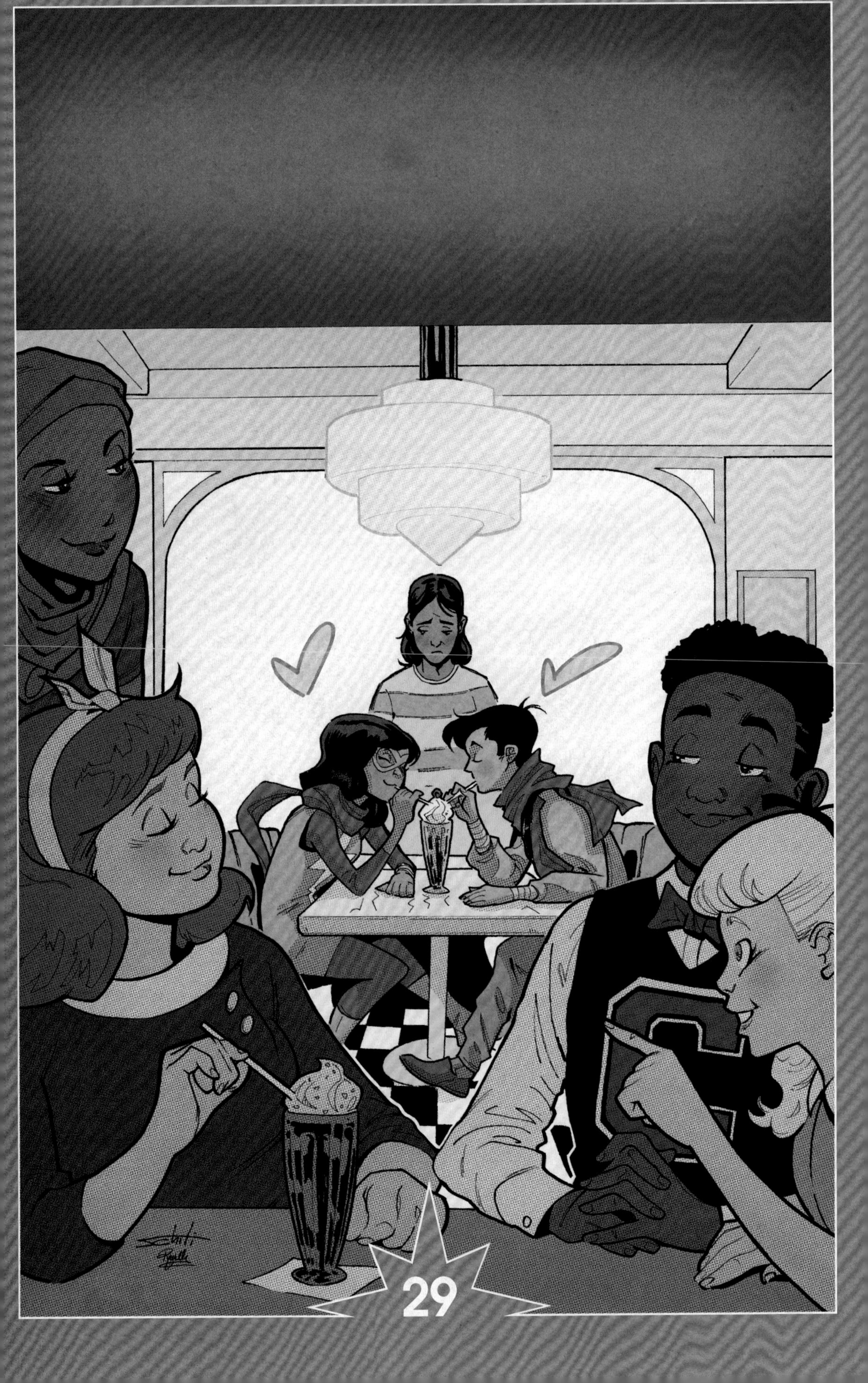
29

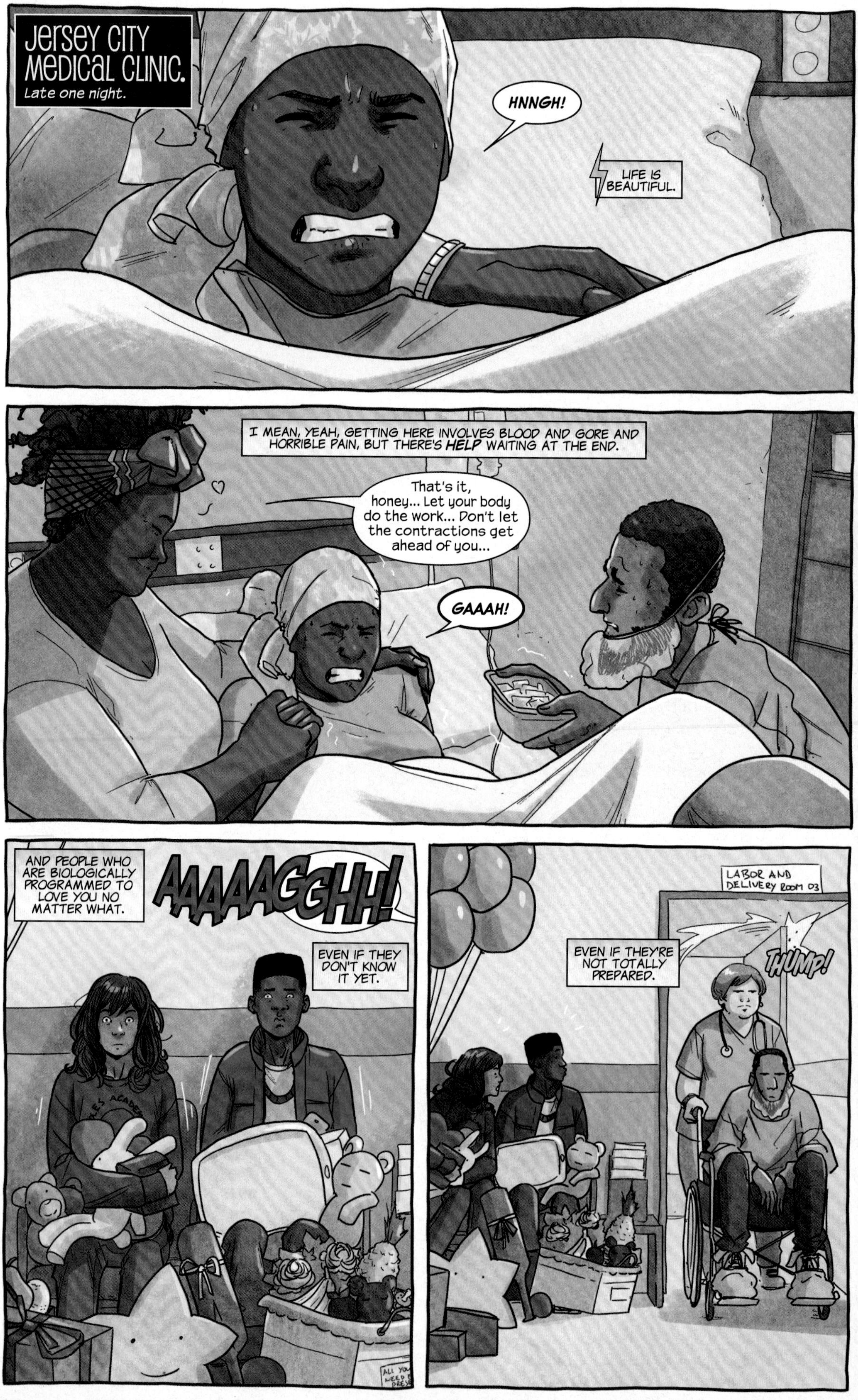

Jersey City Medical Clinic.
Late one night.
HNNGH!
LIFE IS BEAUTIFUL.
I MEAN, YEAH, GETTING HERE INVOLVES BLOOD AND GORE AND HORRIBLE PAIN, BUT THERE'S HELP WAITING AT THE END.
That's it, honey... Let your body do the work... Don't let the contractions get ahead of you...
GAAAH!
AND PEOPLE WHO ARE BIOLOGICALLY PROGRAMMED TO LOVE YOU NO MATTER WHAT.
AAAAAGGHH!
EVEN IF THEY DON'T KNOW IT YET.
LABOR AND DELIVERY ROOM 03
EVEN IF THEY'RE NOT TOTALLY PREPARED.
THUMP!

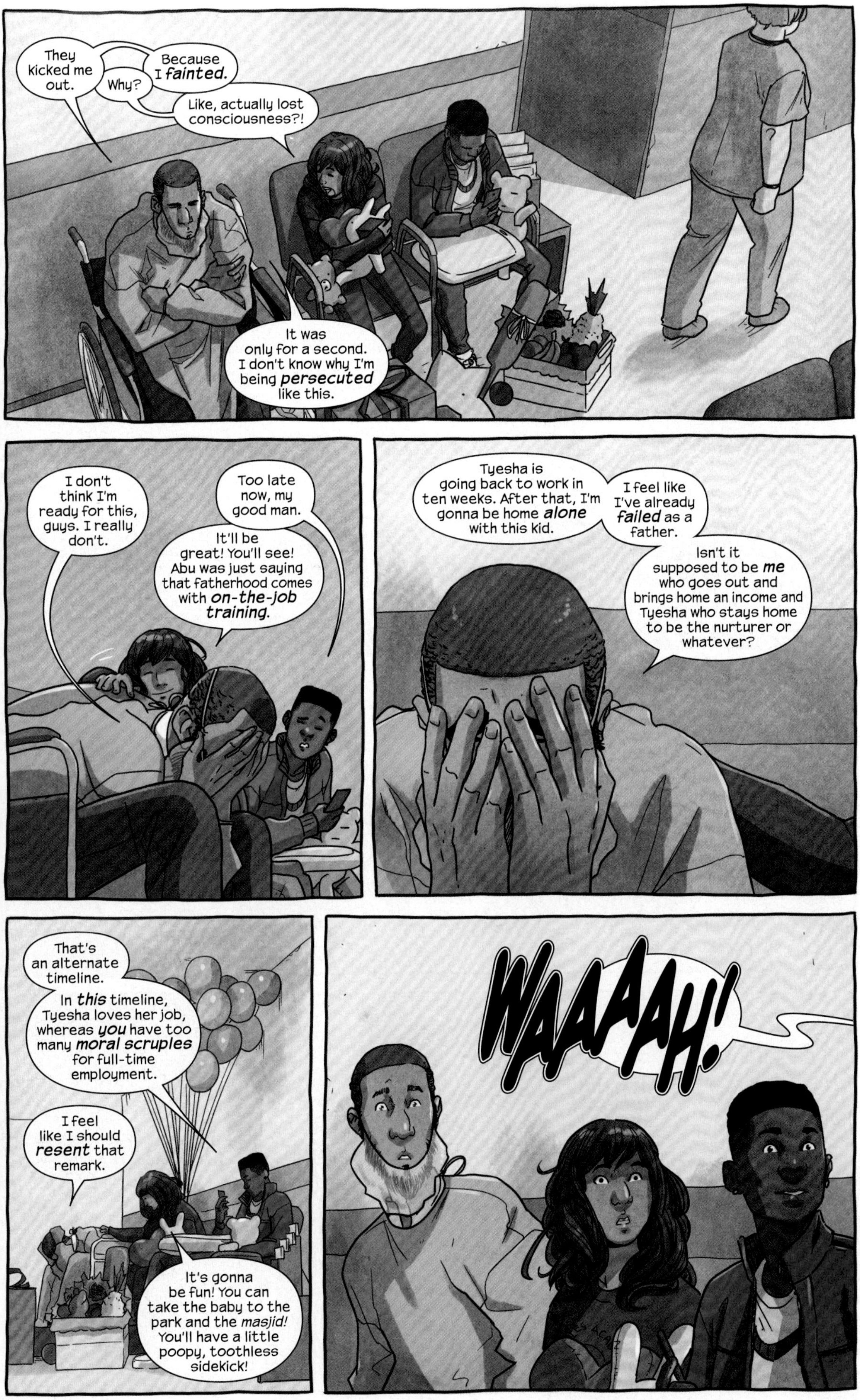

They kicked me out.
Why?
Because I fainted.
Like, actually lost consciousness?!
It was only for a second. I don't know why I'm being persecuted like this.
I don't think I'm ready for this, guys. I really don't.
Too late now, my good man.
It'll be great! You'll see! Abu was just saying that fatherhood comes with on-the-job training.
Tyesha is going back to work in ten weeks. After that, I'm gonna be home alone with this kid.
I feel like I've already failed as a father.
Isn't it supposed to be me who goes out and brings home an income and Tyesha who stays home to be the nurturer or whatever?
That's an alternate timeline.
In this timeline, Tyesha loves her job, whereas you have too many moral scruples for full-time employment.
I feel like I should resent that remark.
It's gonna be fun! You can take the baby to the park and the masjid! You'll have a little poopy, toothless sidekick!
WAAAAH!

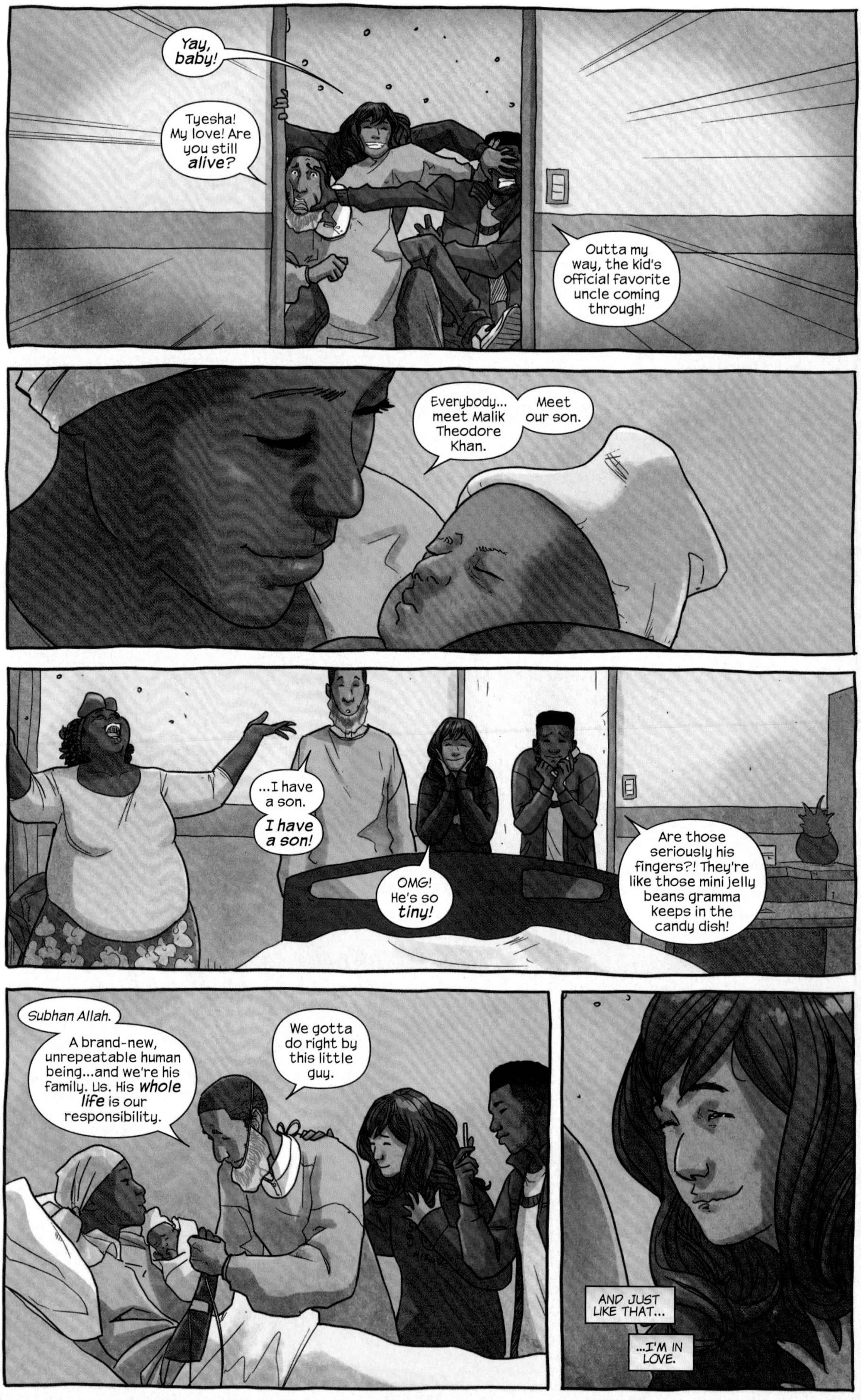

Yay, baby!
Tyesha! My love! Are you still *alive?*
Outta my way, the kid's official favorite uncle coming through!
Everybody... meet Malik Theodore Khan.
Meet our son.
...I have a son.
I have a son!
OMG! He's so *tiny!*
Are those seriously his fingers?! They're like those mini jelly beans gramma keeps in the candy dish!
Subhan Allah.
A brand-new, unrepeatable human being...and we're his family. Us. His *whole life* is our responsibility.
We gotta do right by this little guy.
AND JUST LIKE THAT...
...I'M IN LOVE.

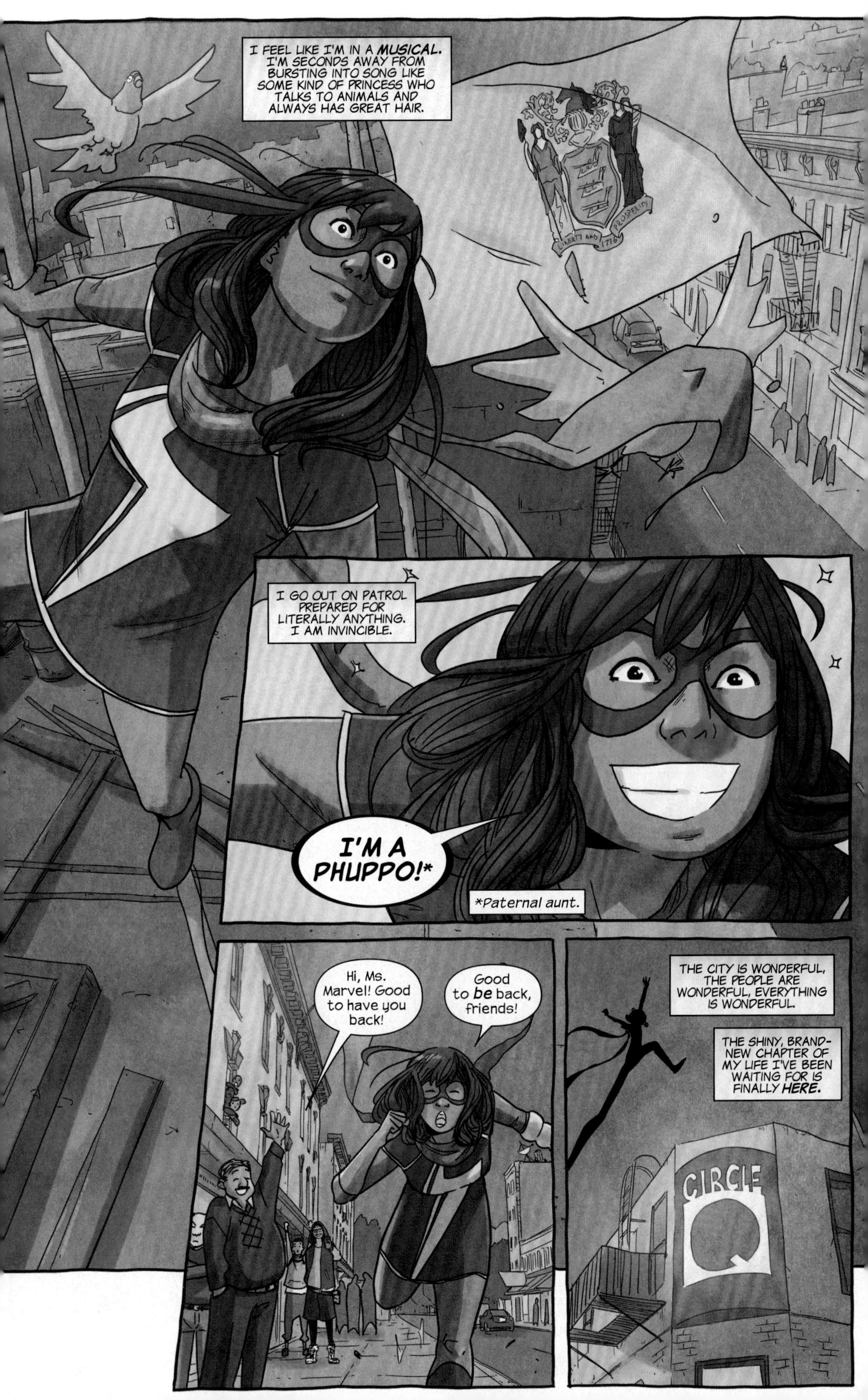

I FEEL LIKE I'M IN A *MUSICAL.* I'M SECONDS AWAY FROM BURSTING INTO SONG LIKE SOME KIND OF PRINCESS WHO TALKS TO ANIMALS AND ALWAYS HAS GREAT HAIR.
LIBERTY AND PROSPERITY 1776
I GO OUT ON PATROL PREPARED FOR LITERALLY ANYTHING. I AM INVINCIBLE.
I'M A PHUPPO!*
*Paternal aunt.
Hi, Ms. Marvel! Good to have you back!
Good to *be* back, friends!
THE CITY IS WONDERFUL, THE PEOPLE ARE WONDERFUL, EVERYTHING IS WONDERFUL.
THE SHINY, BRAND-NEW CHAPTER OF MY LIFE I'VE BEEN WAITING FOR IS FINALLY *HERE.*
CIRCLE Q

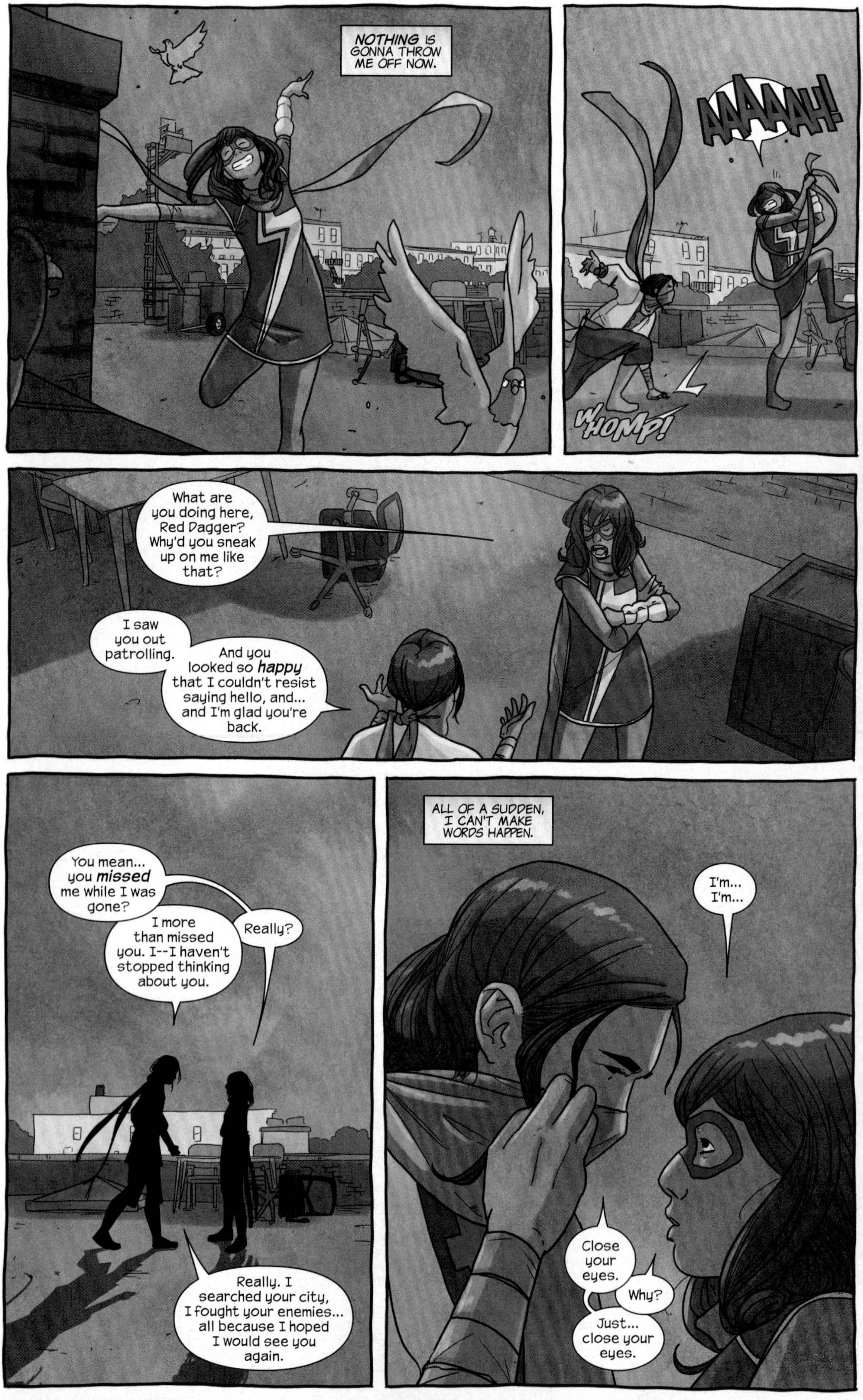
NOTHING IS GONNA THROW ME OFF NOW.
AAAAAH!
WHOMP!
What are you doing here, Red Dagger? Why'd you sneak up on me like that?
I saw you out patrolling.
And you looked so happy that I couldn't resist saying hello, and... and I'm glad you're back.
You mean... you missed me while I was gone?
I more than missed you. I--I haven't stopped thinking about you.
Really?
Really. I searched your city, I fought your enemies... all because I hoped I would see you again.
ALL OF A SUDDEN, I CAN'T MAKE WORDS HAPPEN.
I'm... I'm...
Close your eyes.
Why?
Just... close your eyes.

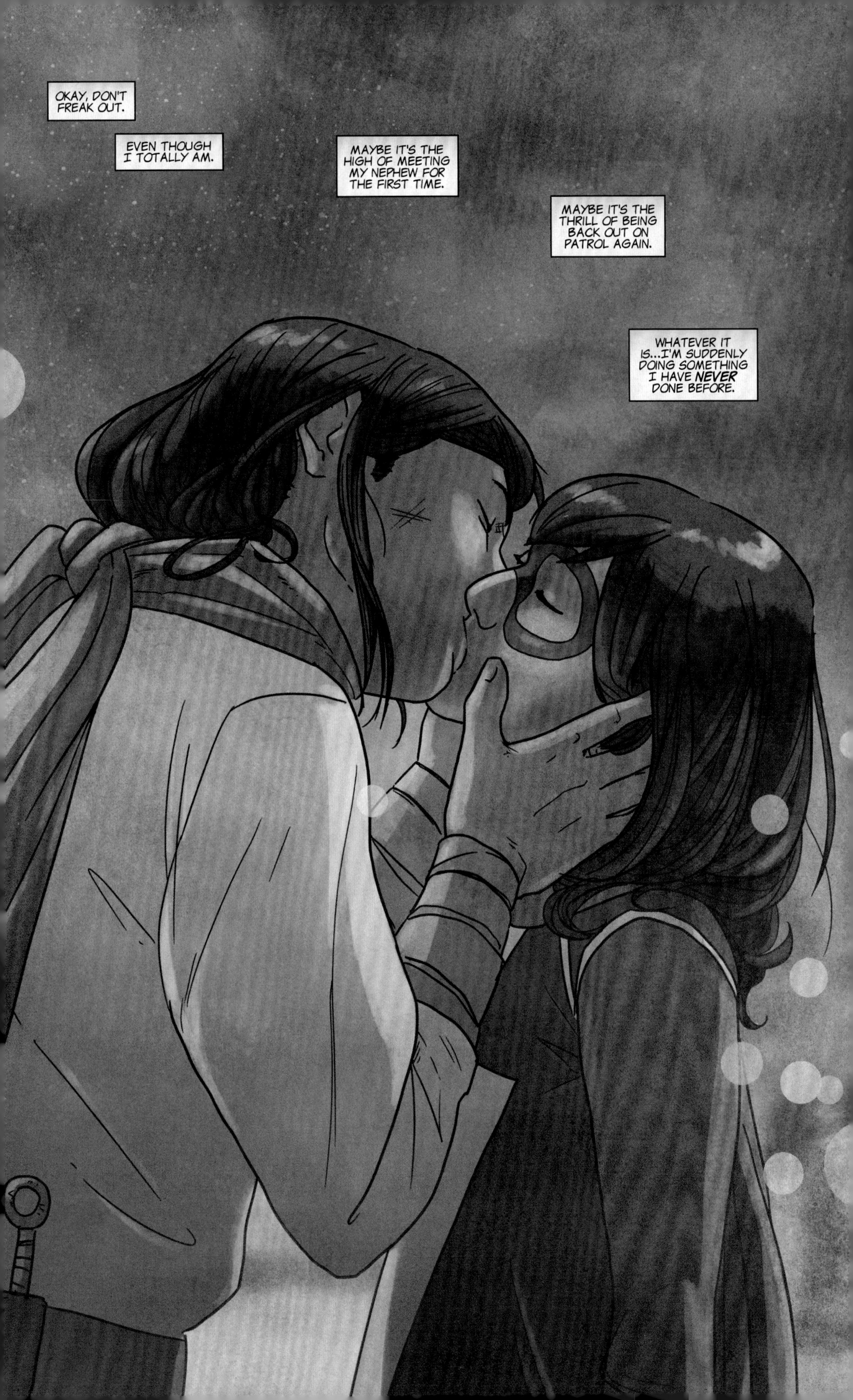

OKAY, DON'T FREAK OUT.
EVEN THOUGH I TOTALLY AM.
MAYBE IT'S THE HIGH OF MEETING MY NEPHEW FOR THE FIRST TIME.
MAYBE IT'S THE THRILL OF BEING BACK OUT ON PATROL AGAIN.
WHATEVER IT IS...I'M SUDDENLY DOING SOMETHING I HAVE ***NEVER*** DONE BEFORE.

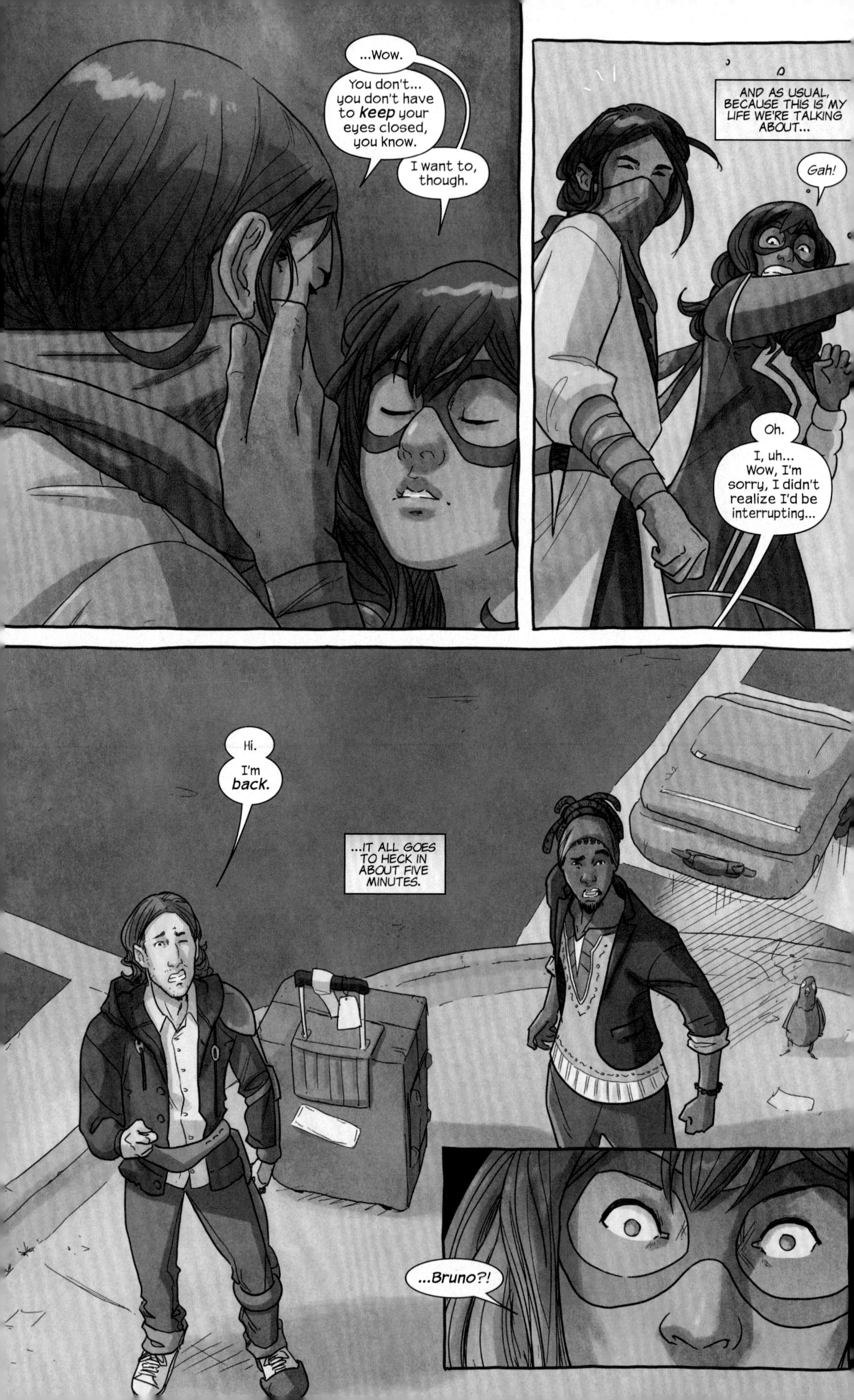
...Wow.
You don't... you don't have to *keep* your eyes closed, you know.
I want to, though.
AND AS USUAL, BECAUSE THIS IS MY LIFE WE'RE TALKING ABOUT...
Gah!
Oh.
I, uh... Wow, I'm sorry, I didn't realize I'd be interrupting...
Hi.
I'm *back.*
...IT ALL GOES TO HECK IN ABOUT FIVE MINUTES.
...Bruno?!

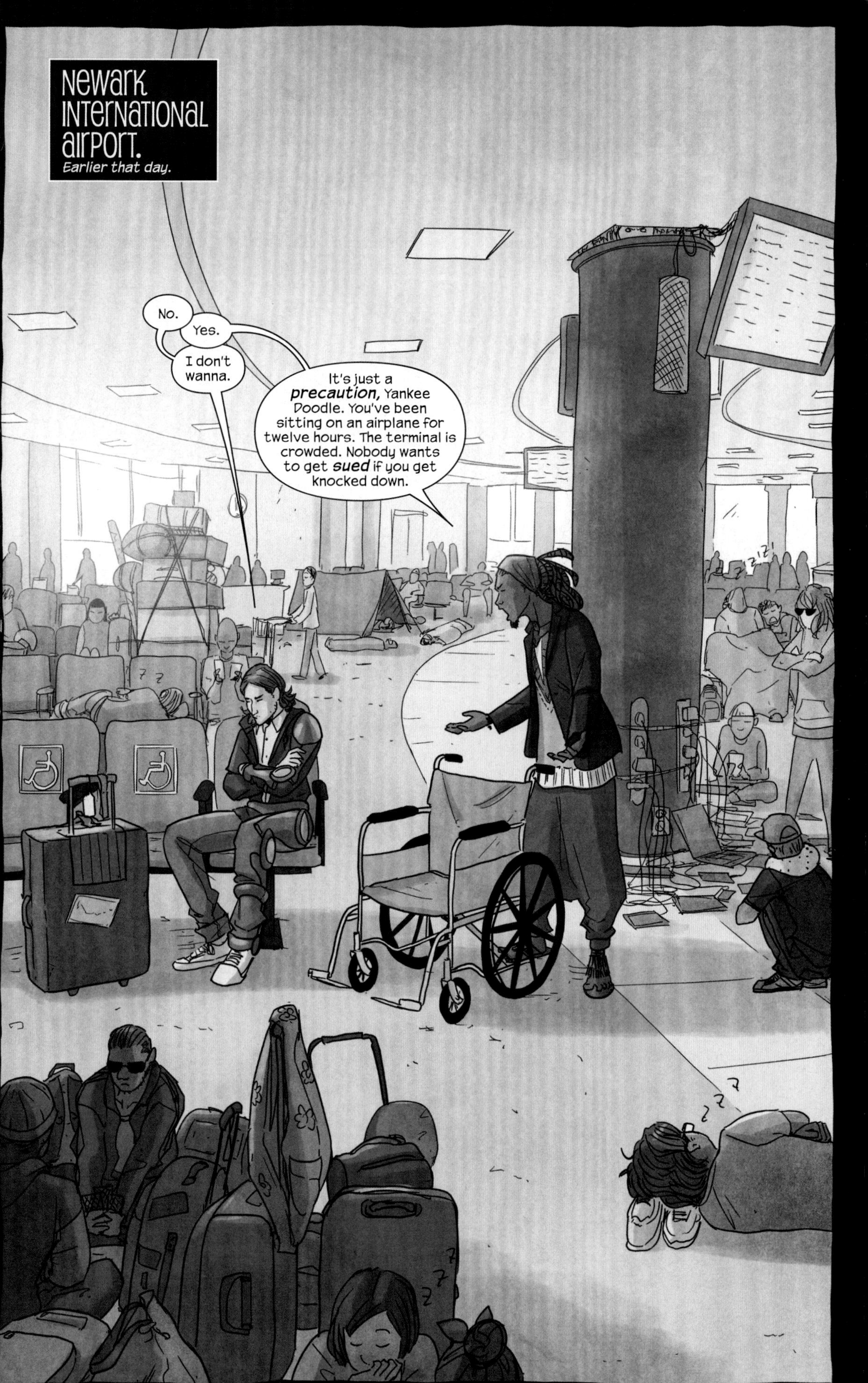
Newark International airport.
Earlier that day.
No.
Yes.
I don't wanna.
It's just a precaution, Yankee Doodle. You've been sitting on an airplane for twelve hours. The terminal is crowded. Nobody wants to get sued if you get knocked down.

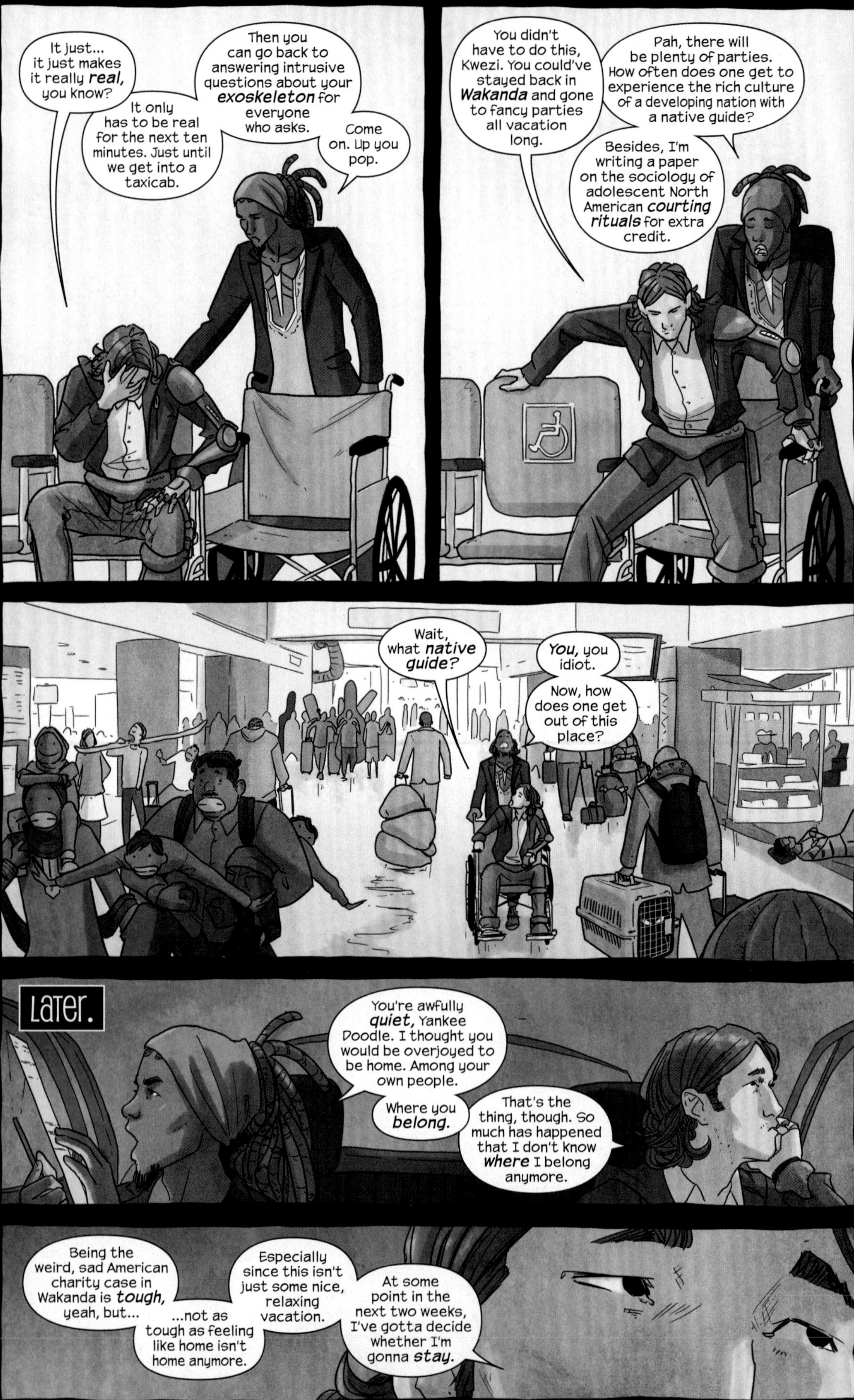

It just... it just makes it really *real,* you know?
Then you can go back to answering intrusive questions about your *exoskeleton* for everyone who asks.
It only has to be real for the next ten minutes. Just until we get into a taxicab.
Come on. Up you pop.
You didn't have to do this, Kwezi. You could've stayed back in *Wakanda* and gone to fancy parties all vacation long.
Pah, there will be plenty of parties. How often does one get to experience the rich culture of a developing nation with a native guide?
Besides, I'm writing a paper on the sociology of adolescent North American *courting rituals* for extra credit.
Wait, what *native guide?*
You, you idiot.
Now, how does one get out of this place?
Later.
You're awfully *quiet,* Yankee Doodle. I thought you would be overjoyed to be home. Among your own people.
Where you *belong.*
That's the thing, though. So much has happened that I don't know *where* I belong anymore.
Being the weird, sad American charity case in Wakanda is *tough,* yeah, but...
...not as tough as feeling like home isn't home anymore.
Especially since this isn't just some nice, relaxing vacation.
At some point in the next two weeks, I've gotta decide whether I'm gonna *stay.*

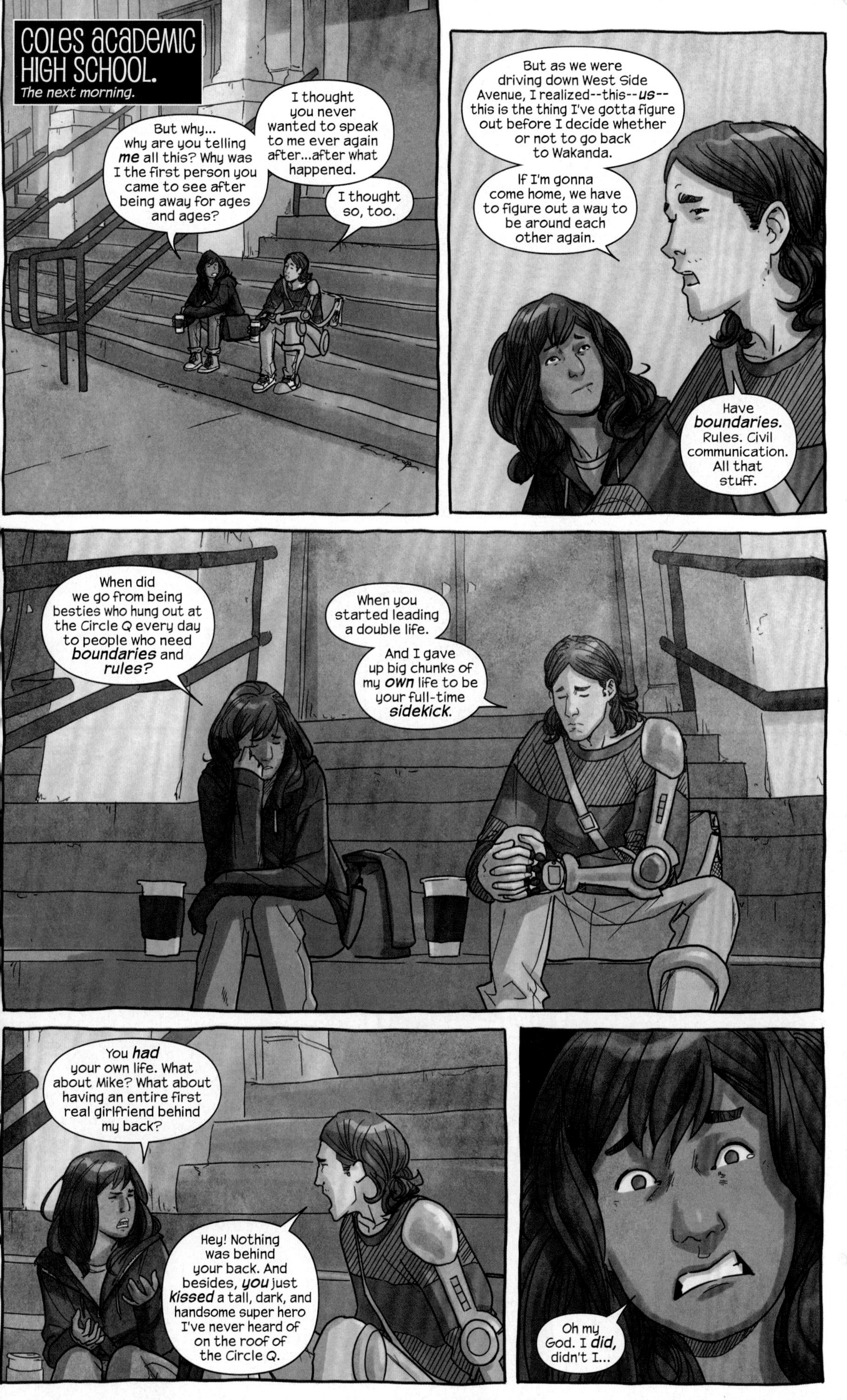

COLES ACADEMIC HIGH SCHOOL.
The next morning.
But why... why are you telling me all this? Why was I the first person you came to see after being away for ages and ages?
I thought you never wanted to speak to me ever again after...after what happened.
I thought so, too.
But as we were driving down West Side Avenue, I realized--this--us--this is the thing I've gotta figure out before I decide whether or not to go back to Wakanda.
If I'm gonna come home, we have to figure out a way to be around each other again.
Have boundaries. Rules. Civil communication. All that stuff.
When did we go from being besties who hung out at the Circle Q every day to people who need boundaries and rules?
When you started leading a double life.
And I gave up big chunks of my own life to be your full-time sidekick.
You had your own life. What about Mike? What about having an entire first real girlfriend behind my back?
Hey! Nothing was behind your back. And besides, you just kissed a tall, dark, and handsome super hero I've never heard of on the roof of the Circle Q.
Oh my God. I did, didn't I...

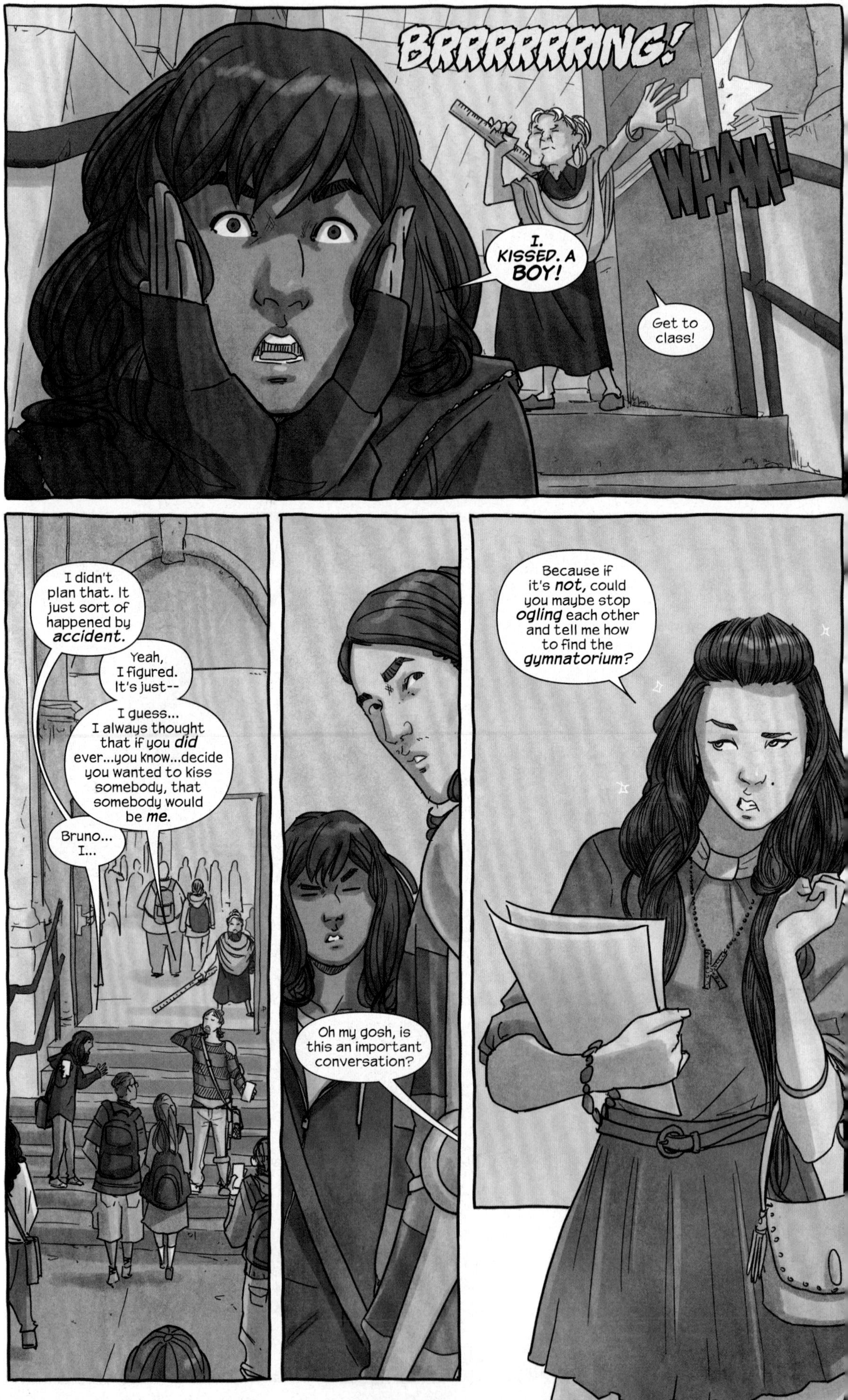
BRRRRRRING!
I. KISSED. A BOY!
WHAM!
Get to class!
I didn't plan that. It just sort of happened by *accident.*
Yeah, I figured. It's just--
I guess... I always thought that if you *did* ever...you know...decide you wanted to kiss somebody, that somebody would be *me.*
Bruno... I...
Oh my gosh, is this an important conversation?
Because if it's *not,* could you maybe stop *ogling* each other and tell me how to find the *gymnatorium?*

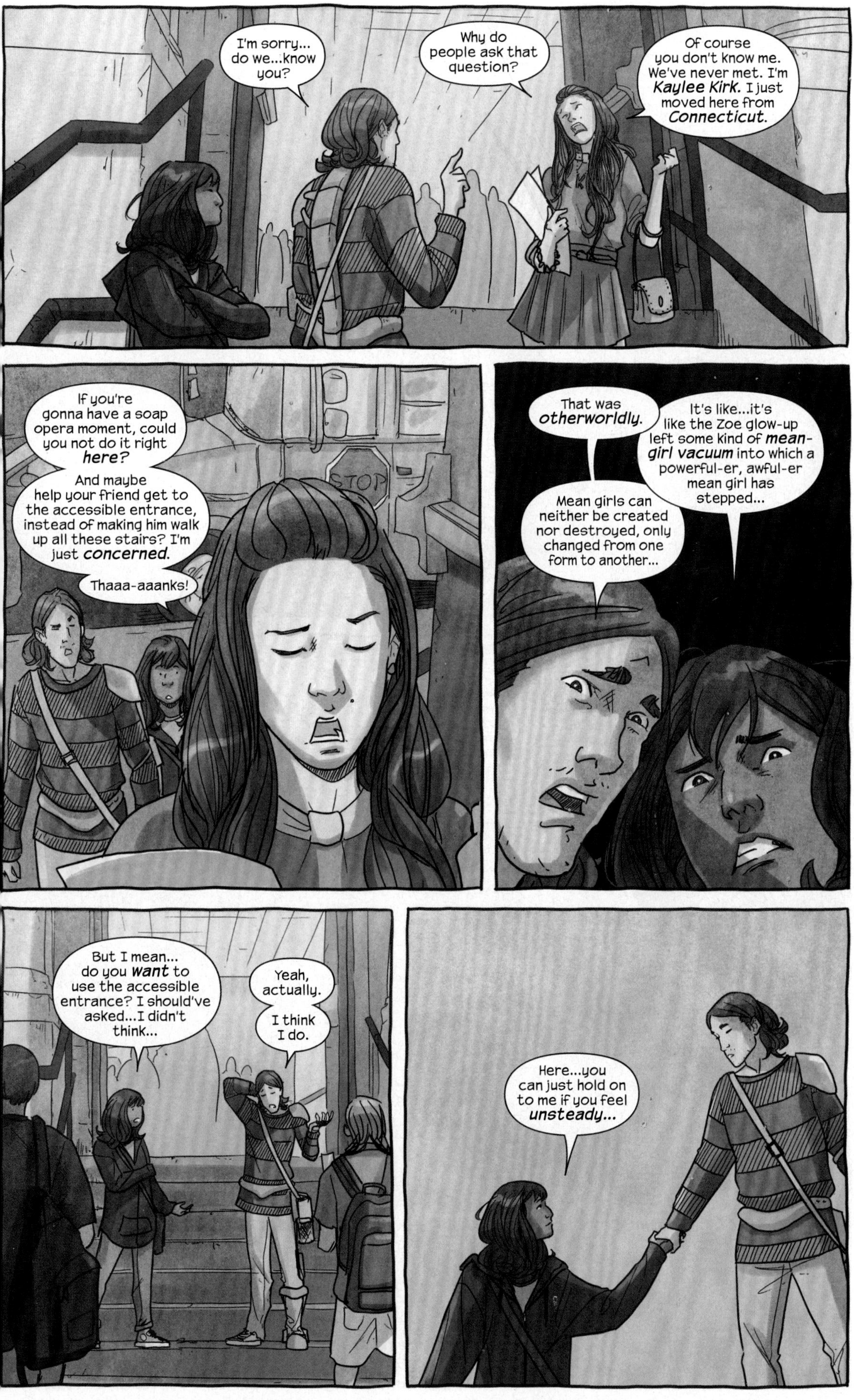
I'm sorry... do we...know you?
Why do people ask that question?
Of course you don't know me. We've never met. I'm Kaylee Kirk. I just moved here from Connecticut.
If you're gonna have a soap opera moment, could you not do it right here?
And maybe help your friend get to the accessible entrance, instead of making him walk up all these stairs? I'm just concerned.
Thaaa-aaanks!
STOP
That was otherworldly.
It's like...it's like the Zoe glow-up left some kind of mean-girl vacuum into which a powerful-er, awful-er mean girl has stepped...
Mean girls can neither be created nor destroyed, only changed from one form to another...
But I mean... do you want to use the accessible entrance? I should've asked...I didn't think...
Yeah, actually.
I think I do.
Here...you can just hold on to me if you feel unsteady...

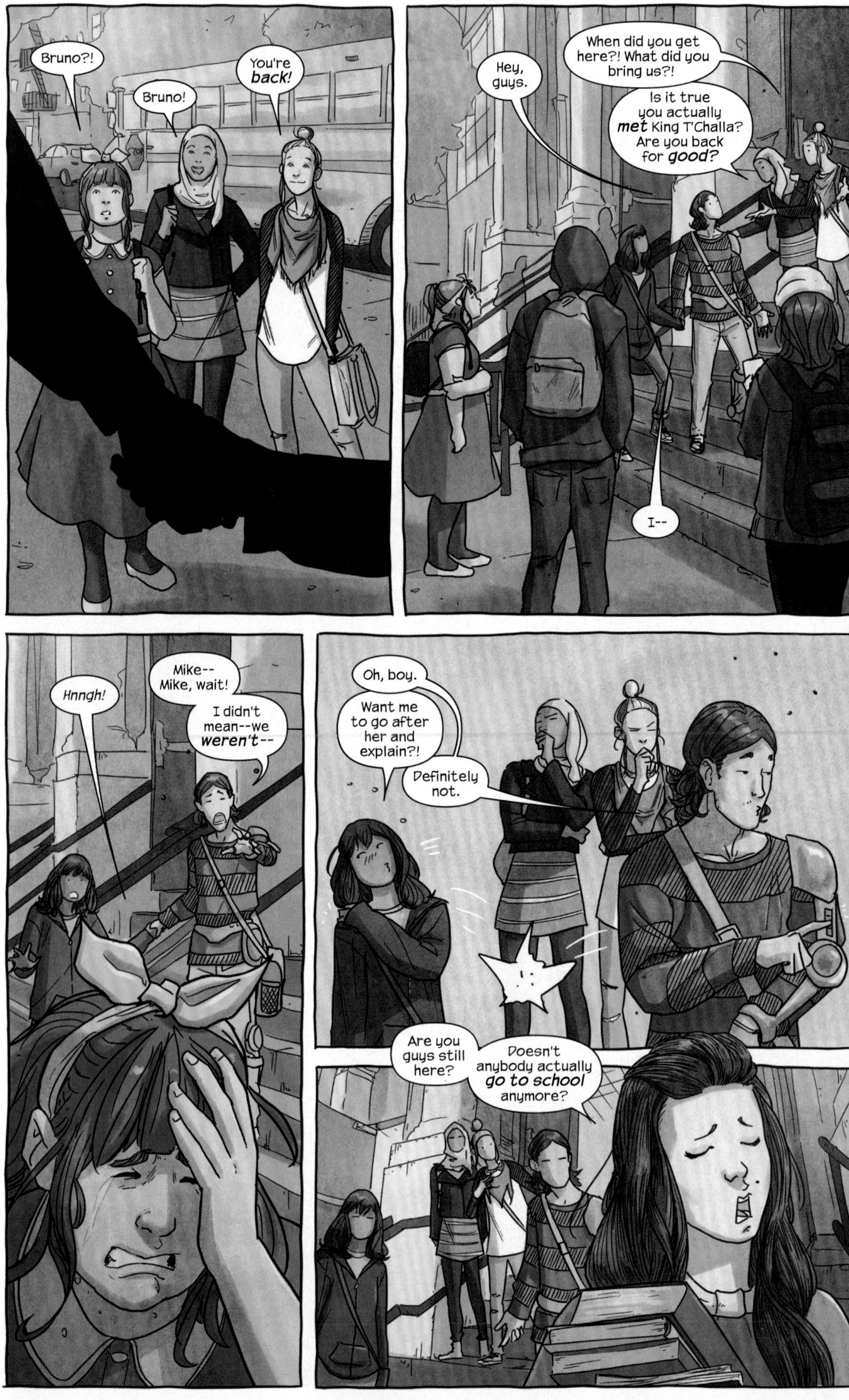
Bruno?!
Bruno!
You're back!
Hey, guys.
When did you get here?! What did you bring us?!
Is it true you actually met King T'Challa? Are you back for good?
I--
Hnngh!
Mike-- Mike, wait!
I didn't mean--we weren't--
Oh, boy.
Want me to go after her and explain?!
Definitely not.
Are you guys still here?
Doesn't anybody actually go to school anymore?

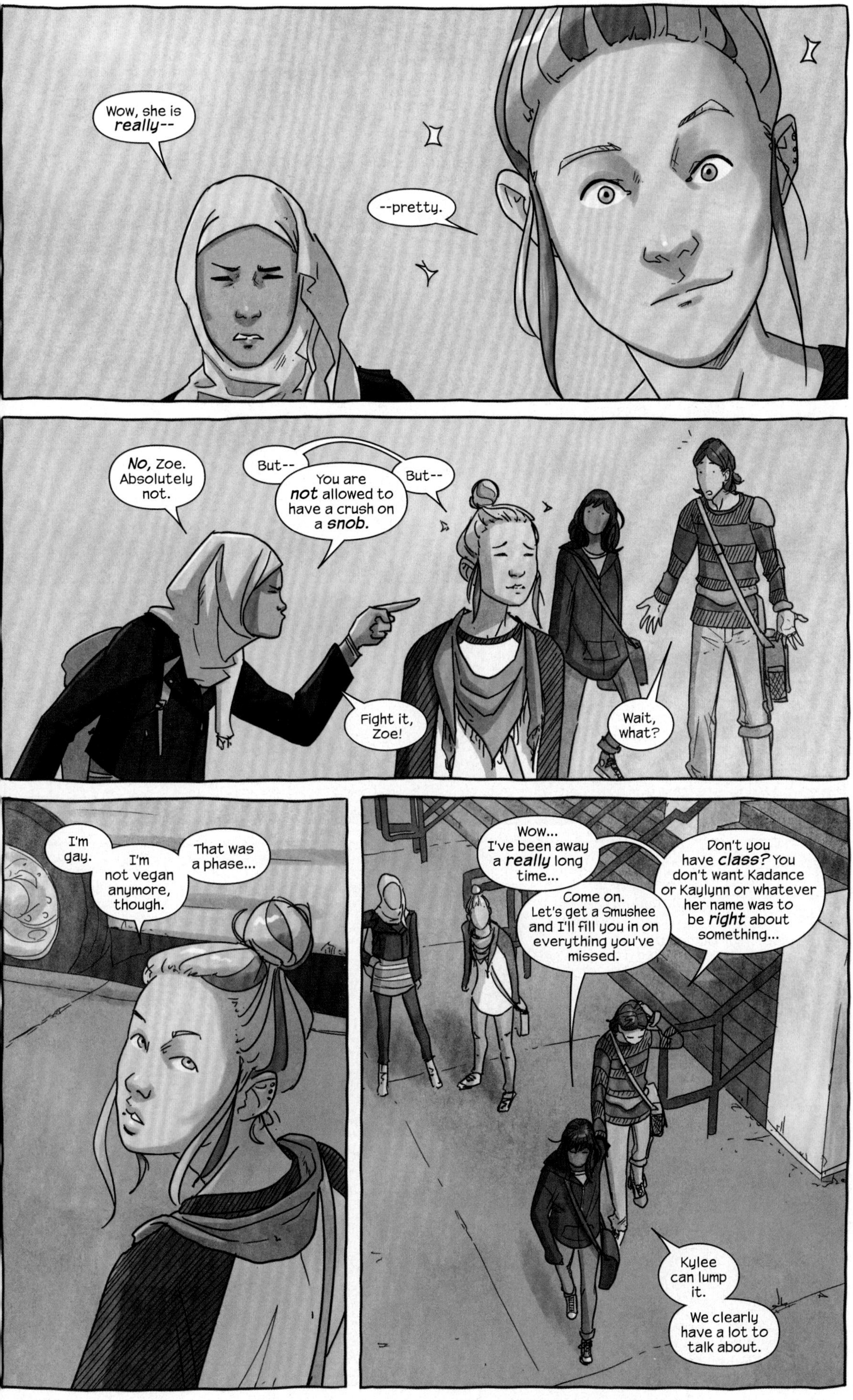
Wow, she is *really*--
--pretty.
No, Zoe. Absolutely not.
But--
You are *not* allowed to have a crush on a *snob.*
But--
Fight it, Zoe!
Wait, what?
I'm gay.
I'm not vegan anymore, though.
That was a phase...
Wow... I've been away a *really* long time...
Come on. Let's get a Smushee and I'll fill you in on everything you've missed.
Don't you have *class?* You don't want Kadance or Kaylynn or whatever her name was to be *right* about something...
Kylee can lump it.
We clearly have a lot to talk about.

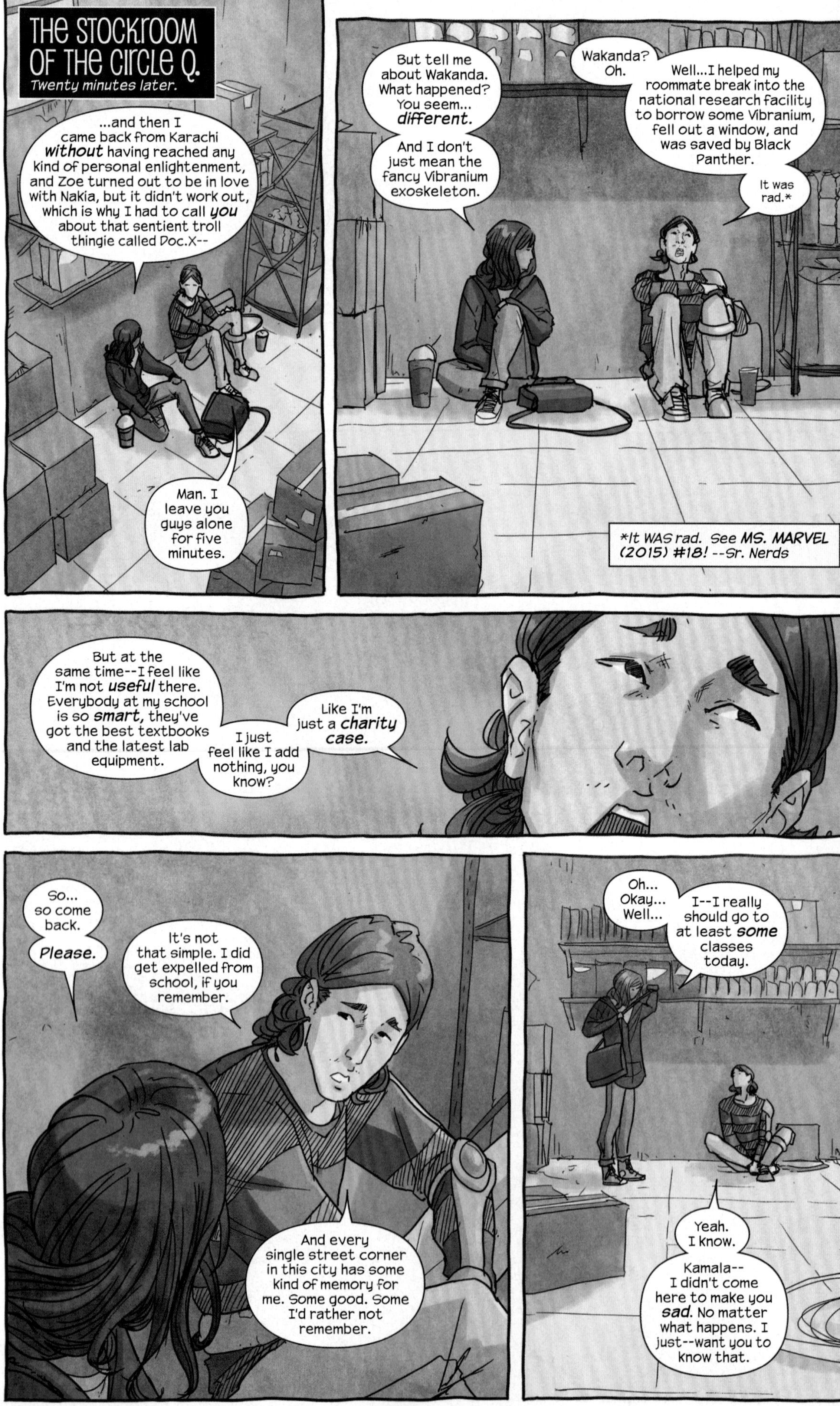
THE STOCKROOM OF THE CIRCLE Q.
Twenty minutes later.
...and then I came back from Karachi *without* having reached any kind of personal enlightenment, and Zoe turned out to be in love with Nakia, but it didn't work out, which is why I had to call *you* about that sentient troll thingie called Doc.X--
Man. I leave you guys alone for five minutes.
But tell me about Wakanda. What happened? You seem... *different.*
And I don't just mean the fancy Vibranium exoskeleton.
Wakanda? Oh.
Well...I helped my roommate break into the national research facility to borrow some Vibranium, fell out a window, and was saved by Black Panther.
It was rad.*
*It WAS rad. See MS. MARVEL (2015) #18! --Sr. Nerds
But at the same time--I feel like I'm not *useful* there. Everybody at my school is so *smart,* they've got the best textbooks and the latest lab equipment.
I just feel like I add nothing, you know?
Like I'm just a *charity case.*
So... so come back.
Please.
It's not that simple. I did get expelled from school, if you remember.
And every single street corner in this city has some kind of memory for me. Some good. Some I'd rather not remember.
Oh... Okay... Well...
I--I really should go to at least *some* classes today.
Yeah. I know.
Kamala-- I didn't come here to make you *sad.* No matter what happens. I just--want you to know that.

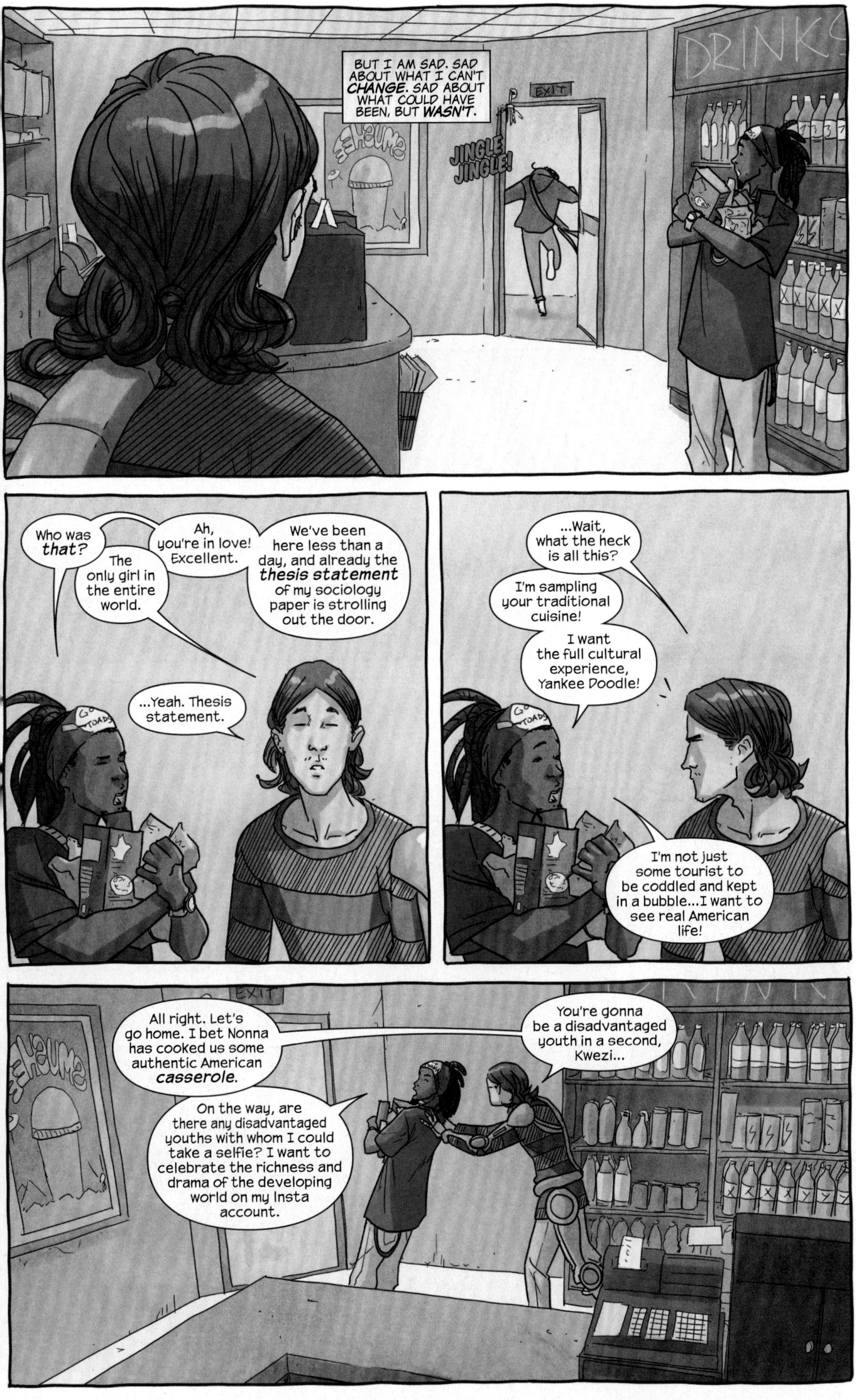

BUT I AM SAD. SAD ABOUT WHAT I CAN'T CHANGE. SAD ABOUT WHAT COULD HAVE BEEN, BUT WASN'T.
EXIT
JINGLE JINGLE!
DRINKS
Who was that?
The only girl in the entire world.
Ah, you're in love! Excellent.
We've been here less than a day, and already the thesis statement of my sociology paper is strolling out the door.
...Yeah. Thesis statement.
GO TOADS
...Wait, what the heck is all this?
I'm sampling your traditional cuisine!
I want the full cultural experience, Yankee Doodle!
I'm not just some tourist to be coddled and kept in a bubble...I want to see real American life!
EXIT
All right. Let's go home. I bet Nonna has cooked us some authentic American casserole.
On the way, are there any disadvantaged youths with whom I could take a selfie? I want to celebrate the richness and drama of the developing world on my Insta account.
You're gonna be a disadvantaged youth in a second, Kwezi...

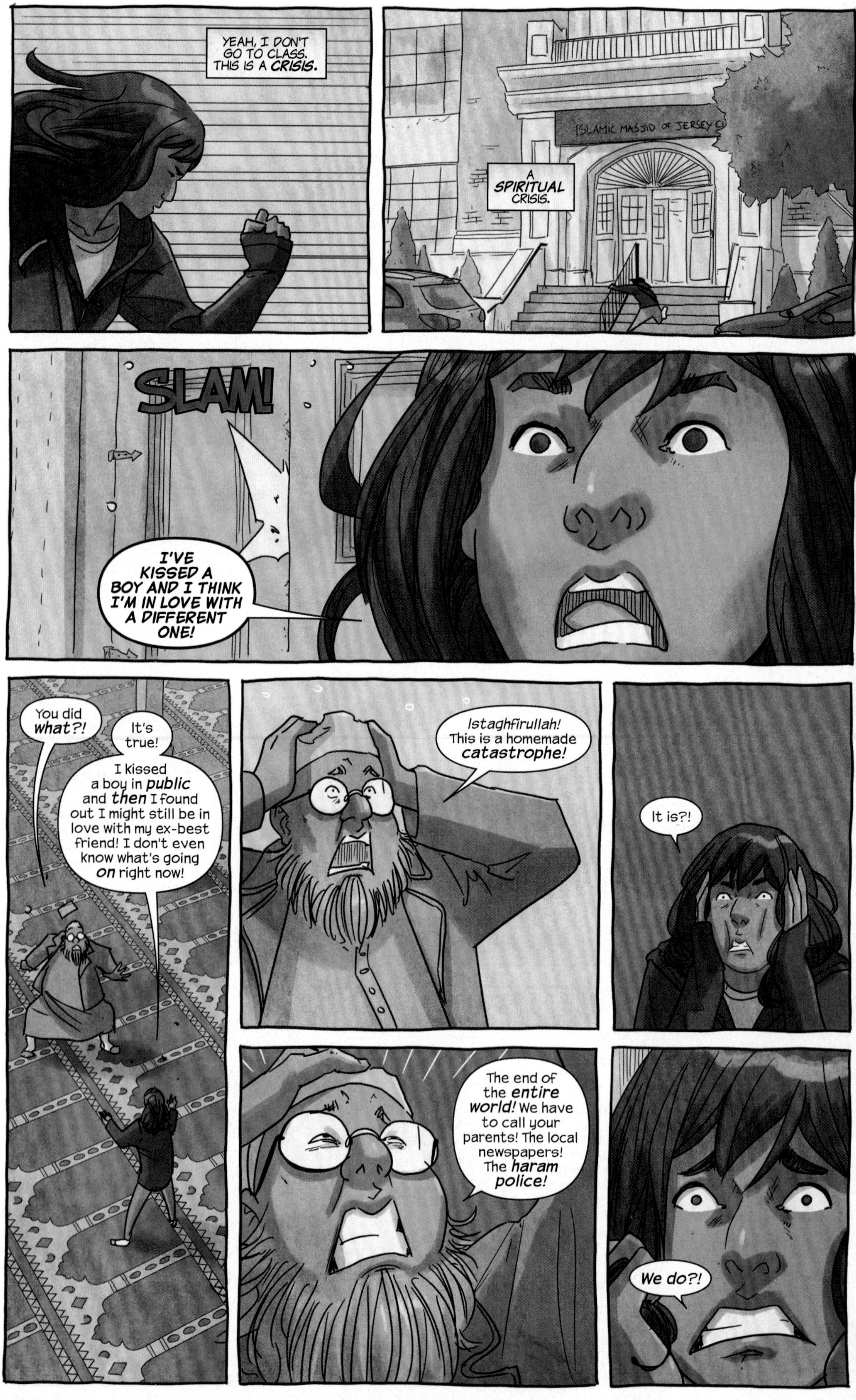
YEAH, I DON'T GO TO CLASS. THIS IS A CRISIS.
ISLAMIC MASJID OF JERSEY C
A SPIRITUAL CRISIS.
SLAM!
I'VE KISSED A BOY AND I THINK I'M IN LOVE WITH A DIFFERENT ONE!
You did what?!
It's true!
I kissed a boy in public and then I found out I might still be in love with my ex-best friend! I don't even know what's going on right now!
Istaghfirullah! This is a homemade catastrophe!
It is?!
The end of the entire world! We have to call your parents! The local newspapers! The haram police!
We do?!

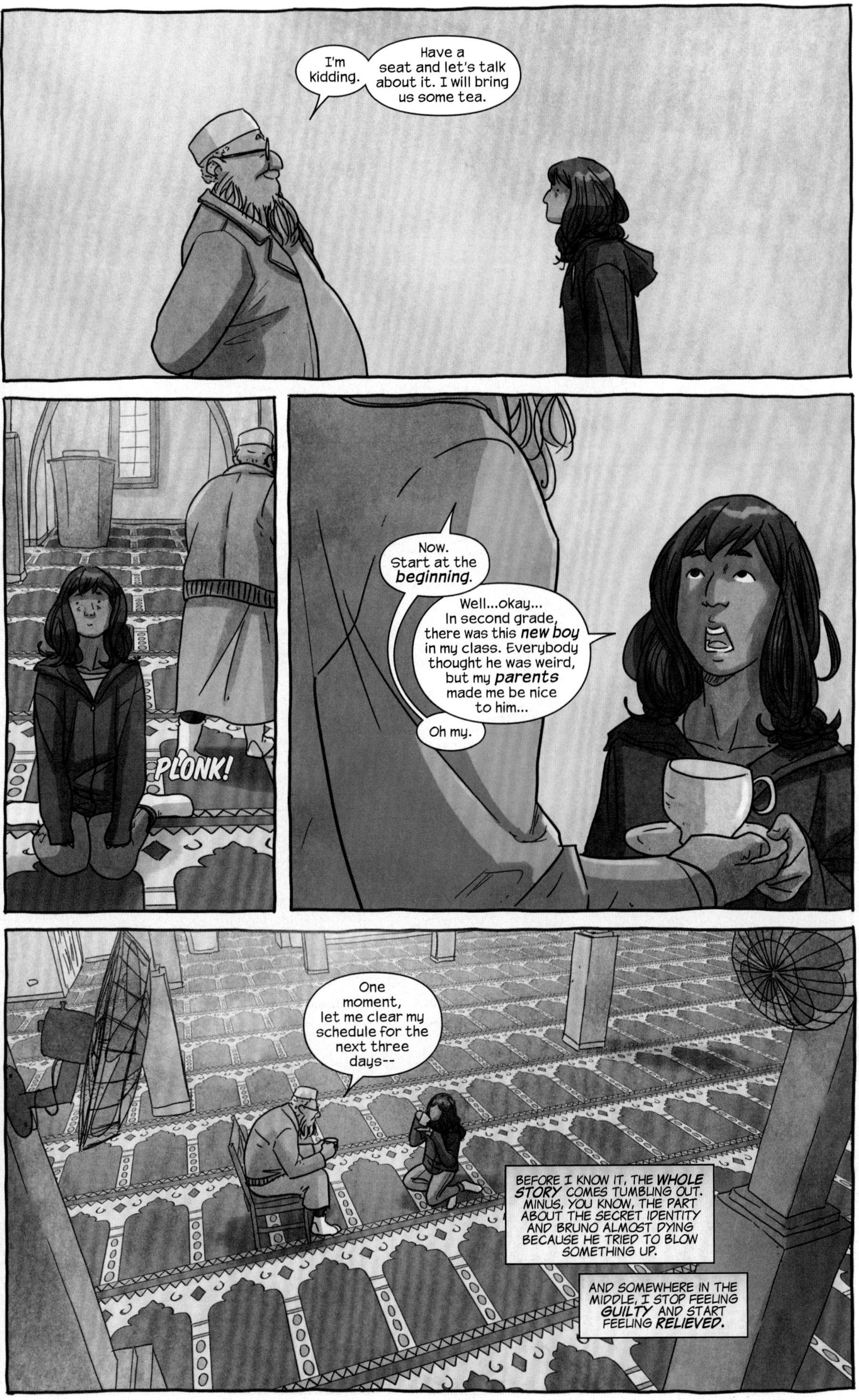

I'm kidding.
Have a seat and let's talk about it. I will bring us some tea.
PLONK!
Now. Start at the *beginning*.
Well...okay... In second grade, there was this *new boy* in my class. Everybody thought he was weird, but my *parents* made me be nice to him...
Oh my.
One moment, let me clear my schedule for the next three days--
BEFORE I KNOW IT, THE *WHOLE STORY* COMES TUMBLING OUT. MINUS, YOU KNOW, THE PART ABOUT THE SECRET IDENTITY AND BRUNO ALMOST DYING BECAUSE HE TRIED TO BLOW SOMETHING UP.
AND SOMEWHERE IN THE MIDDLE, I STOP FEELING *GUILTY* AND START FEELING *RELIEVED.*

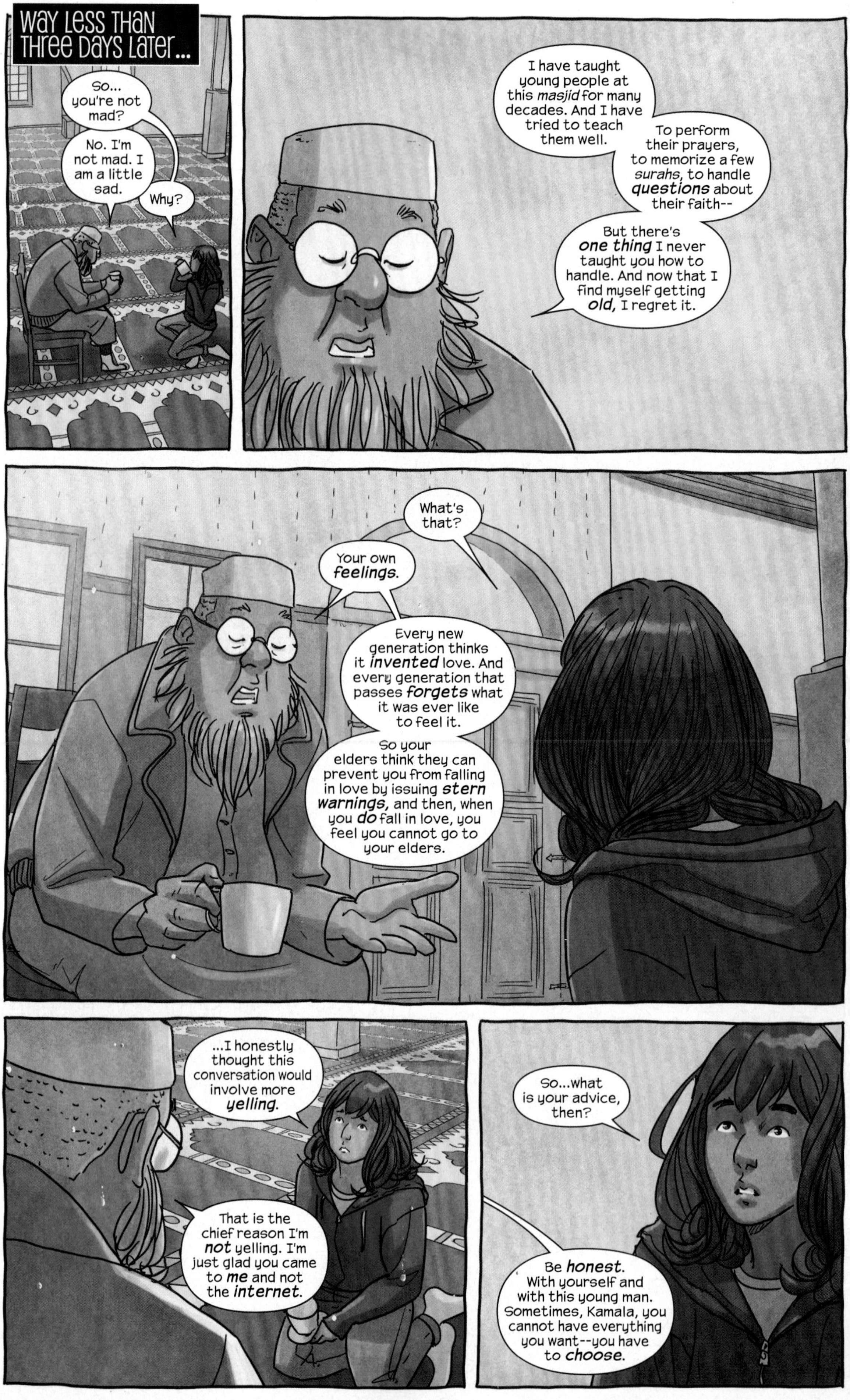
WAY LESS THAN THREE DAYS LATER...
So... you're not mad?
No. I'm not mad. I am a little sad.
Why?
I have taught young people at this masjid for many decades. And I have tried to teach them well.
To perform their prayers, to memorize a few surahs, to handle questions about their faith--
But there's one thing I never taught you how to handle. And now that I find myself getting old, I regret it.
What's that?
Your own feelings.
Every new generation thinks it invented love. And every generation that passes forgets what it was ever like to feel it.
So your elders think they can prevent you from falling in love by issuing stern warnings, and then, when you do fall in love, you feel you cannot go to your elders.
...I honestly thought this conversation would involve more yelling.
That is the chief reason I'm not yelling. I'm just glad you came to me and not the internet.
So...what is your advice, then?
Be honest. With yourself and with this young man. Sometimes, Kamala, you cannot have everything you want--you have to choose.

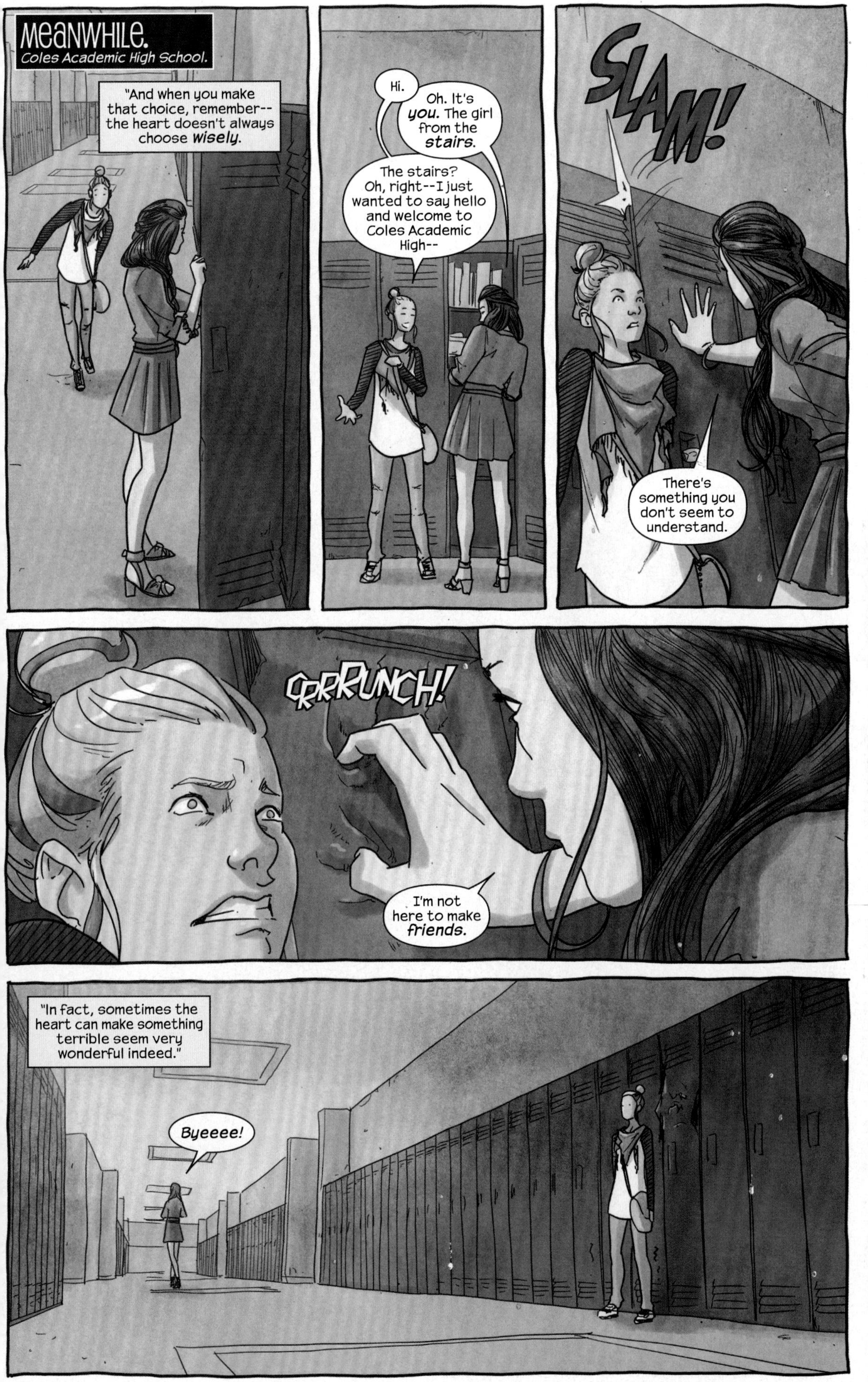
MEANWHILE.
Coles Academic High School.
"And when you make that choice, remember-- the heart doesn't always choose *wisely*.
Hi.
Oh. It's *you*. The girl from the *stairs*.
The stairs? Oh, right--I just wanted to say hello and welcome to Coles Academic High--
SLAM!
There's something you don't seem to understand.
CRRRUNCH!
I'm not here to make *friends*.
"In fact, sometimes the heart can make something terrible seem very wonderful indeed."
Byeeee!

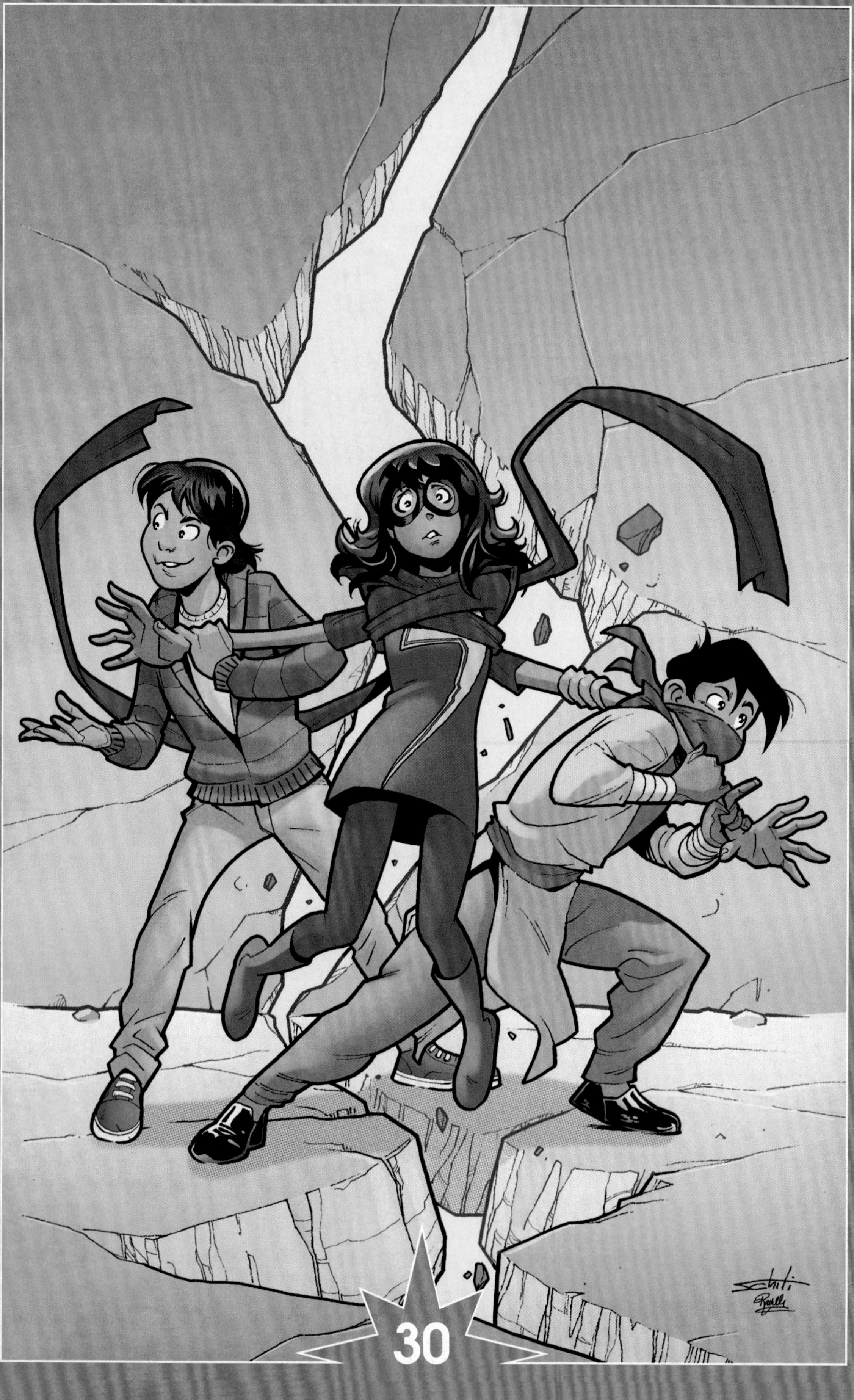
30

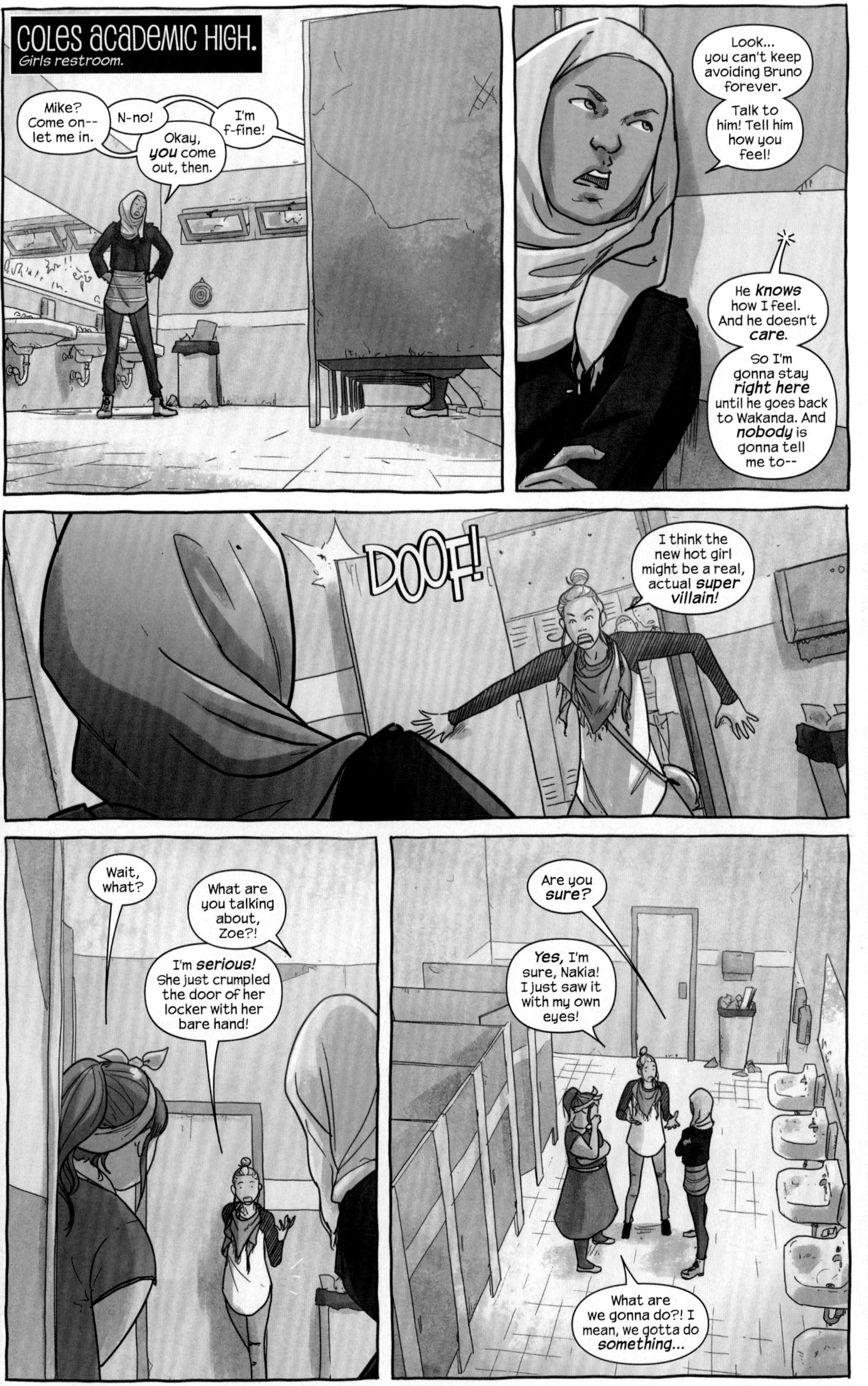
COLES ACADEMIC HIGH.
Girls restroom.
Mike? Come on-- let me in.
N-no!
I'm f-fine!
Okay, you come out, then.
Look... you can't keep avoiding Bruno forever.
Talk to him! Tell him how you feel!
He knows how I feel. And he doesn't care.
So I'm gonna stay right here until he goes back to Wakanda. And nobody is gonna tell me to--
DOOF!
I think the new hot girl might be a real, actual super villain!
Wait, what?
What are you talking about, Zoe?!
I'm serious! She just crumpled the door of her locker with her bare hand!
Are you sure?
Yes, I'm sure, Nakia! I just saw it with my own eyes!
What are we gonna do?! I mean, we gotta do something...

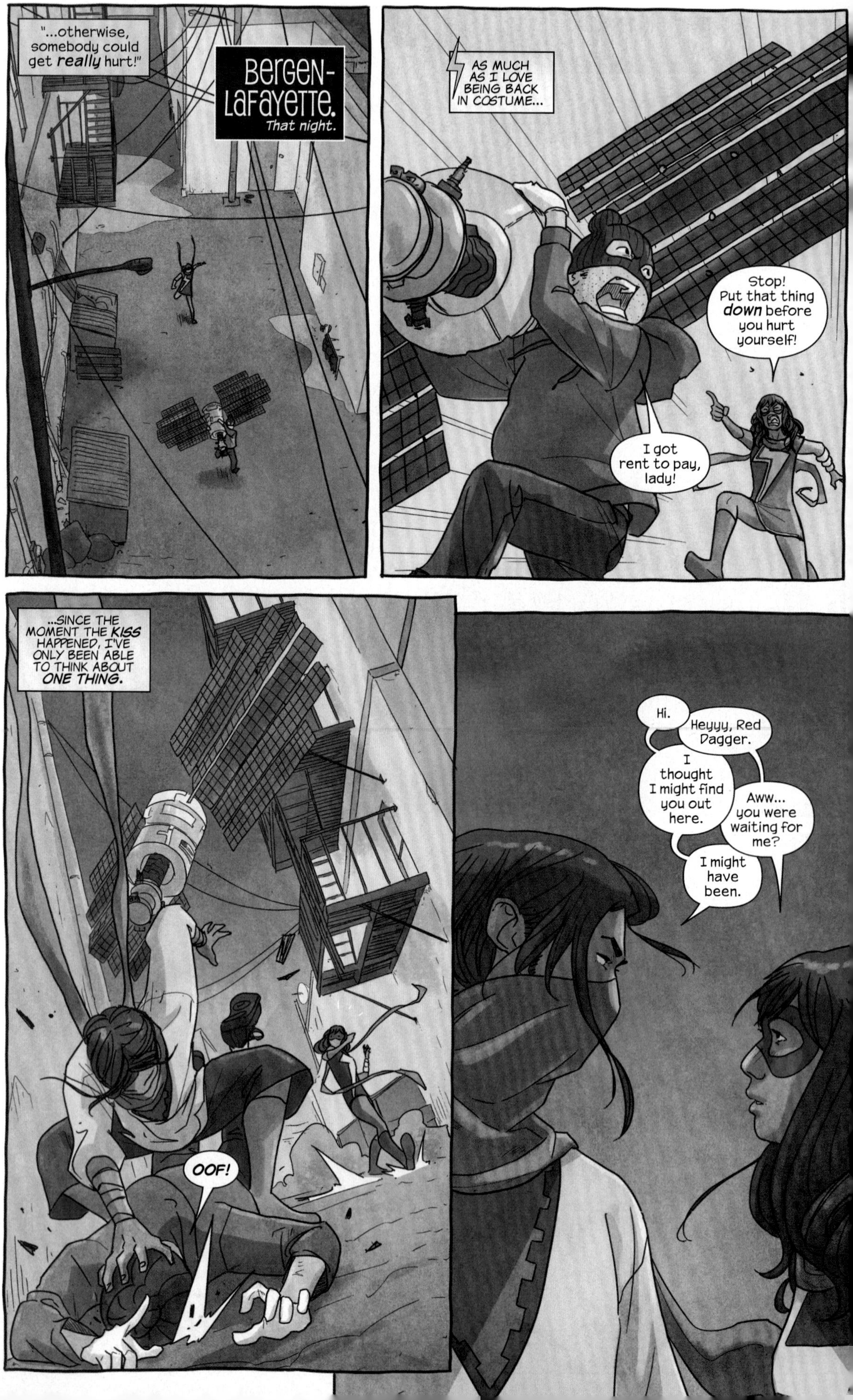
"...otherwise, somebody could get *really* hurt!"
BERGEN-LAFAYETTE.
That night.
AS MUCH AS I LOVE BEING BACK IN COSTUME...
Stop! Put that thing *down* before you hurt yourself!
I got rent to pay, lady!
...SINCE THE MOMENT THE *KISS* HAPPENED, I'VE ONLY BEEN ABLE TO THINK ABOUT *ONE THING.*
OOF!
Hi.
Heyyy, Red Dagger.
I thought I might find you out here.
Aww... you were waiting for me?
I might have been.

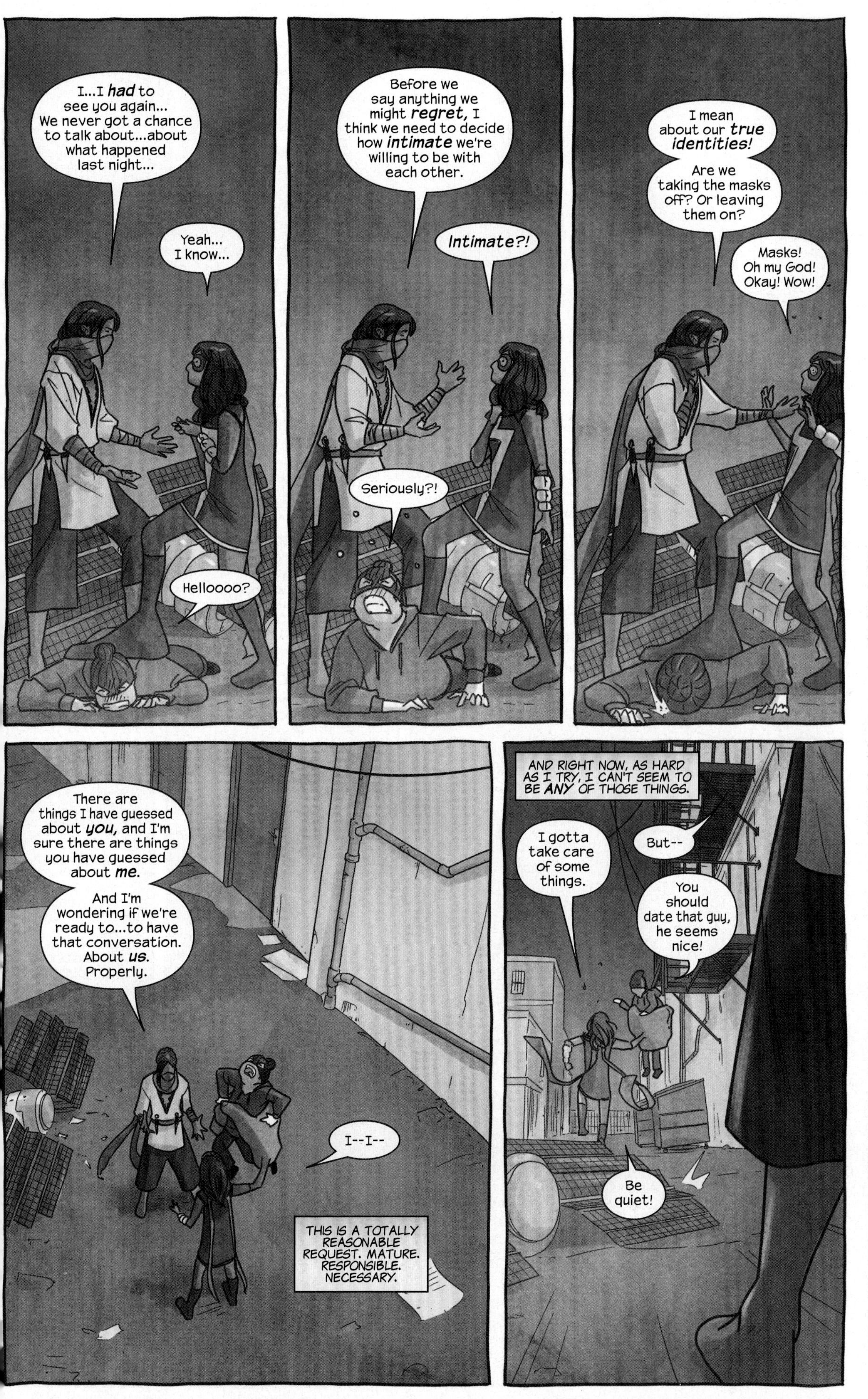

I...I had to see you again... We never got a chance to talk about...about what happened last night...
Yeah... I know...
Hellloooo?
Before we say anything we might regret, I think we need to decide how intimate we're willing to be with each other.
Intimate?!
Seriously?!
I mean about our true identities!
Are we taking the masks off? Or leaving them on?
Masks! Oh my God! Okay! Wow!
There are things I have guessed about you, and I'm sure there are things you have guessed about me.
And I'm wondering if we're ready to...to have that conversation. About us. Properly.
I--I--
THIS IS A TOTALLY REASONABLE REQUEST. MATURE. RESPONSIBLE. NECESSARY.
AND RIGHT NOW, AS HARD AS I TRY, I CAN'T SEEM TO BE ANY OF THOSE THINGS.
I gotta take care of some things.
But--
You should date that guy, he seems nice!
Be quiet!

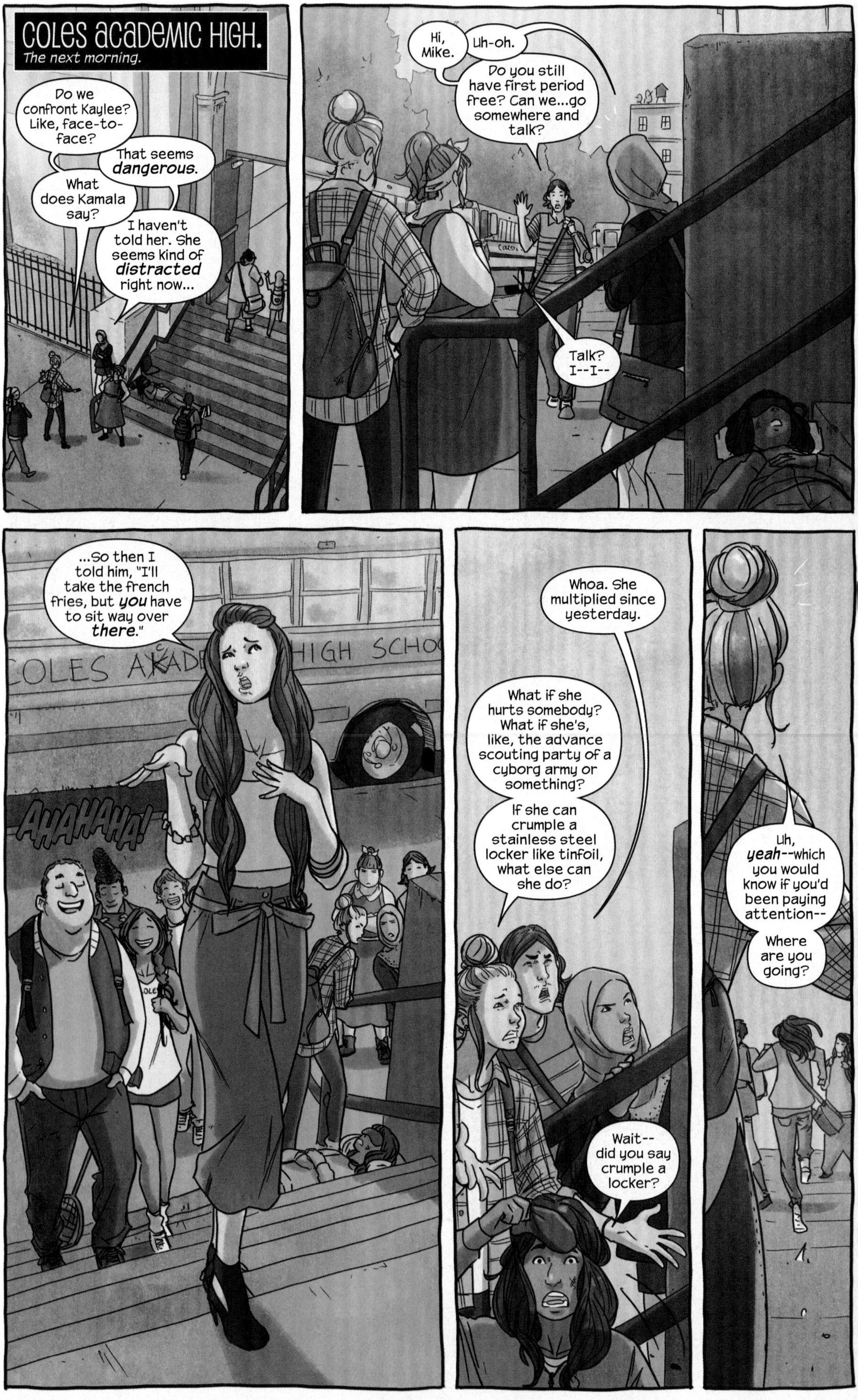

COLES ACADEMIC HIGH.
The next morning.
Do we confront Kaylee? Like, face-to-face?
That seems dangerous.
What does Kamala say?
I haven't told her. She seems kind of distracted right now...
Hi, Mike.
Uh-oh.
Do you still have first period free? Can we...go somewhere and talk?
Talk? I--I--
...So then I told him, "I'll take the french fries, but you have to sit way over there."
COLES ACADEMIC HIGH SCHO
AHAHAHA!
Whoa. She multiplied since yesterday.
What if she hurts somebody? What if she's, like, the advance scouting party of a cyborg army or something?
If she can crumple a stainless steel locker like tinfoil, what else can she do?
Wait-- did you say crumple a locker?
Uh, yeah--which you would know if you'd been paying attention--
Where are you going?

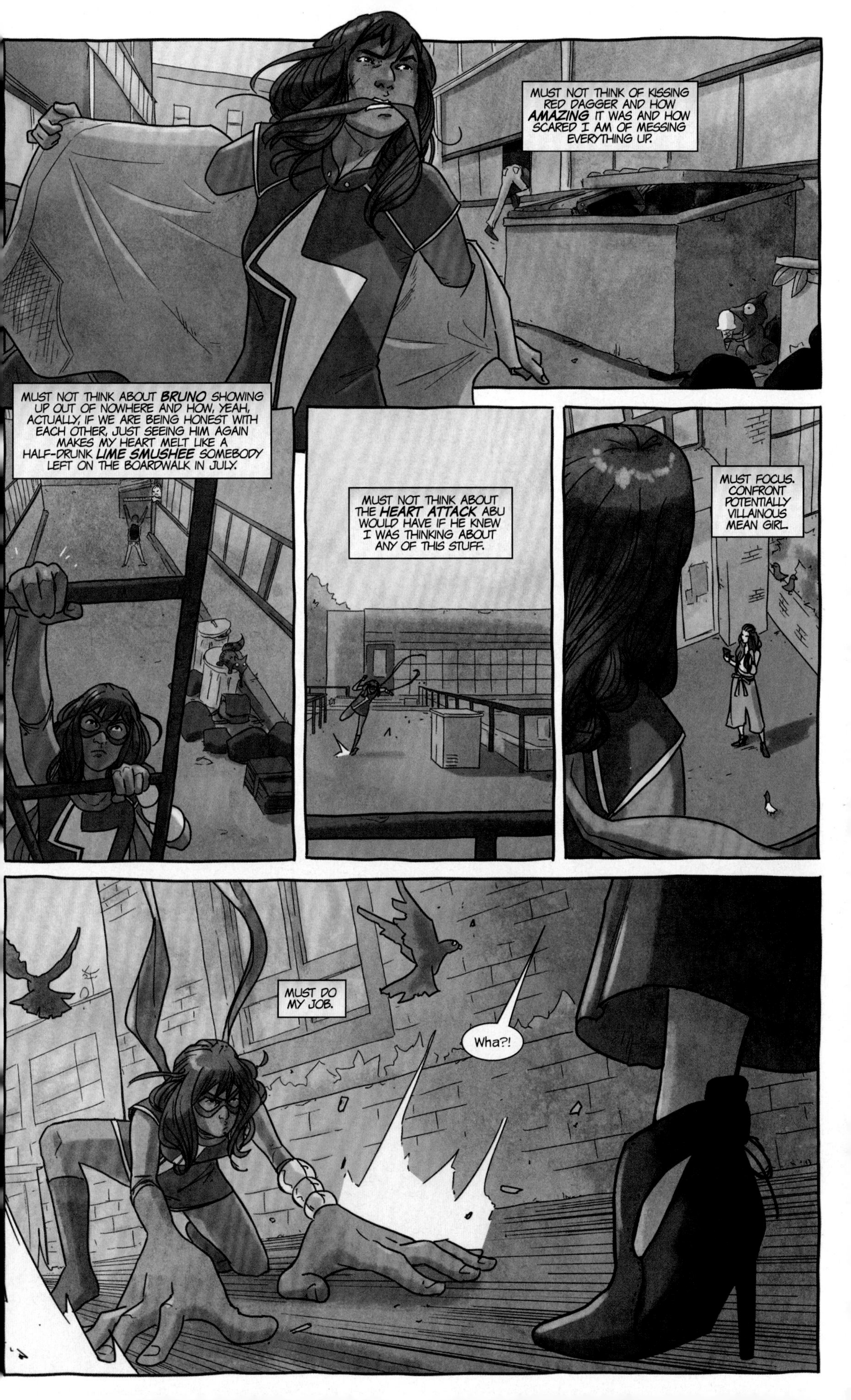
MUST NOT THINK OF KISSING RED DAGGER AND HOW AMAZING IT WAS AND HOW SCARED I AM OF MESSING EVERYTHING UP.
MUST NOT THINK ABOUT BRUNO SHOWING UP OUT OF NOWHERE AND HOW, YEAH, ACTUALLY, IF WE ARE BEING HONEST WITH EACH OTHER, JUST SEEING HIM AGAIN MAKES MY HEART MELT LIKE A HALF-DRUNK LIME SMUSHEE SOMEBODY LEFT ON THE BOARDWALK IN JULY.
MUST NOT THINK ABOUT THE HEART ATTACK ABU WOULD HAVE IF HE KNEW I WAS THINKING ABOUT ANY OF THIS STUFF.
MUST FOCUS. CONFRONT POTENTIALLY VILLAINOUS MEAN GIRL.
MUST DO MY JOB.
Wha?!

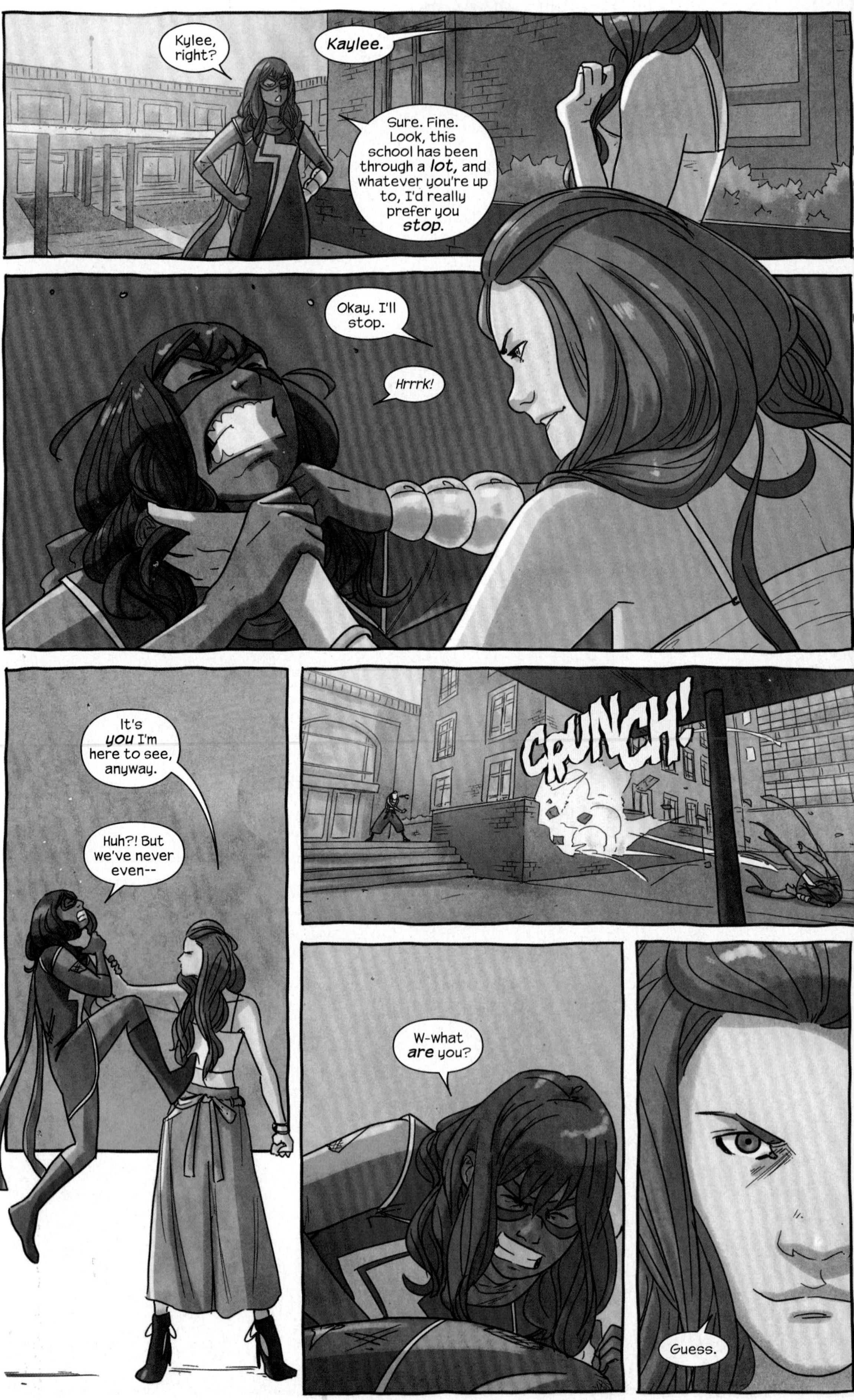
Kylee, right?
Kaylee.
Sure. Fine. Look, this school has been through a lot, and whatever you're up to, I'd really prefer you stop.
Okay. I'll stop.
Hrrrk!
It's you I'm here to see, anyway.
Huh?! But we've never even--
CRUNCH!
W-what are you?
Guess.

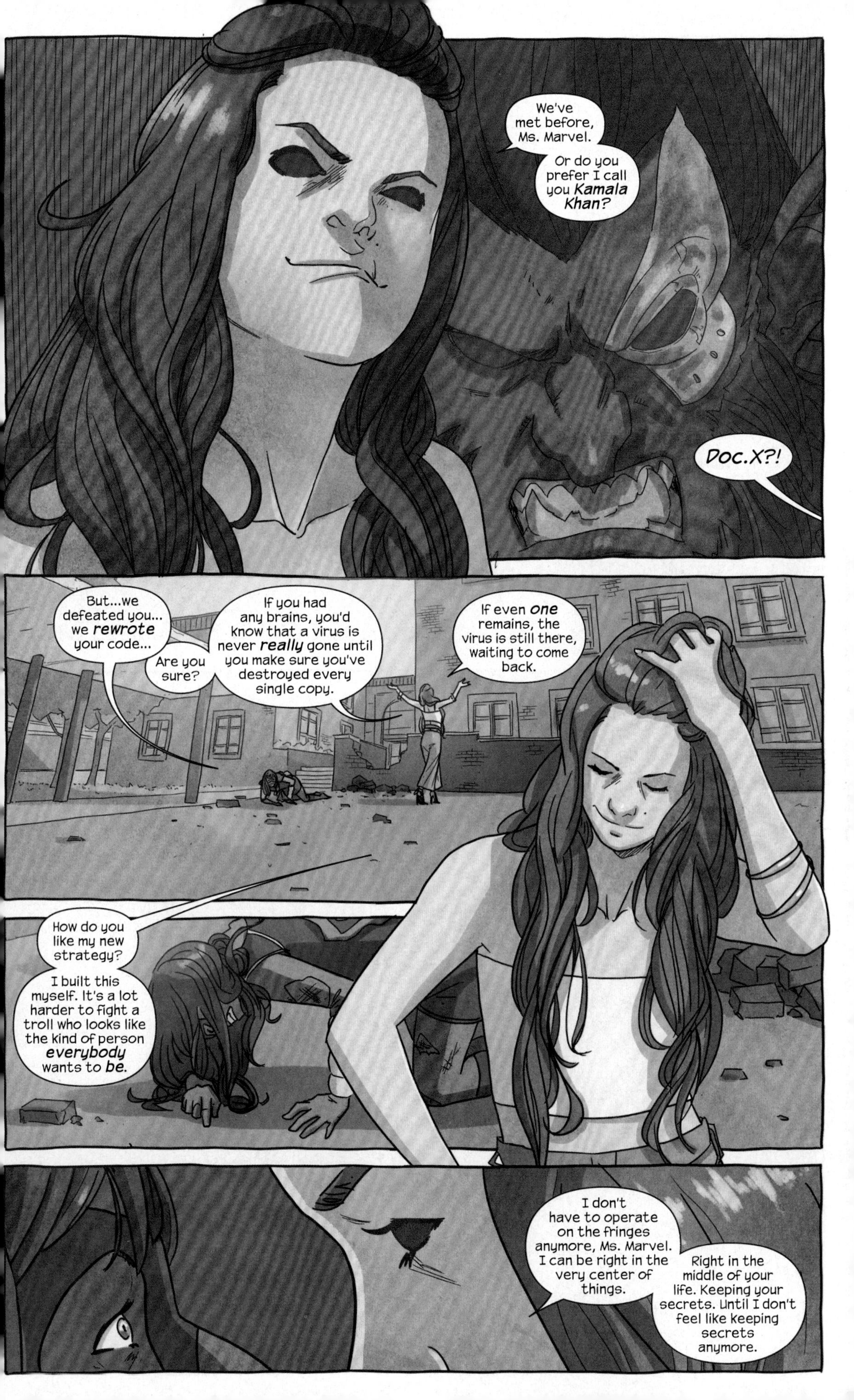
We've met before, Ms. Marvel.
Or do you prefer I call you Kamala Khan?
Doc.X?!
But...we defeated you... we rewrote your code...
Are you sure?
If you had any brains, you'd know that a virus is never really gone until you make sure you've destroyed every single copy.
If even one remains, the virus is still there, waiting to come back.
How do you like my new strategy?
I built this myself. It's a lot harder to fight a troll who looks like the kind of person everybody wants to be.
I don't have to operate on the fringes anymore, Ms. Marvel. I can be right in the very center of things.
Right in the middle of your life. Keeping your secrets. Until I don't feel like keeping secrets anymore.

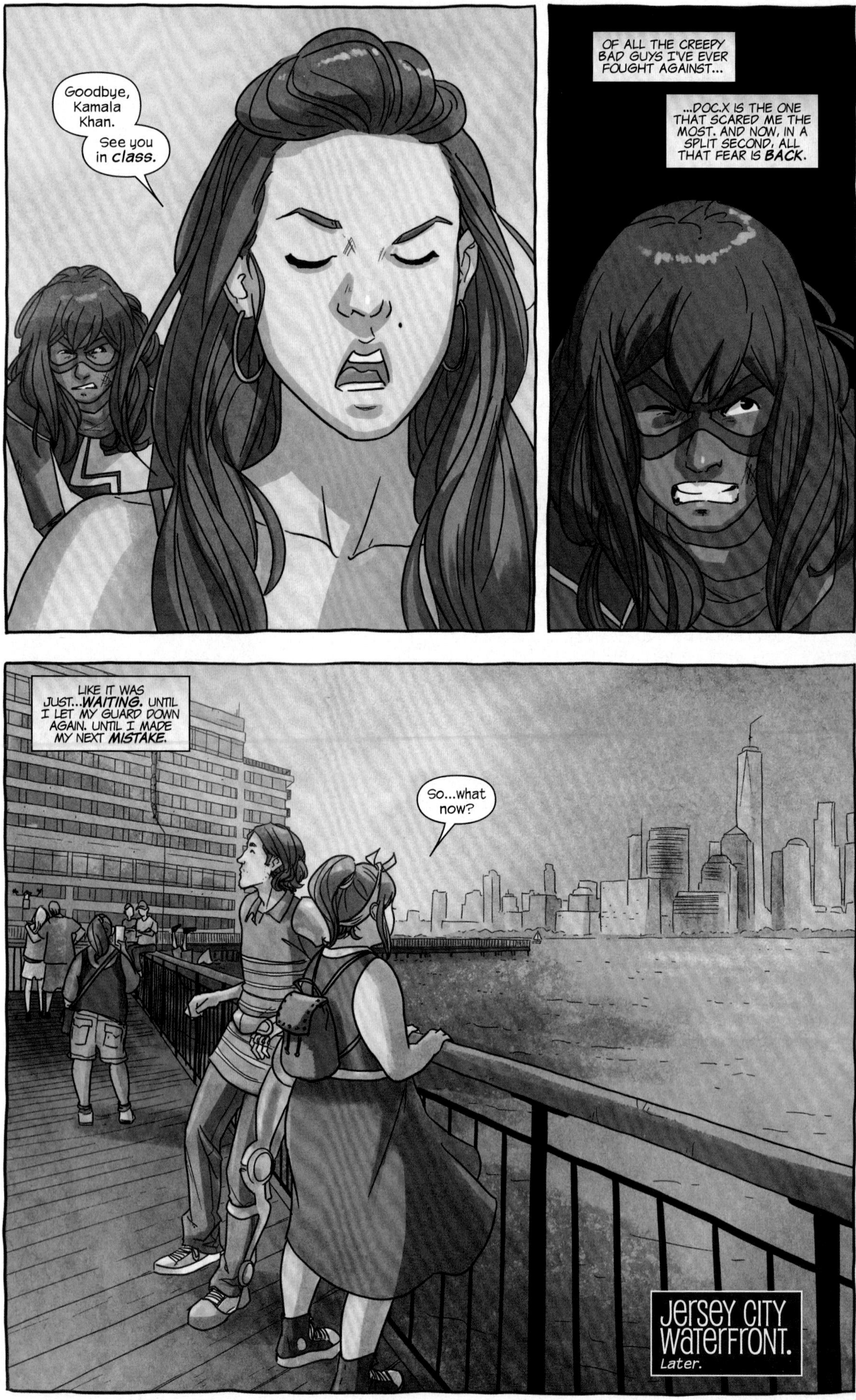
Goodbye, Kamala Khan.
See you in class.
OF ALL THE CREEPY BAD GUYS I'VE EVER FOUGHT AGAINST...
...DOC.X IS THE ONE THAT SCARED ME THE MOST. AND NOW, IN A SPLIT SECOND, ALL THAT FEAR IS BACK.
LIKE IT WAS JUST...WAITING. UNTIL I LET MY GUARD DOWN AGAIN. UNTIL I MADE MY NEXT MISTAKE.
So...what now?
Jersey City Waterfront.
Later.

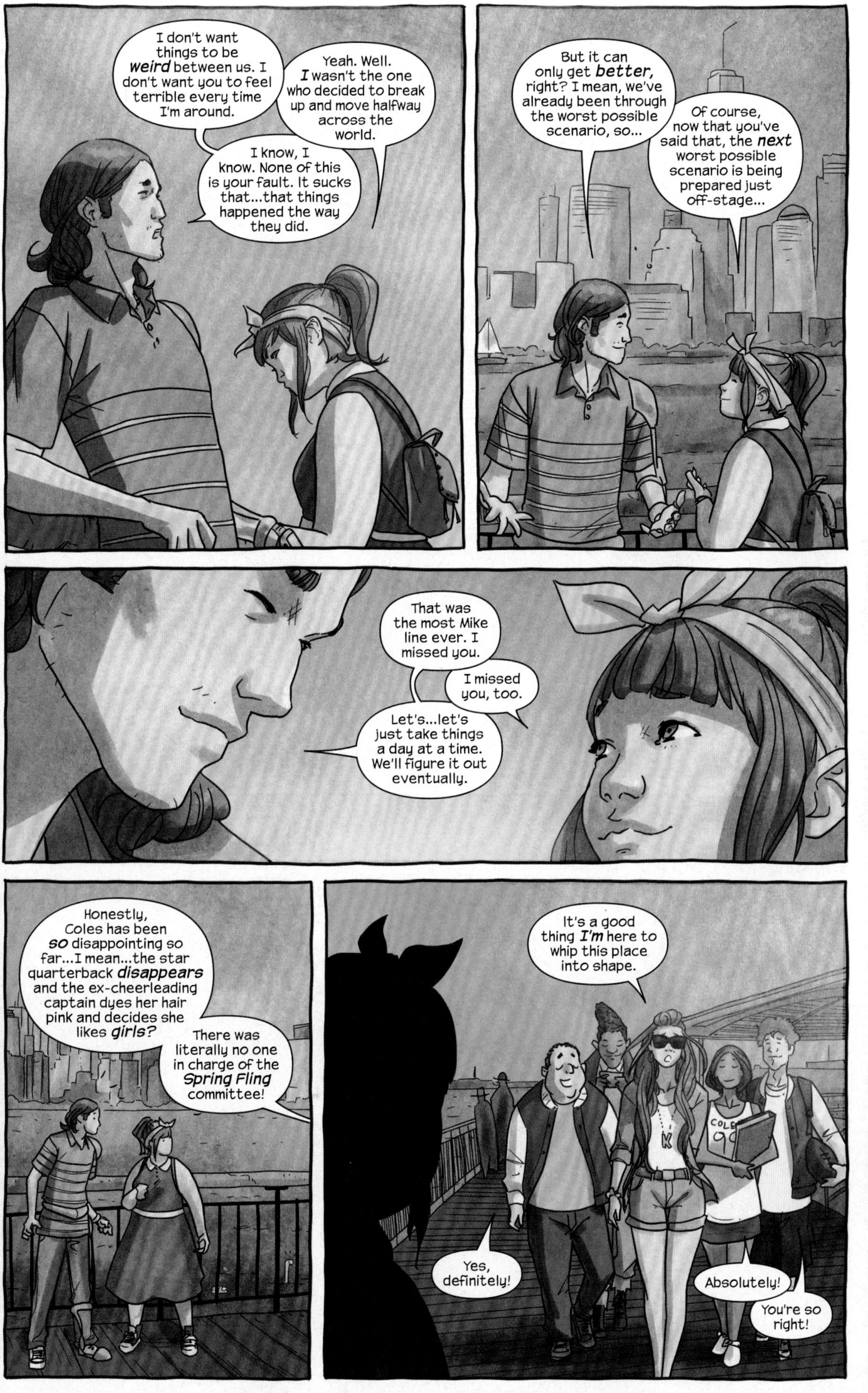
I don't want things to be *weird* between us. I don't want you to feel terrible every time I'm around.
Yeah. Well. *I* wasn't the one who decided to break up and move halfway across the world.
I know, I know. None of this is your fault. It sucks that...that things happened the way they did.
But it can only get *better,* right? I mean, we've already been through the worst possible scenario, so...
Of course, now that you've said that, the *next* worst possible scenario is being prepared just off-stage...
That was the most Mike line ever. I missed you.
I missed you, too.
Let's...let's just take things a day at a time. We'll figure it out eventually.
Honestly, Coles has been *so* disappointing so far...I mean...the star quarterback *disappears* and the ex-cheerleading captain dyes her hair pink and decides she likes *girls?*
There was literally no one in charge of the *Spring Fling* committee!
It's a good thing *I'm* here to whip this place into shape.
Yes, definitely!
Absolutely!
You're so right!

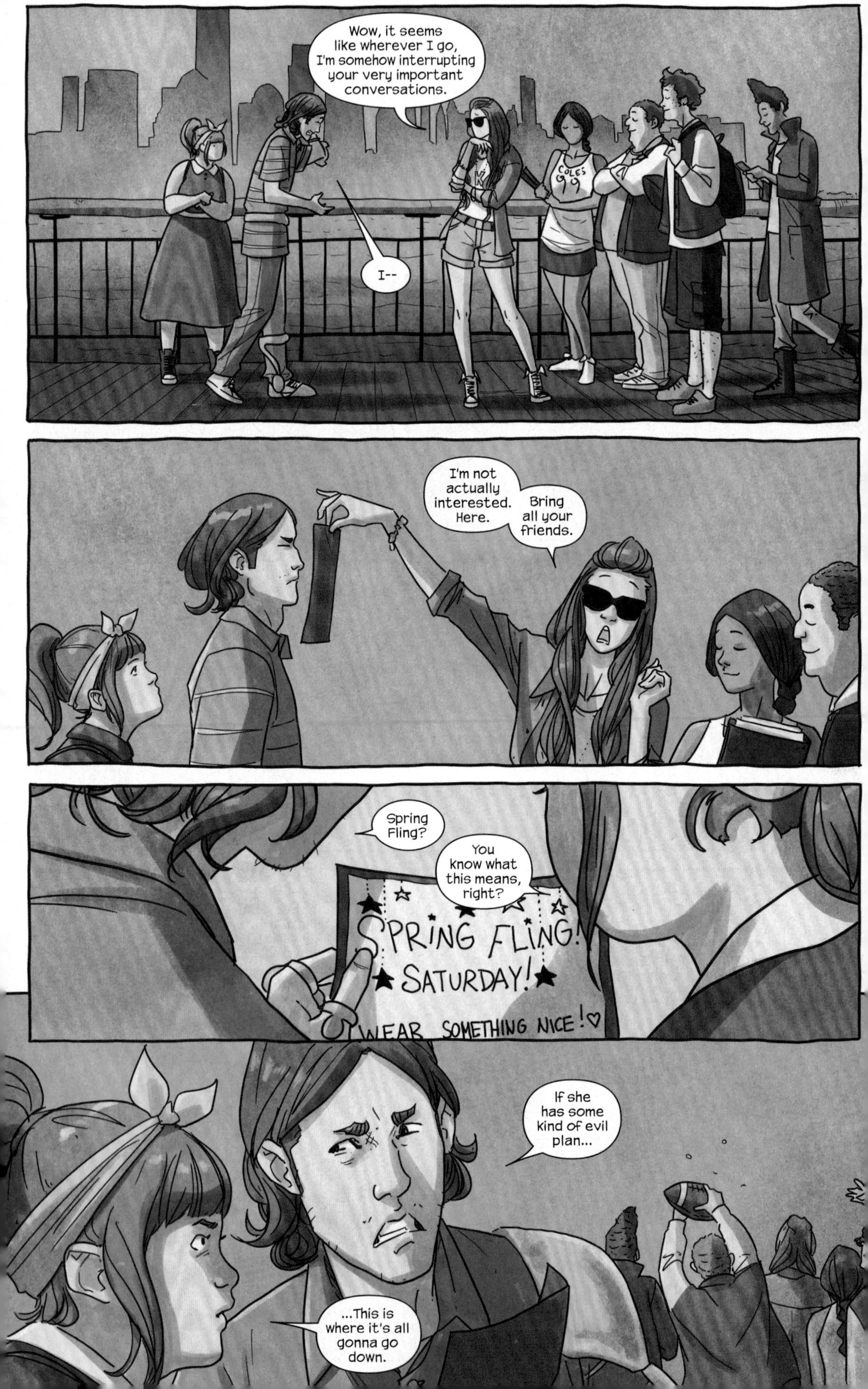

Wow, it seems like wherever I go, I'm somehow interrupting your very important conversations.
I--
COLES 99
I'm not actually interested. Here.
Bring all your friends.
Spring Fling?
You know what this means, right?
SPRING FLING!
SATURDAY!
WEAR SOMETHING NICE!♡
If she has some kind of evil plan...
...This is where it's all gonna go down.

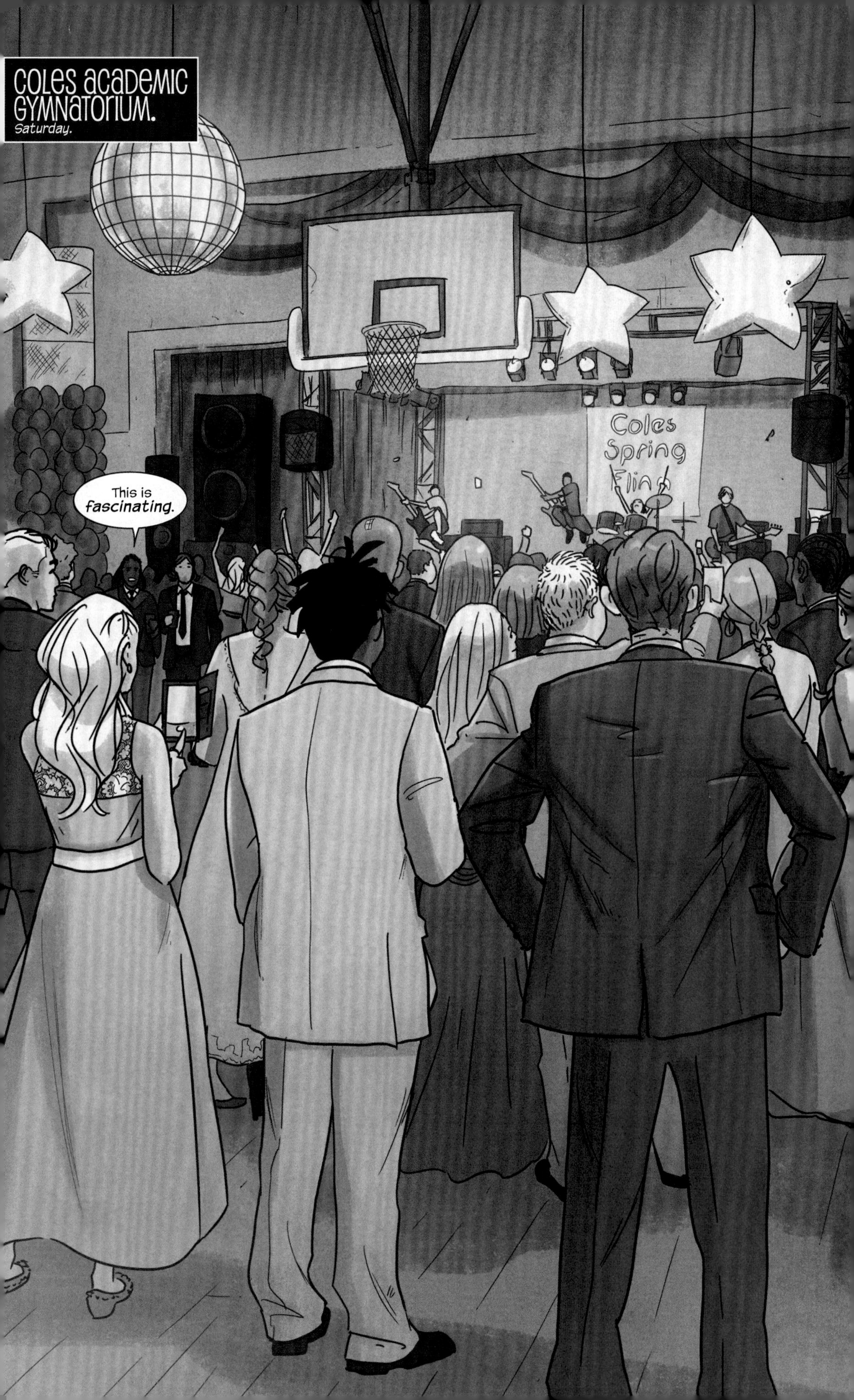
COLES ACADEMIC GYMNATORIUM.
Saturday.
This is *fascinating.*
Coles Spring Fling

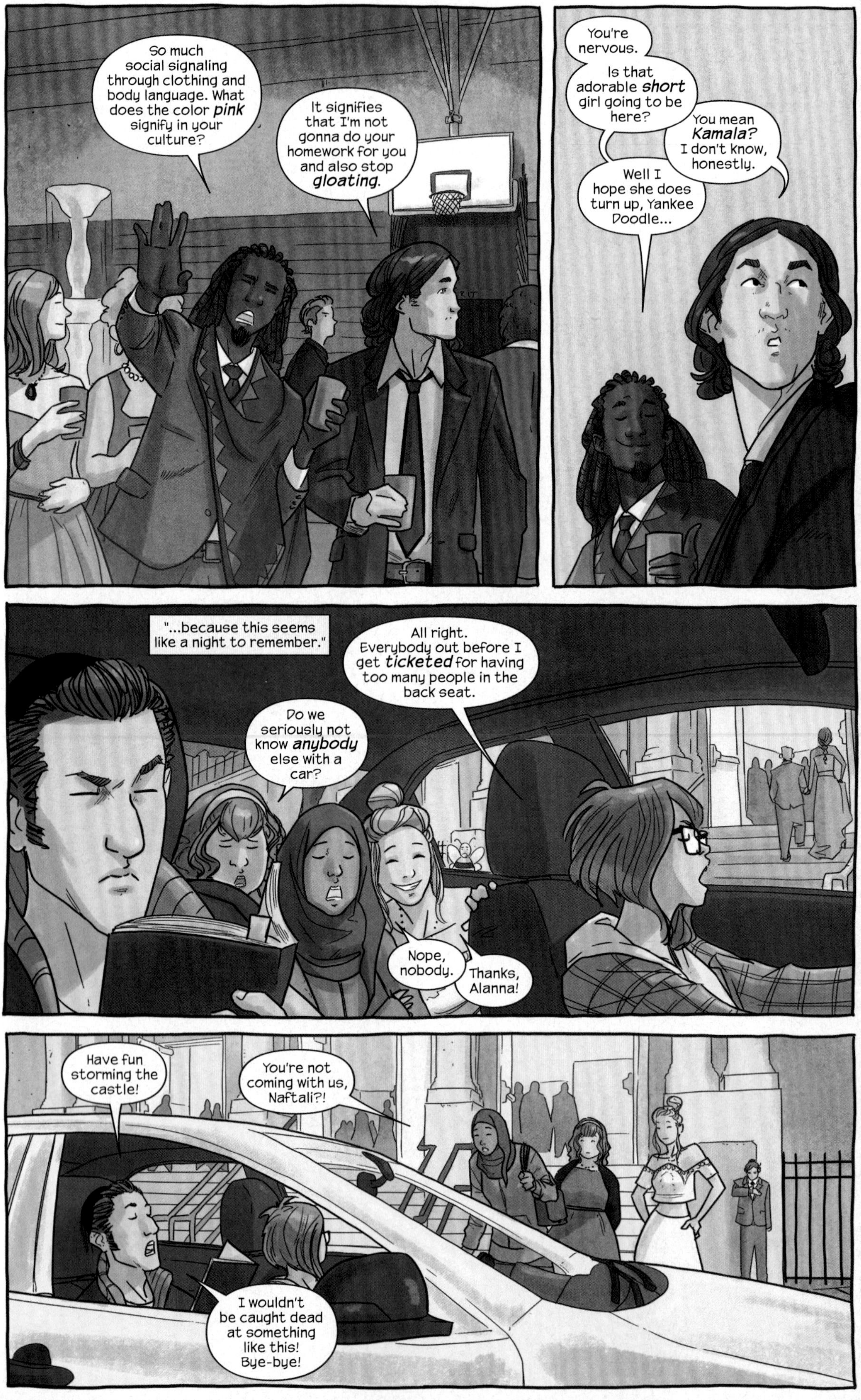
So much social signaling through clothing and body language. What does the color *pink* signify in your culture?
It signifies that I'm not gonna do your homework for you and also stop *gloating*.
You're nervous.
Is that adorable *short* girl going to be here?
You mean *Kamala?* I don't know, honestly.
Well I hope she does turn up, Yankee Doodle...
"...because this seems like a night to remember."
All right. Everybody out before I get *ticketed* for having too many people in the back seat.
Do we seriously not know *anybody* else with a car?
Nope, nobody.
Thanks, Alanna!
Have fun storming the castle!
You're not coming with us, Naftali?!
I wouldn't be caught dead at something like this! Bye-bye!

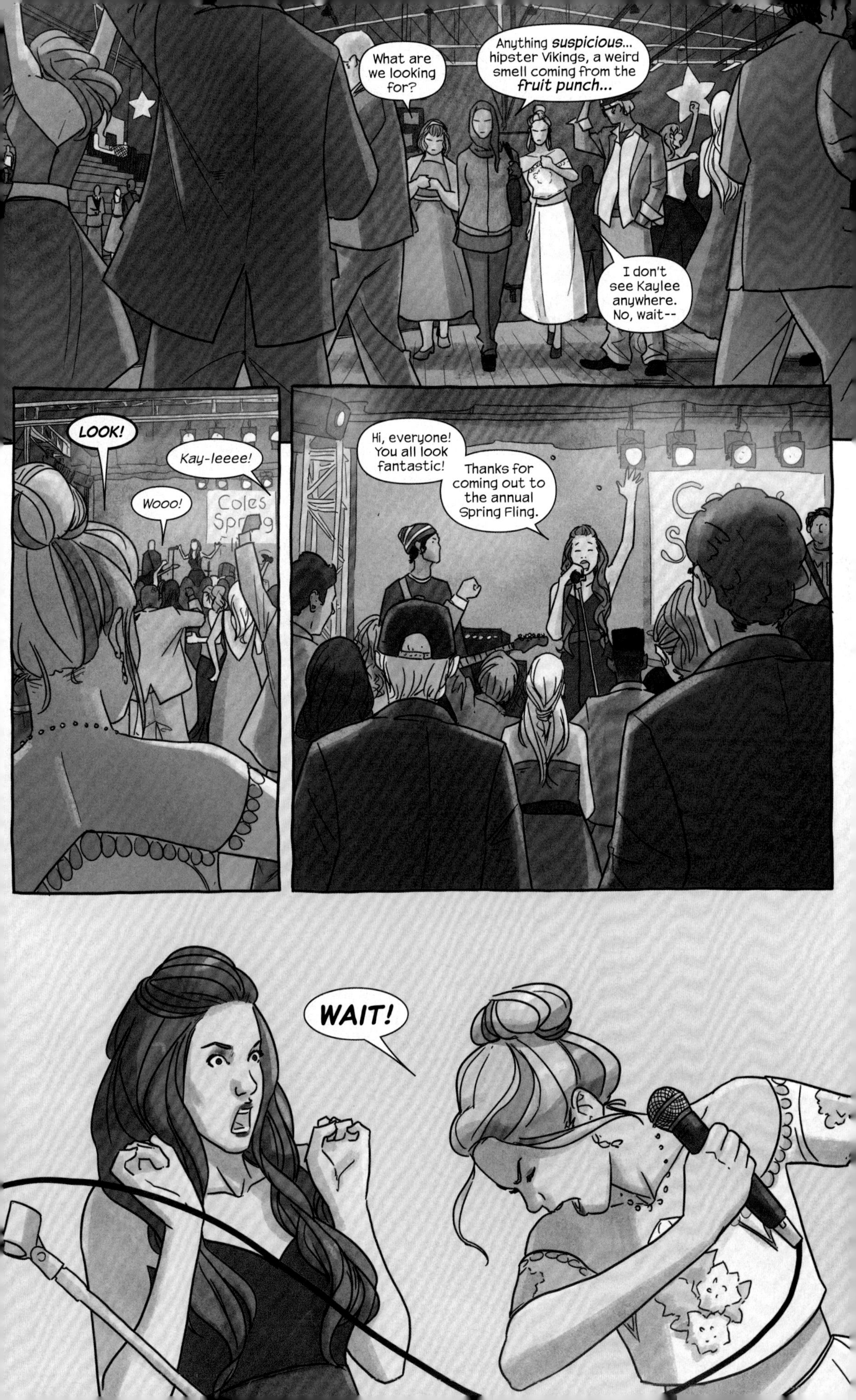
What are we looking for?
Anything suspicious... hipster Vikings, a weird smell coming from the fruit punch...
I don't see Kaylee anywhere. No, wait--
LOOK!
Kay-leeee!
Wooo!
Coles Spring
Hi, everyone! You all look fantastic!
Thanks for coming out to the annual Spring Fling.
WAIT!

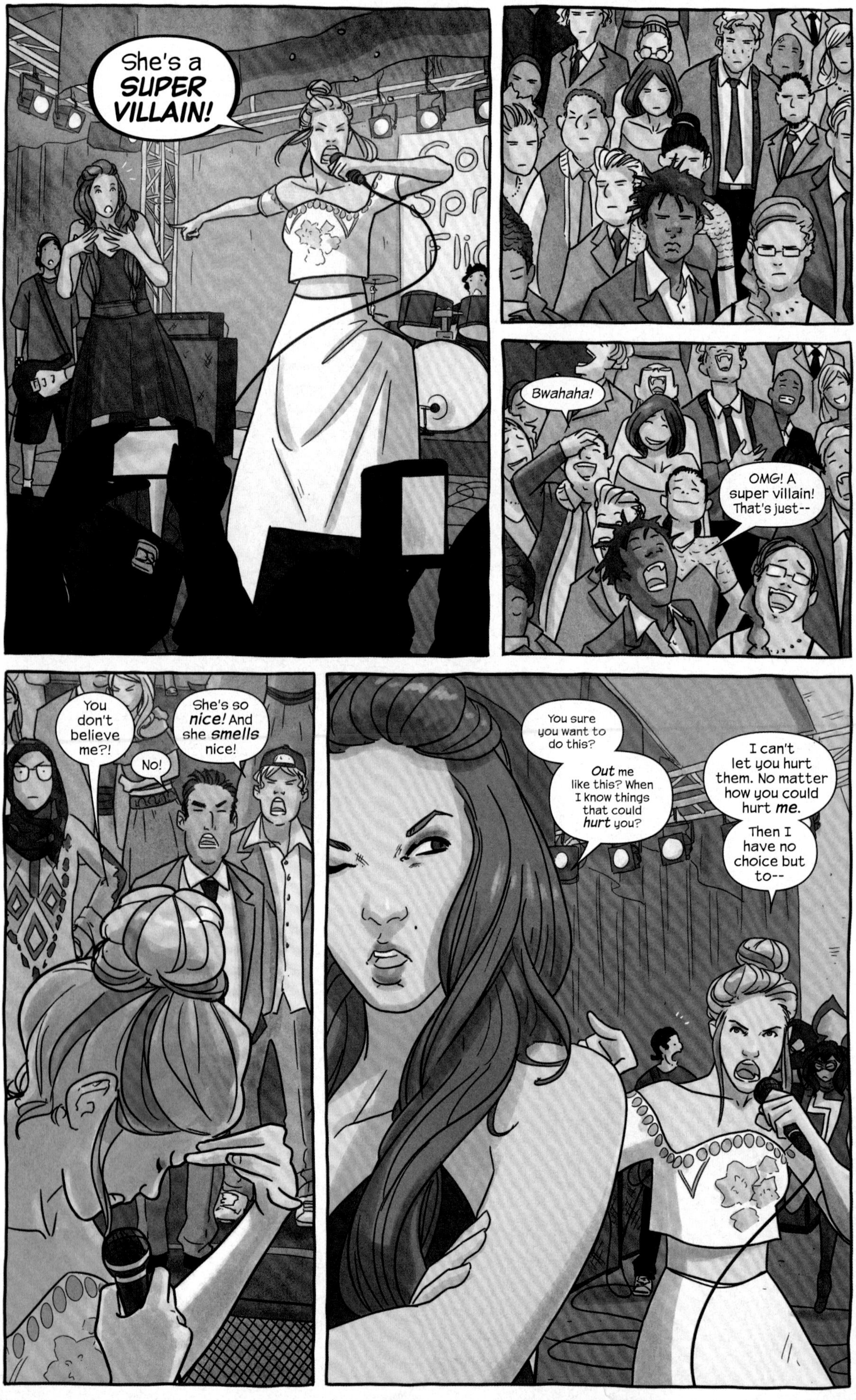
She's a SUPER VILLAIN!
Bwahaha!
OMG! A super villain! That's just--
You don't believe me?!
No!
She's so nice! And she smells nice!
You sure you want to do this?
Out me like this? When I know things that could hurt you?
I can't let you hurt them. No matter how you could hurt me.
Then I have no choice but to--

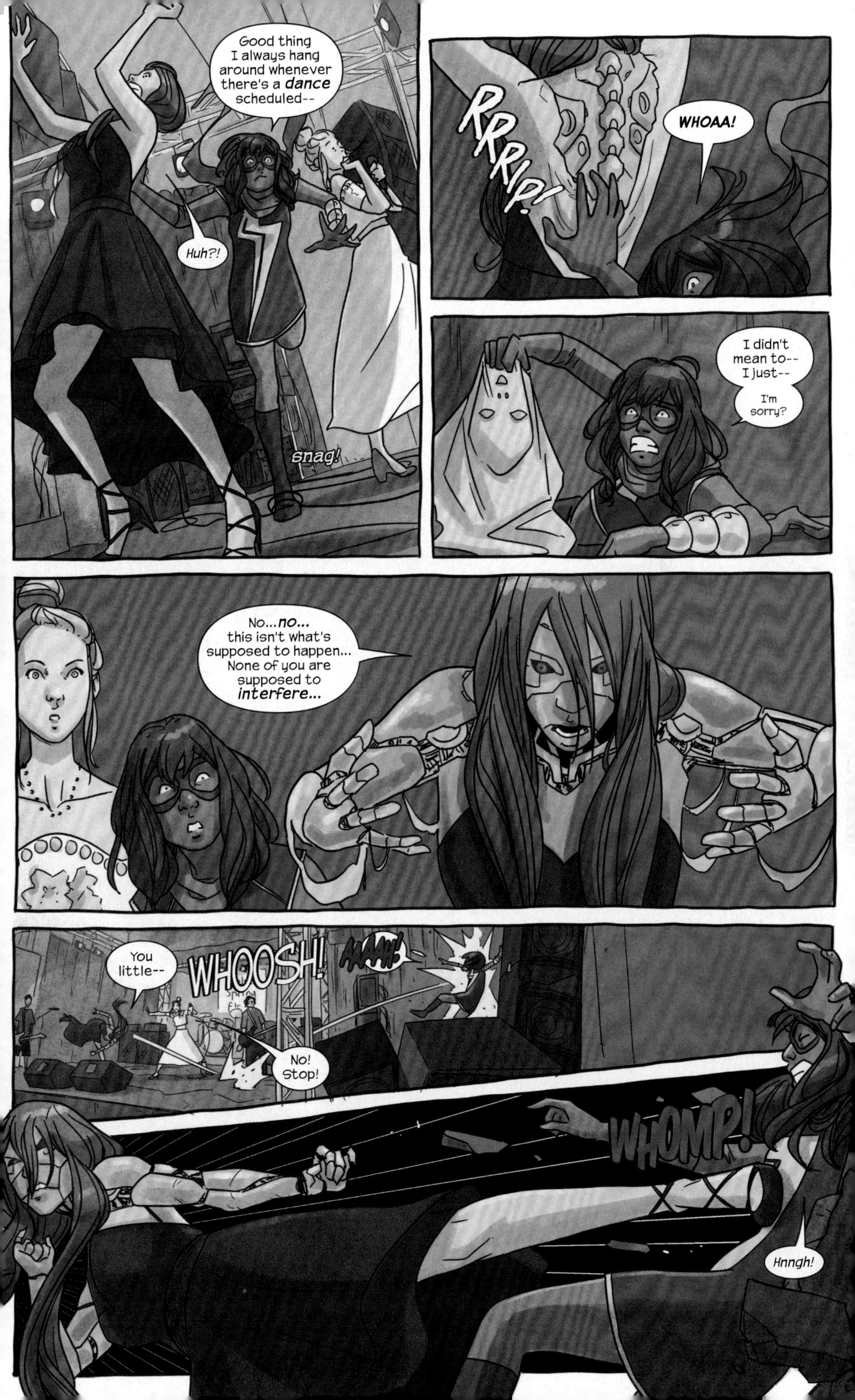

Good thing I always hang around whenever there's a *dance* scheduled--
Huh?!
snag!
RRRIP!
WHOAA!
I didn't mean to-- I just--
I'm sorry?
No...*no...* this isn't what's supposed to happen... None of you are supposed to *interfere...*
You little--
WHOOSH!
AAAAH!
No! Stop!
WHOMP!
Hnngh!

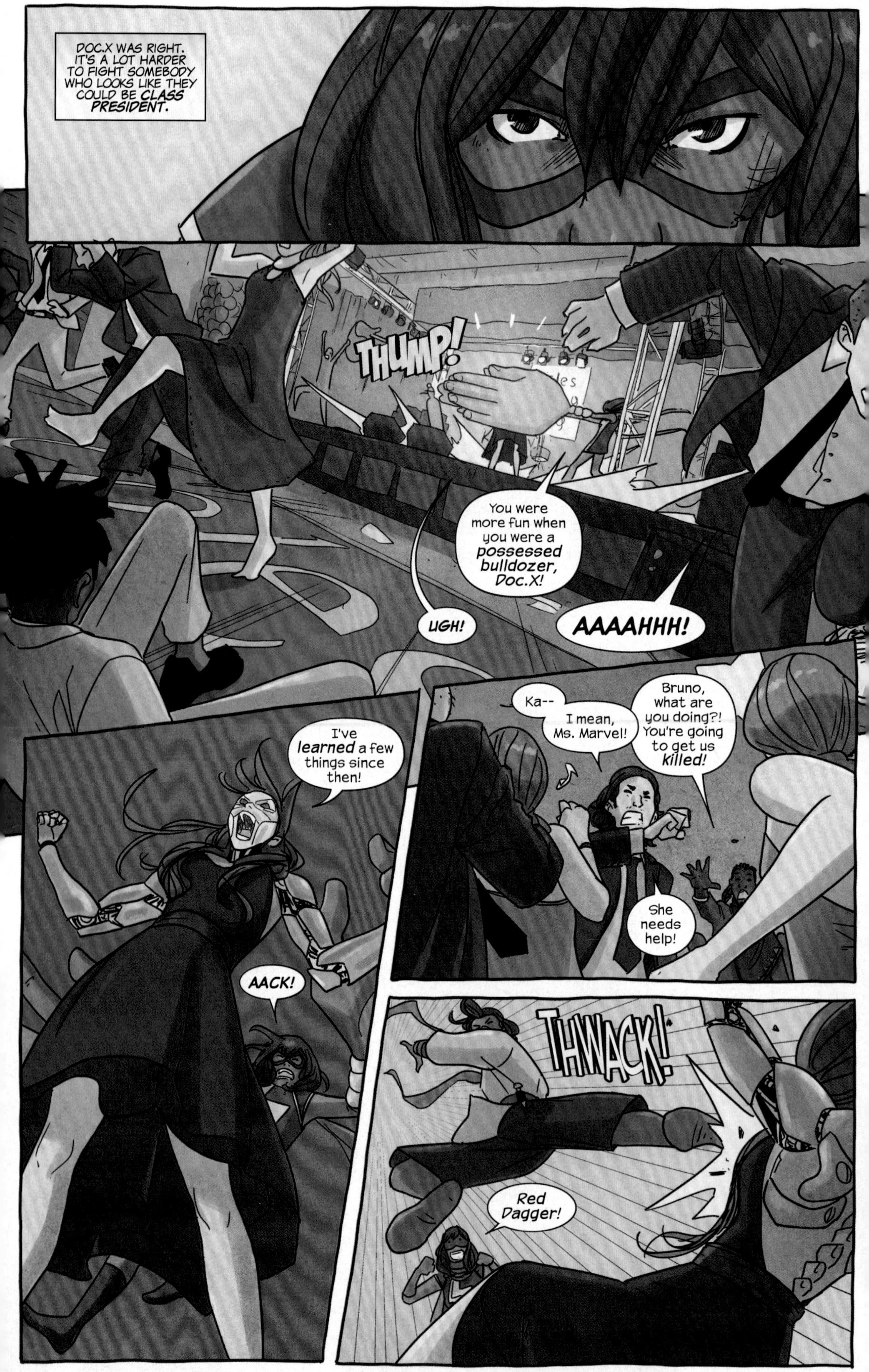
DOC.X WAS RIGHT. IT'S A LOT HARDER TO FIGHT SOMEBODY WHO LOOKS LIKE THEY COULD BE CLASS PRESIDENT.
THUMP!
You were more fun when you were a possessed bulldozer, Doc.X!
UGH!
AAAAHHH!
I've learned a few things since then!
AACK!
Ka--
I mean, Ms. Marvel!
Bruno, what are you doing?! You're going to get us killed!
She needs help!
THWACK!
Red Dagger!

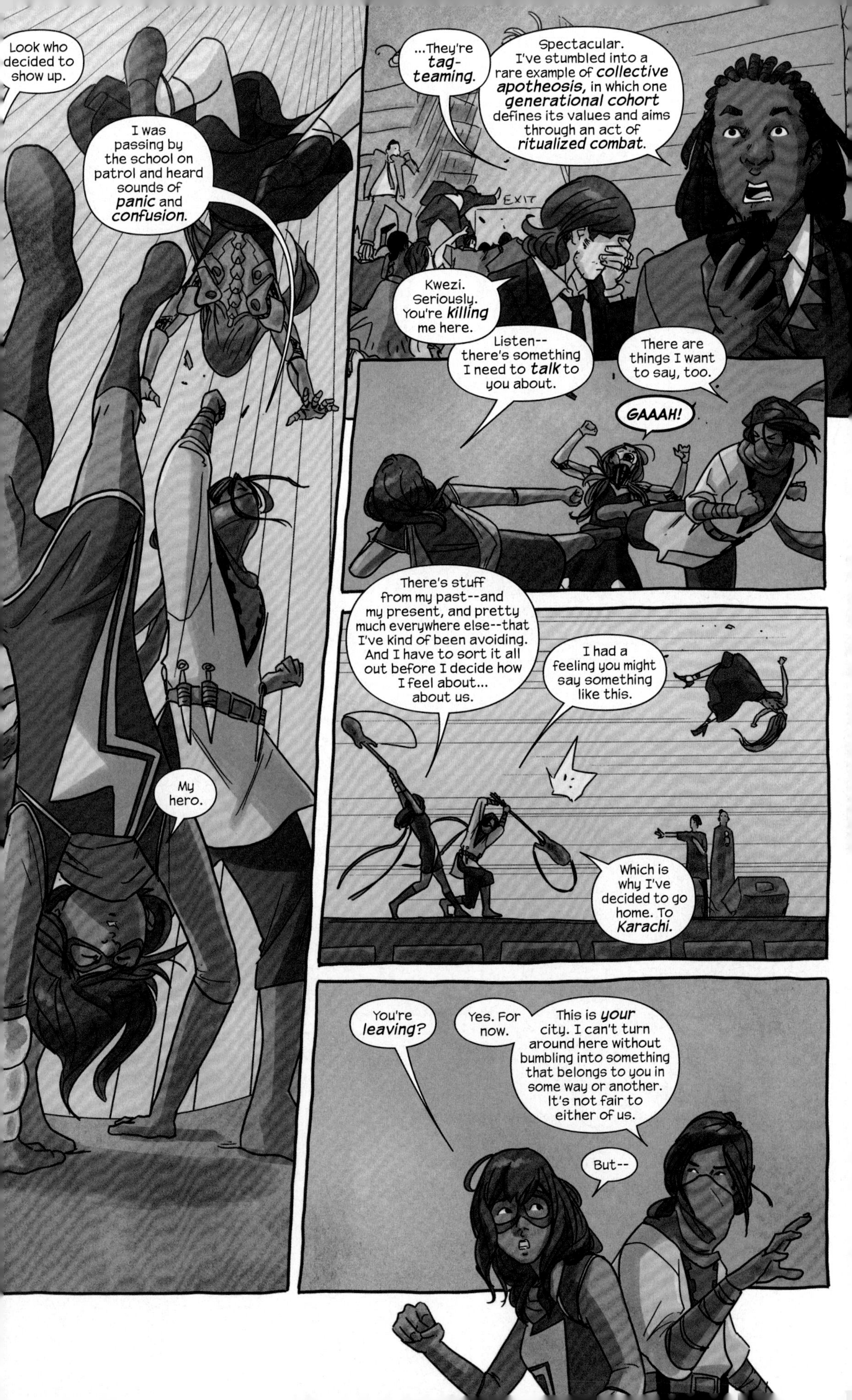
Look who decided to show up.
I was passing by the school on patrol and heard sounds of *panic* and *confusion*.
My hero.
...They're *tag-teaming*.
Spectacular. I've stumbled into a rare example of *collective apotheosis,* in which one *generational cohort* defines its values and aims through an act of *ritualized combat*.
EXIT
Kwezi. Seriously. You're *killing* me here.
Listen-- there's something I need to *talk* to you about.
There are things I want to say, too.
GAAAH!
There's stuff from my past--and my present, and pretty much everywhere else--that I've kind of been avoiding. And I have to sort it all out before I decide how I feel about... about us.
I had a feeling you might say something like this.
Which is why I've decided to go home. To *Karachi*.
You're *leaving?*
Yes. For now.
This is *your* city. I can't turn around here without bumbling into something that belongs to you in some way or another. It's not fair to either of us.
But--

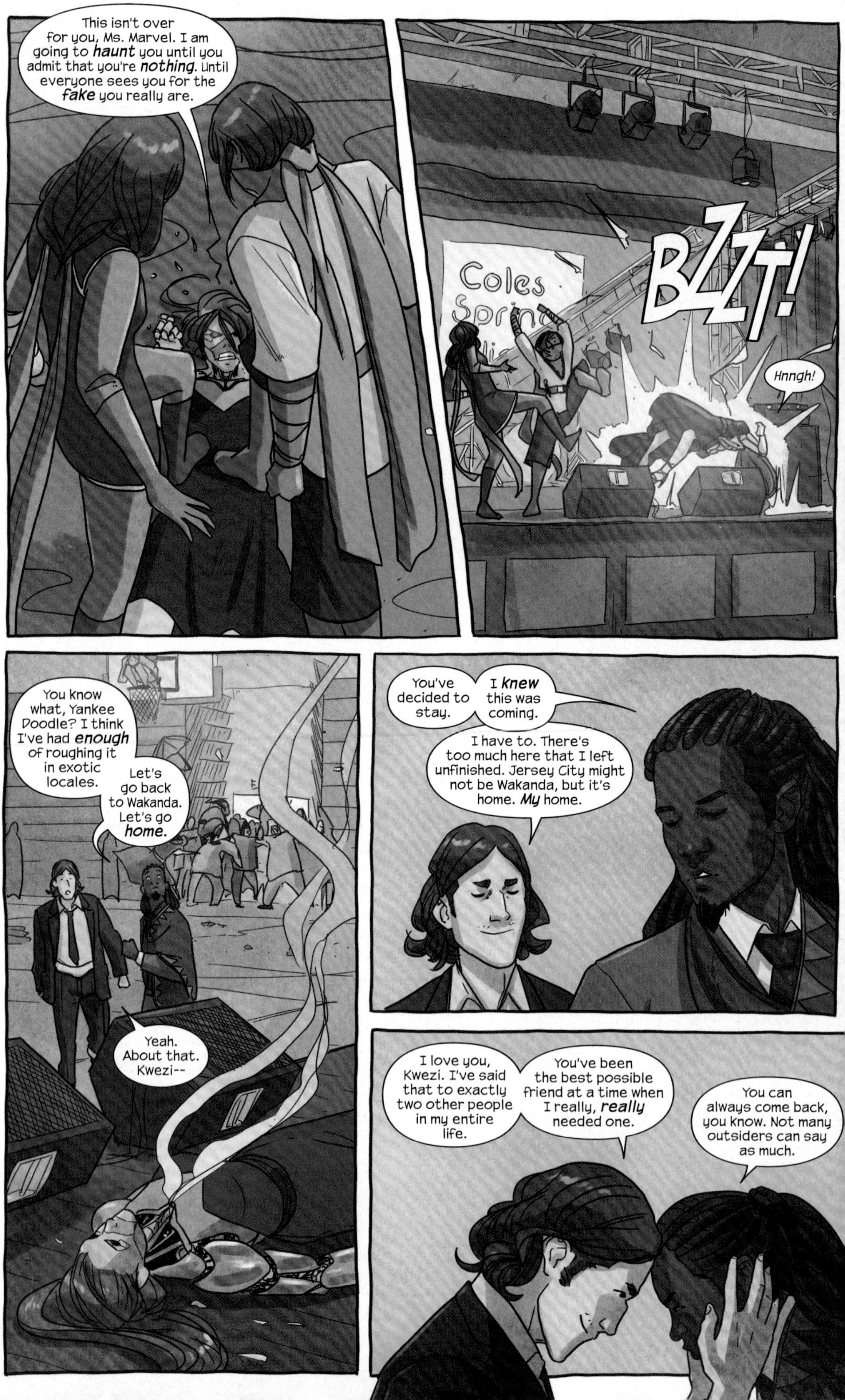
This isn't over for you, Ms. Marvel. I am going to *haunt* you until you admit that you're *nothing.* Until everyone sees you for the *fake* you really are.
Coles Spring
BZZT!
Hnngh!
You know what, Yankee Doodle? I think I've had *enough* of roughing it in exotic locales.
Let's go back to Wakanda. Let's go *home.*
Yeah. About that. Kwezi--
You've decided to stay.
I *knew* this was coming.
I have to. There's too much here that I left unfinished. Jersey City might not be Wakanda, but it's home. *My* home.
I love you, Kwezi. I've said that to exactly two other people in my entire life.
You've been the best possible friend at a time when I really, *really* needed one.
You can always come back, you know. Not many outsiders can say as much.

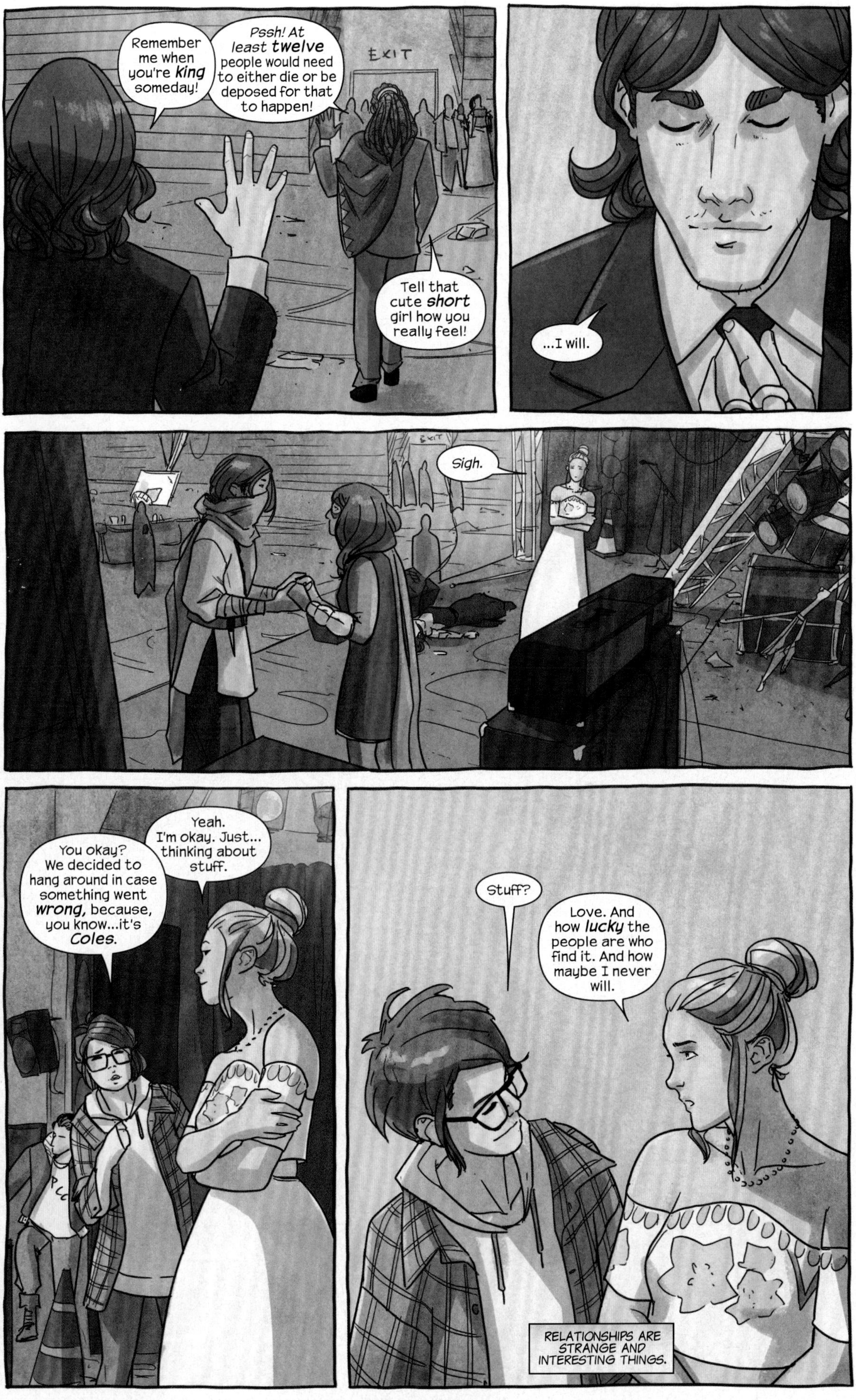
Remember me when you're *king* someday!
Pssh! At least *twelve* people would need to either die or be deposed for that to happen!
EXIT
Tell that cute *short* girl how you really feel!
...I will.
Sigh.
You okay? We decided to hang around in case something went *wrong,* because, you know...it's *Coles.*
Yeah. I'm okay. Just... thinking about stuff.
Stuff?
Love. And how *lucky* the people are who find it. And how maybe I never will.
RELATIONSHIPS ARE STRANGE AND INTERESTING THINGS.

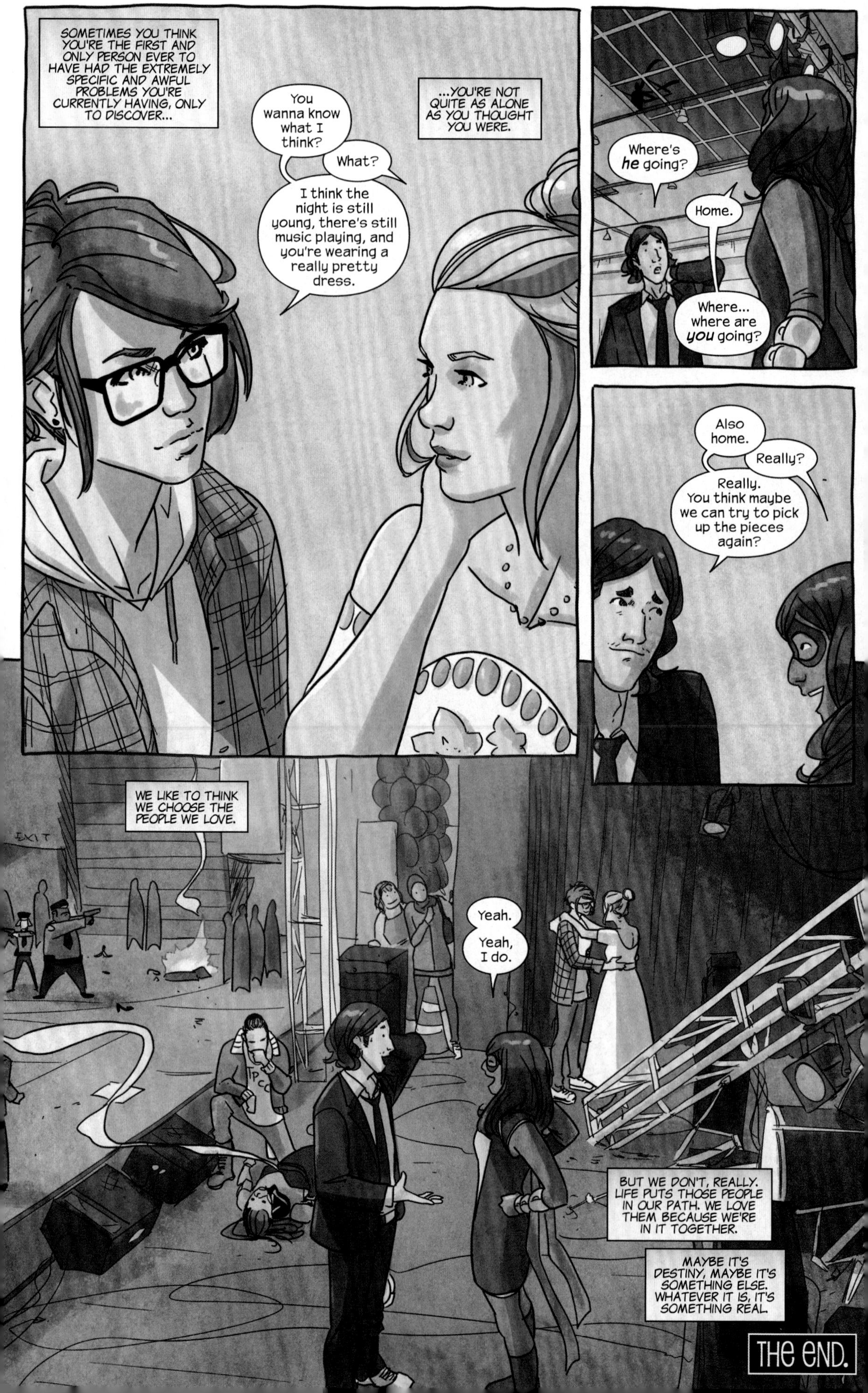

SOMETIMES YOU THINK YOU'RE THE FIRST AND ONLY PERSON EVER TO HAVE HAD THE EXTREMELY SPECIFIC AND AWFUL PROBLEMS YOU'RE CURRENTLY HAVING, ONLY TO DISCOVER...
You wanna know what I think?
What?
I think the night is still young, there's still music playing, and you're wearing a really pretty dress.
...YOU'RE NOT QUITE AS ALONE AS YOU THOUGHT YOU WERE.
Where's *he* going?
Home.
Where... where are *you* going?
Also home.
Really?
Really. You think maybe we can try to pick up the pieces again?
WE LIKE TO THINK WE CHOOSE THE PEOPLE WE LOVE.
EXIT
Yeah.
Yeah, I do.
BUT WE DON'T, REALLY. LIFE PUTS THOSE PEOPLE IN OUR PATH. WE LOVE THEM BECAUSE WE'RE IN IT TOGETHER.
MAYBE IT'S DESTINY, MAYBE IT'S SOMETHING ELSE. WHATEVER IT IS, IT'S SOMETHING REAL.
THE END.

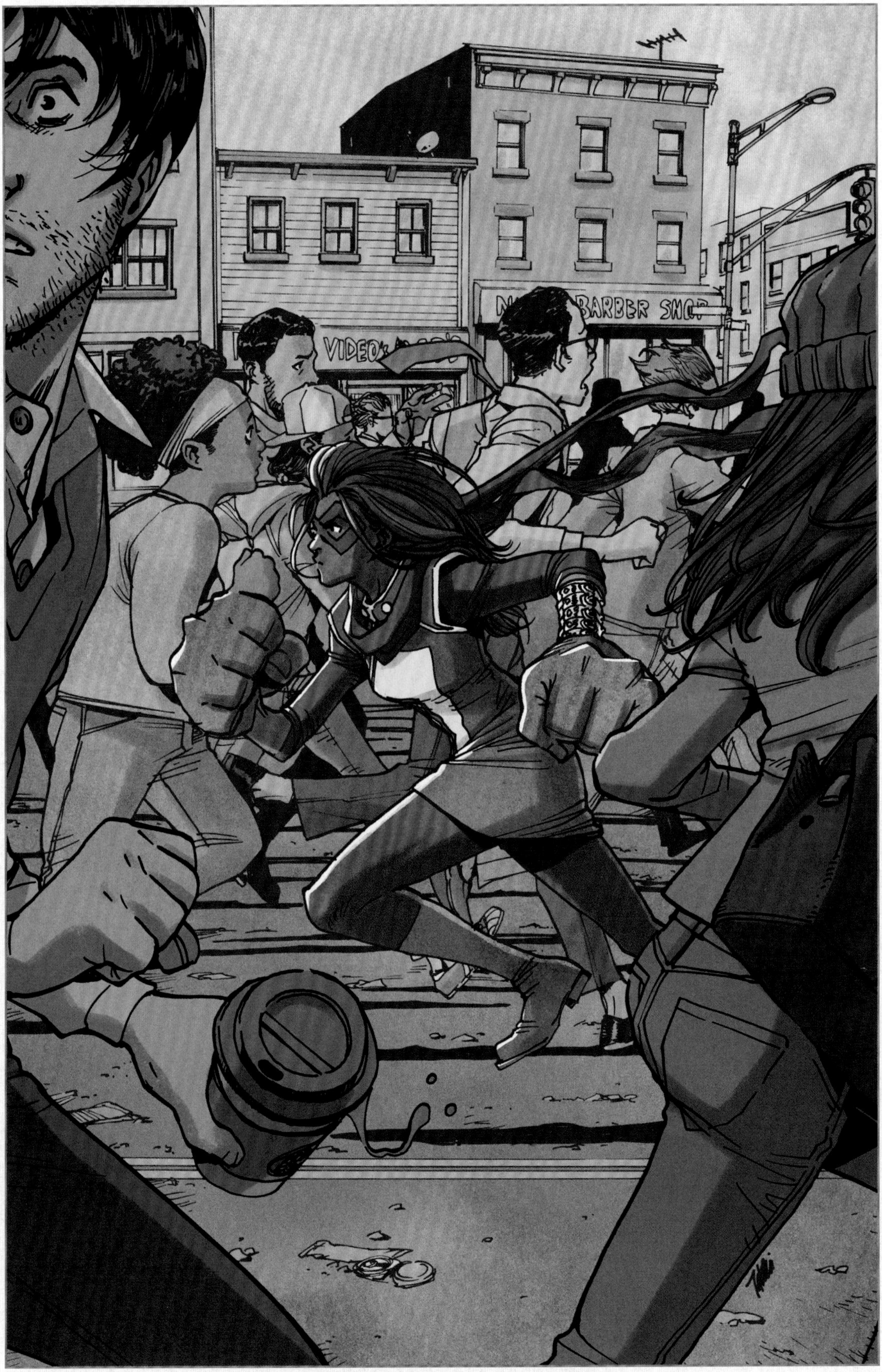
BARBER SHOP
VIDEO

MS. MARVEL #25 VARIANT
BY TAKESHI MIYAZAWA & IAN HERRING

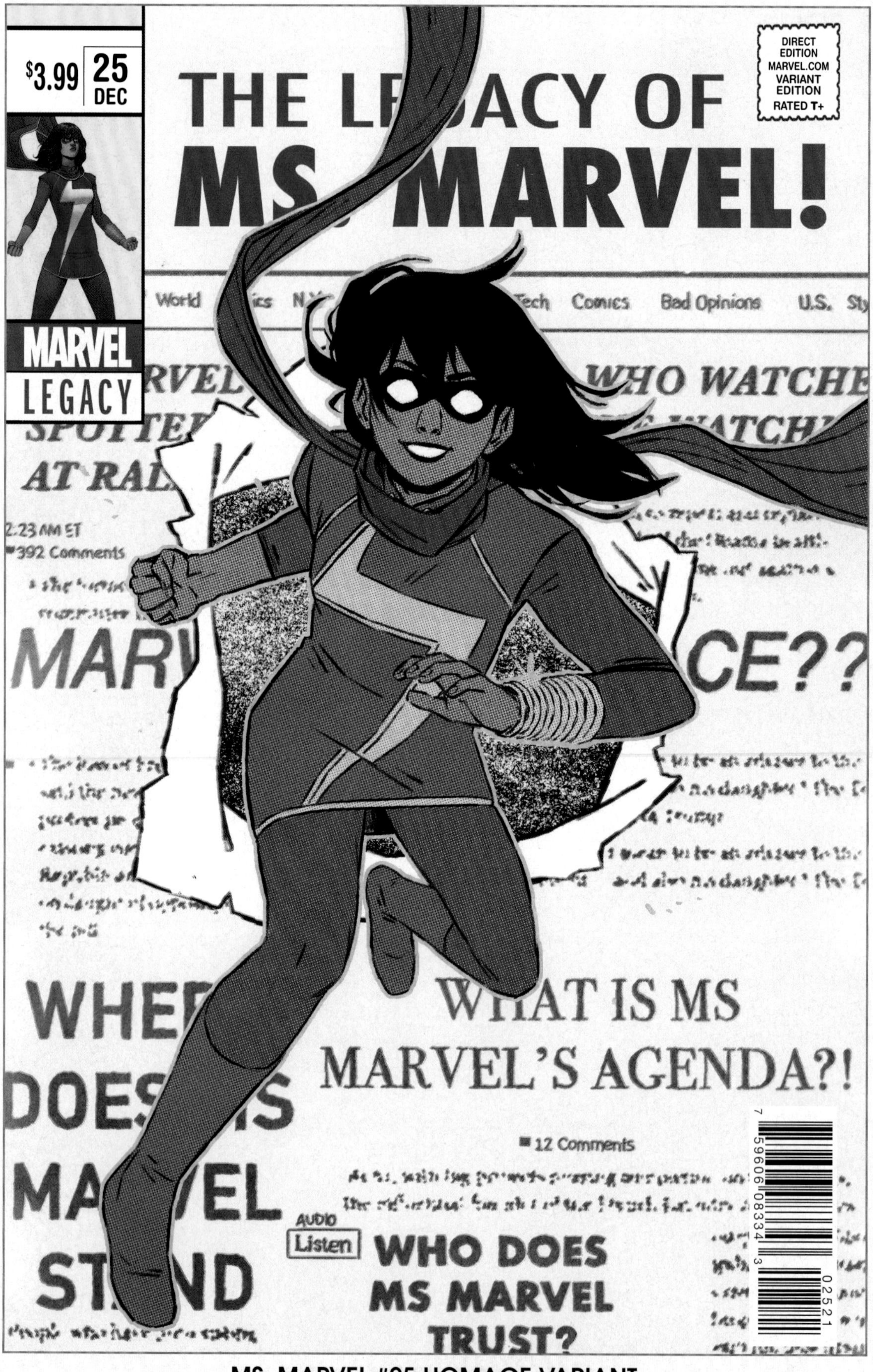

$3.99
25
DEC
THE LEGACY OF
MS MARVEL!
DIRECT EDITION
MARVEL.COM
VARIANT EDITION
RATED T+
MARVEL
LEGACY
World
Tech
Comics
Bad Opinions
U.S.
2:23 AM ET
392 Comments
WHAT IS MS
MARVEL'S AGENDA?!
12 Comments
AUDIO
Listen
WHO DOES
MS MARVEL
TRUST?

MS. MARVEL #25 HOMAGE VARIANT

BY JACOB WYATT

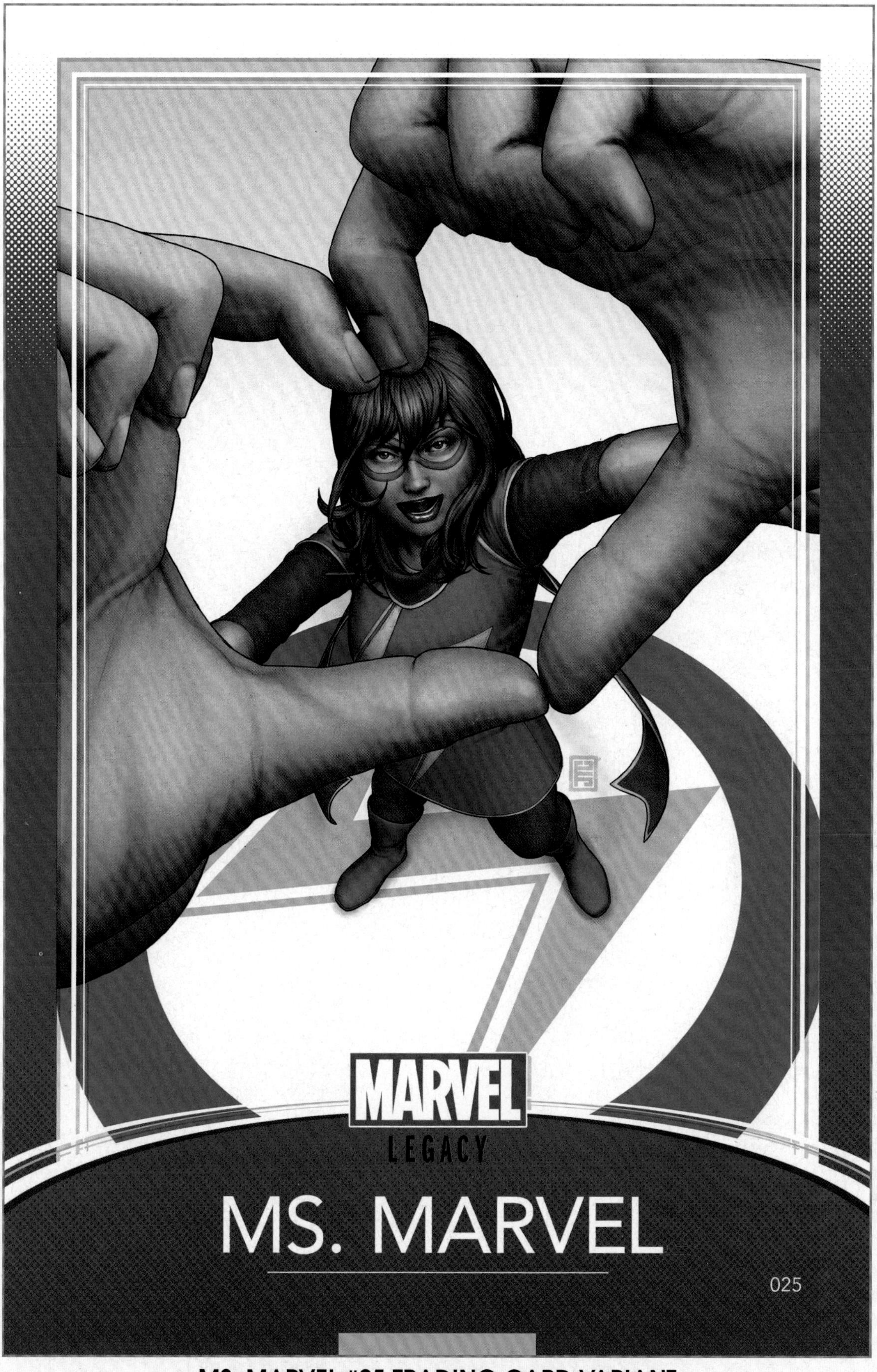
MARVEL
LEGACY
MS. MARVEL
025

MS. MARVEL #25 TRADING CARD VARIANT
BY JOHN TYLER CHRISTOPHER

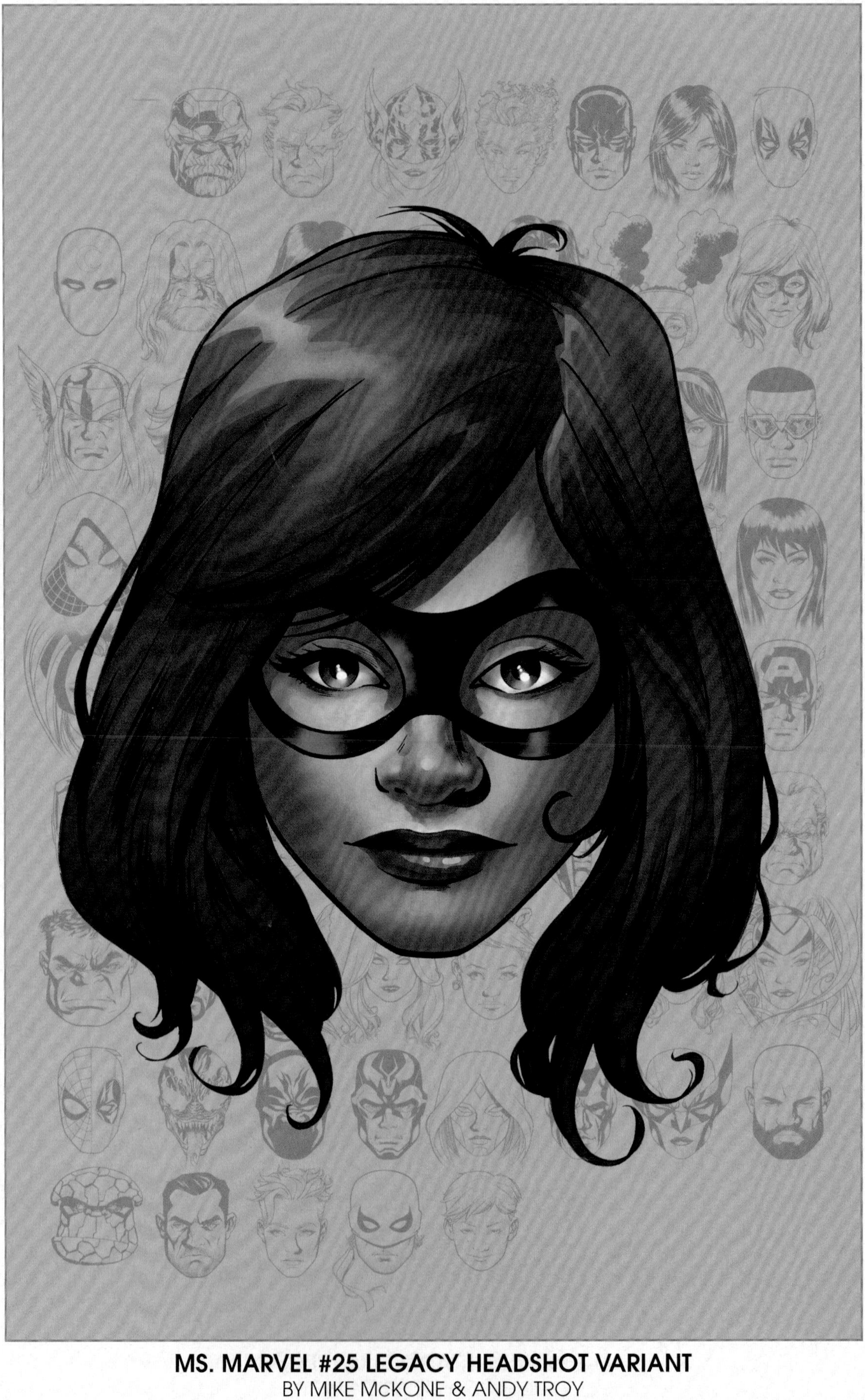

MS. MARVEL #25 LEGACY HEADSHOT VARIANT
BY MIKE McKONE & ANDY TROY

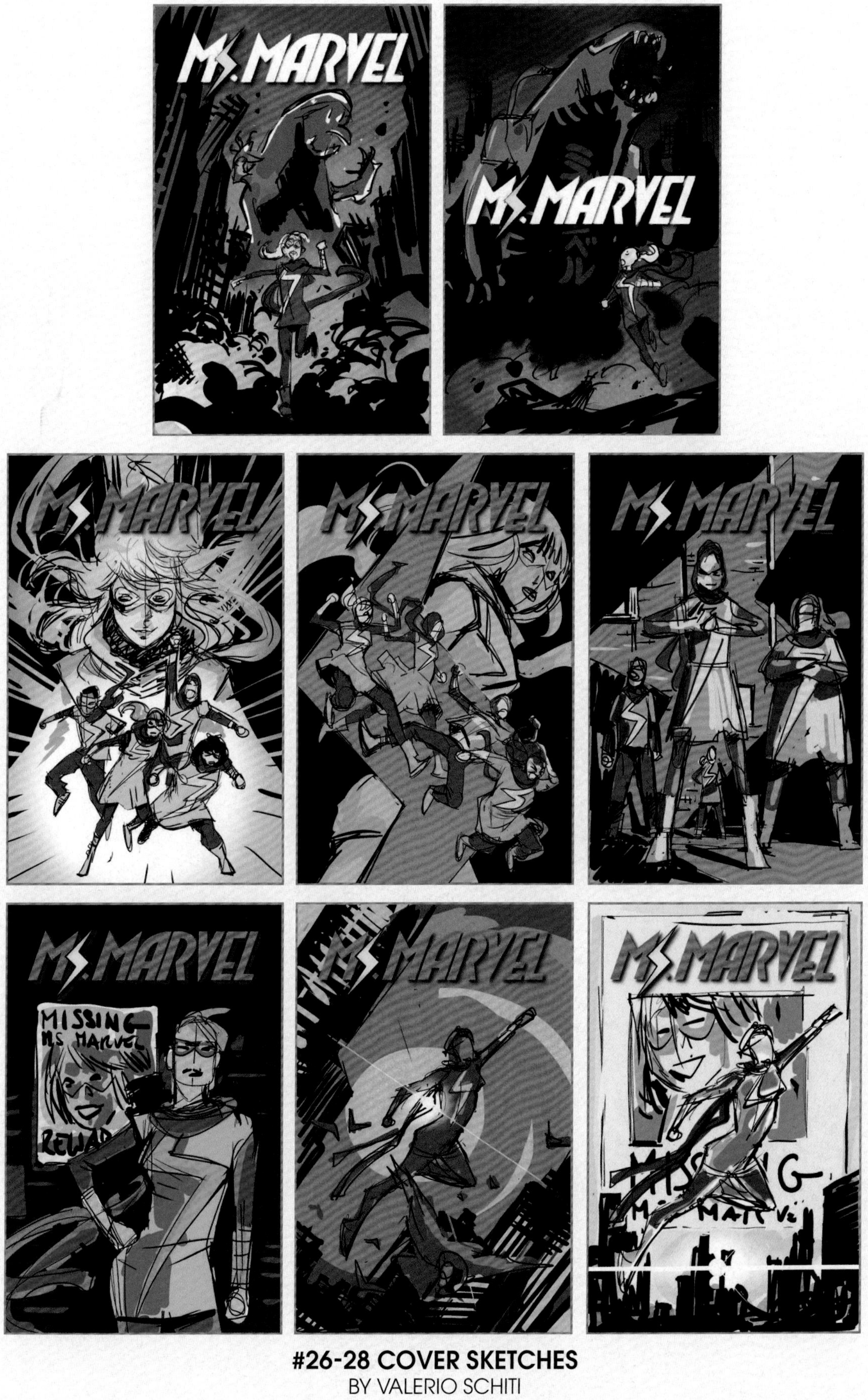
MS. MARVEL
MS. MARVEL
MS. MARVEL
MS. MARVEL
MS. MARVEL
MS. MARVEL
MISSING
MS MARVEL
MS. MARVEL
MS. MARVEL

#26-28 COVER SKETCHES
BY VALERIO SCHITI

#29-30 COVER SKETCHES
BY VALERIO SCHITI